Pricing Guide
for Web Services

How to Make Money on the Information Superhighway

by

Robert C. Brenner, MSEE, MSSM

Pricing Guide for Web Services
How to Make Money on the Information Superhighway

ISBN 0-929535-18-9

©1997, 1998 Robert C. Brenner. All rights reserved. Brief quotations of statements or other material in this book may be used in other books, broadcast and print media, Web sites, house organs, term papers and presentations, provided full prominent credit is given as follows: "from *Pricing Guide for Web Services* by Robert C. Brenner. Published by Brenner Information Group, San Diego, California." For larger excerpts or reprint rights, contact the publisher.

SECOND PRINTING

Published in the United States of America

by

BRENNER INFORMATION GROUP
P.O. Box 721000
San Diego, CA 92172-1000 U.S.A.
(619) 538-0093
info@brennerbooks.com

www.brennerbooks.com
Printed in Canada

Tables of Contents

Introduction - Internet Opportunities - 1

Chapter 1 - Web Services for Sale- 5
    Web Consulting 5
    Site Design & Development... 6
    Page Design & Layout 8
    Site Promotion 10
    Site Maintenance & Management 11
    Can Web Service be Profitable? 13

Chapter 2 - Cost and Price - 15
    Determining Cost 16
    Fixed Costs 18
    Variable Costs 20
    Direct Costs 21
    Indirect Costs & Overhead 22
    Overhead Factor 24
    Burden Rate 24
    General & Administrative (G&A) 25
    Cost of Services Sold 27
    Calculating the Cost of Sales & Support 28
    Productivity 29
    Calculating Productivity 30
    Measuring Productivity by $/FTE 32
    Factors That Affect Productivity 38
    Budgeting Costs by the Hour 39
    Calculating Budgeted Hourly Costs 44
    Example 1 - Single Home Page Design 57
    Example 2 - Six Page Site Design 60
    How Costs Vary During a Project 64

Chapter 3 - Marketplace and Price - 65
    Market Analysis 66
    Market Type 67
    Market Size 69
    Estimating Demand for Your Services 75
    Elasticity of Demand.. 78
    How to Evaluate Demand 82

Chapter 4 - Competition and Price - 85
    Collecting Competitor Information 86
    With Results in Hand 93

Chapter 5 - Understanding Business Numbers - 95
- General Accounting Principles 95
- So What is Profit? 98
- Return on Investment (ROI) 102
- Return on Assets (ROA) 104
- Markup 107
- Break-Even Analysis 110
- Finding Break-Even on Advertising 116
- Margin Analysis 118

Chapter 6 - Pricing Strategies - 123
- Selecting Which Services to Offer 127
- Pricing Strategies to Consider 130
- Cost-Oriented Pricing 131
- Shop-Oriented Pricing 141
- Competitor-Oriented Pricing 146
- Market-Oriented Pricing 150
- Smart Strategies 163

Chapter 7 - Pricing Tactics - 183
- Charging by Page, Hour, etc. 183
- Incorporating 'Other' Charges 185
- Tactical Pricing Actions 186
- Reducing Your Prices 192
- Raising Your Price 209

Chapter 8 - Managing by the Numbers - 223
- The Critical Number 225
- Cash on Hand 225
- Income 226
- Expenses 226
- Accounts Receivable 227
- Gross Profit 232
- Revenue Per Employee 234
- Monitoring Schedule 236
- Cash Flow 237
- Analyzing Profit in Competitor Bids 240
- How Much Can You Actually Earn? 241

Chapter 9 - Street Smarts - 247
- Networking for Business 247
- Listening for Profit 253
- Body Language in Business 260
- Getting Paid 267

Index 277

INTRODUCTION
Internet Opportunities

"Our world will never be the same again."

This book is a no-nonsense approach to making money at the on and off-ramps of the information data highway. It's about pricing for business success beyond your wildest dreams.

The Future is On-Line

The Internet is driving a fundamental change in the way we communicate. Everyone seems to be "going on-line." Every major company in the country has or is developing a unique Internet presence to communicate with customers, vendors, and each other. So are government offices, libraries, radio and TV stations, newspapers, magazines, and professionals in the workplace. These employees are drawn to the Internet by a desire to give and receive information. Individuals are also developing their own identities on the Internet.

Skeptics tell us that few people are making money on the Web. They claim that only the marketing types, seminar presenters, and advertising account sales reps are successfully selling on-line. Yet we see a brighter view. Thousands of businesses are beginning to sell products and services using this medium. And the first place that most young people go to find answers is on-line through their computers. The growth of access to the Internet has consistently increased and improved. And everyone feels a need to be involved.

A sidebar in *INC* magazine described a recent Internet use survey that concluded that half of the people who use the Web, do so for the following business purposes:

- gather information
- collaborate with others
- provide vendor support and communication
- research competitors
- communicate internally
- provide customer service and support
- publish information
- purchase products or services
- sell products or services

There is significant money to be made helping companies conduct electronic commerce on the Internet. Those entrepreneurs that drag their feet may find themselves eating the digital dust of visionaries who sweep past them to the gold medals at the end of electronic paths.

The on-line evolution-revolution is providing fantastic opportunities for Web service providers. According to *Computer Reseller News*, "It is no secret that the Internet has grown over the past year like a spider web in an abandoned garage, giving birth to dozens of one- or two-person shops that specialize in building [Web] sites."

While thousands of people experiment with their own Web pages, in the end, good design and good content determine who wins the economic war for business on the Web. A recent study by Gartner Group and reported in *Infoworld* concluded that most Web sites fall short of what customers want. In fact, 75% of the sites surveyed need a major redesign. What an opportunity for you!

The Web offers enormous profit for those who know how to design and present information for on-line use. Graphic designers, desktop publishers, animators, and multimedia artists are nicely positioned to exploit this huge and growing market. There's also a profit place for the technicians who understand servers and networks. And service providers who can write Internet-related code, develop Web animation, handle Web page editors and design good-looking Web sites are worth their weight in gold. Web authoring has become the desktop publishing of the 90s, and the Internet is a profit goldmine for those with the skills to do Web site development right.

A recent survey showed a wide range in the billing rates for Web service. This is typical of a new business model and much like what we saw in the early stages of the desktop publishing revolution. New Web service providers are not sure how to price their work. We found Web page development going for $29 to $1,500 each, Home Page design going for $17 - $150 an hour, Web consulting for $25 - $150 an hour, and HTML programming for $40 - $135 an hour. Like desktop publishing, Web service prices will settle out as owner-operators become more experienced and learn the true value of what they offer.

Just about anyone with a technical skill can discover and mine a niche in the Internet gold field. Carve out your own niche in this huge profit pie by creating value for potential customers. Develop the skills and then find ways to generate higher value relationships for your clients—relationships with their customers, their suppliers and with their investors. Then charge what you're worth. Remember. Value is not what you think your services are worth. Value is what a customer will buy.

The Internet is the ultimate "revenge of the nerds." And many are being richly rewarded for their knowledge and abilities.

This book is designed to help professionals who live and work at the on and off-ramps of the information data highway. It's designed for those who seek their fortunes on the crest of the "4th Wave." This book is designed to make Web service a profitable money-maker for you.

How to Use This Book

This "meat and potatoes" reference is full of pricing tips, tricks, and techniques designed to help you make money. Use it to develop strategy and tactics. Use it to set prices that work to return high profits.

But also use it to help educate others. This rich market has room for everyone, even your competitors. One of the major complaints of Web designers concerns "propeller-heads," "technophiles," and "newbies" who do work at low prices or for free. The best way to counter cutthroat pricing is to educate these amateurs about value and profit.

Show them this book. Call them. Suggest that they buy their own copy. There's plenty of business for everyone. By helping others approach Web service as a business, correct value signals are passed to the marketplace, and all Web designers and developers can make good money while enjoying their work. Web service is a profession. It's not a hobby. This book shows you how to make it a profitable business.

1
Web Service For Sale

"The whole idea of Web publishing is new to all of us."

The Web Services Menu

Stripped of its hype and mystique, Web services involve those actions that you take to help individuals and businesses gain competitive advantage using modems and on-line resources. Specifically, web services can be partitioned into:

> consulting
> site design
> site development
> page design
> page layout
> page & site linking
> site maintenance
> site promotion

Web Consulting

A Web consultant can help clients understand and define the purpose for a planned site. They help define the target, content, organization and look of the client's site. They also help them decide how the site will be found and when it will be updated. They analyze and advise on the best place to locate their site, how much information should be made available and how much storage should be reserved for interaction at the site.

With changes in technology driving changes in business models, consultants help clients integrate and adopt their business practices to the new world of electronic commerce. Consultants explain how to use technology to create new, higher valued relationships with prospects and customers.

Web commerce requires radical rethinking of the role of traditional print advertising. This is frightening to many companies whose income depends on reaching out to customers. The whole concept of selling is changing, and a Web consultant is a key link in guiding companies into the next century. Today, print ads are used to sell a Web site, not a product. Product selling occurs when prospects click onto the site's Home Page.

This is a challenging area, because not only must a consultant bean expert in good site design, they must also be expert at marketing and selling on-line. Many Web sites today are poorly designed. They don't present the right message in the best way. And many are slow and dull. This is an opportunity for consultants and designers who can revitalize deficient sites.

And Web consulting is not limited by geography. You can support companies anywhere in the world. Everyone recognizes good design when they see it. And visitors don't care where a design came from except that it works well for on-line commerce.

The advice of a good Web consultant can be worth its weight in gold. And you can bill high rates. Our survey on Web service pricing found consulting rates exceeding $100 an hour—$150 an hour is common. Good advice is worth the cost.

Site Design & Development

Web site design isn't just the look of a Home Page. It includes developing a consistent image on each page, providing quality text, graphics, animation, audio and/or video content, optimizing the speed of access and use by site visitors, and establishing links to other pages and related sites. Figure 1-1 shows the components of Web site design.

Web Site Design
- Text
- Graphics
- Animation
- Video
- Audio
- Interactive content
- Telephony
- Common Gateway Interface (CGI)*
- Browser access
- Download access
- Storage required
- Accounting
    - # hits
    - e-cash
    - order processing
- Security required
- Copyright to elements of page

Fig. 1-1. The components of site design.

Site design can also include constructing ways to count the hits (accesses) and actual transactions at the site, building interactive e-mail feedback and constructing on-line order forms. It can involve the design of secure electronic transactions and data exchange. And it can include designing ways to collect customer/client information from the site visitor so target marketing and one-to-one marketing can occur.

As the person who will design the form of information content, you must understand the options available for presenting and sharing information using a display screen as the visual medium. A customer may decide that they want a simple text-only display. Or they may want a full multimedia event linked to every page on their site. The Web site is actually a visual presentation of the customer. They may want photos, illustrations and graphic logos on each page.

Page Design & Layout

Whether your client has a single Home Page or multiple pages linked to the site, each page must be individually designed to produce the response desired of visitors. Page design involves generating a storyboard of how the site will look and how each page will interact. Each page is drawn in rough and the designer attempts to instill a consistent look to the complete site package.

For example, the Home Page could have navigation buttons or icons that a visitor can click on to access downline pages that provide specific information or capability. The top of the page could have a banner advertising the latest offering from the business. And one of the linked pages could be new or upcoming products.

Developing the content could involve writing, illustration, graphic design, animation, video production, audio production and re-purposing content for electronic distribution. Web publishing software may include an editor, image mapping to link graphics to hot spots, a database to Web page connection, and templates to help in site design. By linking a database to a Web site, a client can publish and maintain a current on-line catalog.

Getting the information onto a Web page is a technical issue. Getting the content together is an organizational issue. The most difficult part of Web publishing is collecting the information that the world will want to see.

When the design is completed on paper and shared with the client, get the client to sign off on the design. Then your services shift to page layout. Page layout involves the actual implementation of the design—from the Home Page to other linked pages at the same or subordinate sites. Here is where the actual software tools come into play. Here is where the graphic designer and desktop publisher operate. Here is where the rubber meets the road.

Every aspect of desktop service can be involved—from scanning, to graphic design, to page layout, to integration of multimedia elements. And each skill can have a different value.

Layout also involves the actual programming that produces the look of the design. Each page must be formed with a consistent look and be able to interact as intended. Simple HTML programming differs from VRML coding in that the latter requires much more education and experience. Figure 1-2 shows the components of Web page design.

>
> Web Page Design
> Text
> Graphics
> Animation
> Video
> Audio
> Interactive content
> Screen layout
> HTML programming
> Java/JavaScript programming
> ActiveX programming
> OLE
> Visual Basic
> Networked Multimedia
> Networked Video
> Networked Audio
> Scanning
> Update frequency

Fig. 1-2. Components of page design.

The result is a set of Web pages that attract and hold visitors during the selling process.

Before a Home Page design is given a site address and uploaded to a site server so browsers and prospective customers can find it, the design should be reviewed in detail. The same goes for each page linked to the site.

Carefully check each page for legibility (text, text-over-background-graphics, color compatibility, etc.) Then check all links - "hyperlink" is a command to let a user jump between Web pages of a site.

Customers of your clients are likely more interested in content than in glitz. Thus for every site that will be loaded with graphics, encourage your client to have a twin "text-only" site designed for those users who only seek textual information and don't want to wait for graphics to download.

The Web pages are uploaded to the ISP using an FTP client program. This places the web page files into the server of the ISP.

Finally, check the site using various browsers. The display will vary, requiring tweaking of the design for optimum viewing. Often a Home Page will include a statement describing the best browser to use when viewing the site.

Site Promotion

Next comes site promotion. A company can have a great Web site, but it can't be effective if visitors don't come. To make a site work, it must be promoted.

Show your client how to promote the URL address for their site. Have them include the Home Page URL address on their business cards and in every display ad and printed brochure that they produce. Also suggest that they encourage their customers to log on and visit the site.

As a Web service provider, you will also help get their site listed on search engines that contain directories to various sites. Some search engines require monthly or annual payments. Some are free. You as the expert must know which are which, and you must recommend to your client the best search engines to be listed on.

This means that you must develop, not only your technical skills, you must also develop your Internet marketing skills. As a Web service provider, your education is ongoing and continuous. As new capabilities arrive, you must seek out and adopt those that will benefit your customer base. In this way you create value and you create income potential for your customers. You also keep them loyal and continuously sending money your way. They need your skills and they need your knowledge. As long as you can help them earn more money, you, too, will profit. Everyone wins in this formula.

Site Maintenance & Management

The position of the client's site in a list of keywords that can be accessed by search engines is important to increasing the number of visits to the site. When a search engine is engaged, a number of matches to a keyword can be found.

Typically the search software lists 10 sites on each display page. The position of the client's site on the list determines if and how prospective customers will stop by for a look. If the client's site is on page 14 and number 134 in a list of 1,267, there is less likelihood that the client will get many visits (hits).

The position of the client's site on search engine directories depends on several factors. If the site is consistently updated and new keywords are produced, it is kept close to the top of the list since the position is determined based on when a site was last changed.

Since most clients have little experience in site management, you can negotiate a nice continuing income by handling this for your client.

You provide a valuable service to your customer by paying attention to the audience and planning for growth, including upgrades in hardware and network bandwidth.

Bandwidth is especially important. You can clog a 56k line quickly. And one hundred 14.4 kbps users will fill a T1 channel differently than ten T1 users. Anything more than 40 simultaneous connections will clog a T1 line. Users on 28.8 kbps links need about 1 second to download 1 kB of a page. So design for 28.8k, and faster modem users will love your site.

Many clients initially want all the bells and whistles connected to their design. But, speed and access are important, so help the client understand the affect of bells and whistles such as image resolution and size on download time—a 14.4 kbps modem takes 1 second per kB to download a picture into the browser.

Manage the traffic and performance of your client's site. Keep the end-user in mind when you design the look and feel of their site. Help the client consistently update and change the content of their site. You could also develop and use logs and stats with a script to count the number of accesses or downloads.

The payoff to your client is in lower costs per sale. You can help your client calculate the value of lower printing, technical support and telephone costs; better customer relations; improved information collection and distribution; and increased direct sales.

Help your client measure the site on the basis of fulfilling business results. Determine how much it costs them to get a new customer and to maintain customer relationships. Server logs can help. Use the log statistics to adjust the structure of your client's site.

When it's appropriate, put multimedia on the site. Consider adding sound and video using clips and streams. Clips are large files. They are used where high quality is required. They can be created at any resolution. Streams convert the Net into a broadcast medium. The sound quality is only fair, but they do work on high-speed links.

Then work to create new services. Consider new search engine strategies, site upgrades and discussion groups and mailing lists. Create ties. According to *MacWEEK*, "The Web browser is emerging as a universal graphic user interface client for all legacy data systems." This means that a Web browser can be used to access a company's internal databases, catalogs, inventory and shipping records. Federal Express lets customers track their own packages through their Web site. New tools are being introduced that help a Webmaster integrate Web sites with SQL databases.

As the designer and maintainer of a site, you can help optimize the client's site. For this you can (and should) be well compensated.

Can Web Services be Profitable?

A good Web site developer can earn a handsome income while having fun at the same time. Lynn Bremner of Digital WestMedia in San Diego was quoted in the *San Diego Business Journal* as saying, "Pricing for the creation of a Web site can begin as low as $2,500 for a simple three to five page Web site, and rise to $20,000 and above for a site spanning 50 pages or more with many high tech elements. If there's a database included on the site, the cost can rise even higher."

Web service is one of the best professions with high earning potential. In our recent nationwide survey on Web service pricing, we found Web page development going for $39 - $1,500 per page, Home Page design billing out at $17 - $100 an hour, Web consulting going for $25 to $150 an hour, HTML programming billing out at $40 - $135 an hour, and Web site maintenance running $100 - $650 a month.

A recent article in *Digital Chicago* magazine described a custom masthead graphic with logo going for $100 - $600, text navigation buttons going for $20 - $100 each, graphic navigation buttons priced at $50 - $400 a set, image map navigation buttons going for $50 - $400 a set, HTML programming billing out at $50 - $400 a page, horizontal navigation bars with text links going for $20 - $100 a bar, custom graphic buttons for $100 each, feedback forms for $50 - $200+ each, menu links for $20 - $50 each, graphic button links for $50 - $200, and FTP uploading to a server for $10 - $50 per group of files.

And a recent article in *INC* magazine listed the prices of Web site design as $500 - $50,000 per site. The article also listed site hosting at $30 - $3,500 a month (for businesses). They report that a Web site designer could charge $100 an hour.

One Web developer in Pennsylvania charges $80 an hour for Home Page design and layout, $15 each for scanning images to GIF or JPEG files, $100 an hour for Internet consulting and $100 an hour for custom programming (CGI, Java, etc.).

In Maine, we found a service provider charging $70 an hour for computer graphic design, $55 an hour for desktop publishing page layout, and $100 an hour for Web page design and layout.

Is there money to be made on the Web? You bet! As long as you have the right formula and price with confidence.

Summary

Web service covers a wide range of activities. For each service activity, there is a cost and a price. In the next chapter you'll discover the three faces of price and how each can be used to generate the most revenue for your time and effort.

2
Cost and Price

"As a rule of thumb, new web pages will probably cost about 30% more than the same content prepared for desktop publishing formats."
Jack Powers, Computer Publisher Magazine

The relationship between cost and price is direct and important. Price is driven by four things — costs, customers, competitor and the amount of return (compensation) that you hope to receive.

Cost involves all the money that you spend in reaching customers and selling your service. It comes in a variety of flavors.

Customers can be anyone and come from anywhere. Clients are contacting Web service providers thousands of miles away. Shop owners in Australia are selling design services to clients in Canada. There is no barrier to trade in this global economy.

This means that competitors can also come from places that you never expect. Do an Internet search on Web services and you'll see what I mean.

The fourth factor in price is compensation, or the net profit that you hope to gain by selling service. If you can make more return by investing in stocks and bonds, then you'd better have a good reason for starting and operating a business other than return on investment.

Each of these four factors—cost, customer, competition, and compensation influence what you can charge. Together, they become the basis for your marketing strategy. As shown in Figure 2-1 on the next page, the process to setting price has a distinct path. First collect data. Then analyze the data to generate useful information. Finally, use this information to formulate a pricing strategy that works for you.

> Collect Data
>> Measure your costs
>> Identify your customer
>> Identify your competitors
> Analyze the Data
>> Costs —> Financial Analysis
>> Customers —> Segment customers and analyze
>> Competitors —> Competitive Analysis
> Formulate a Strategy
>> Which Market
>> What Prices
>> How to Be Better

Fig. 2-1. How prices are established.

In this chapter, you'll learn how to use cost, customers, competition and compensation to establish prices that work.

Determining Costs

What is cost? And how does cost relate to price? No consideration of service pricing should occur without a clear understanding of cost. Knowing your costs lets you find break-even. And it enables you to determine a cost basis for each service. From this you can add profit, and return on investment, and then quote a project price.

Street smart shop owners know their actual costs. Sadly, when some owner-operators calculate their true costs, they discover to their dismay that, given their pricing structure, their operating costs exceed revenue. They are actually paying more to earn less. In essence, they are paying for the privilege of being in business.

Figure 2-2 shows the many costs that must be considered in forming a pricing strategy.

> Management Costs
>   Administration
>   Planning
>   Evaluating
>
> Sales & Marketing Costs
>
> Order Fulfillment Costs
>   purchase orders
>   following project
>   expediting project
>
> Accounting Costs
>   invoice preparation
>   invoice delivery
>   getting paid
>
> Client Costs
>   meetings
>   telephone calls
>   fax and e-mail
>
> Design Costs
>
> Production Costs
>   quality
>   re-work

Fig. 2-2. The cost elements of Web services.

These costs also include wages, overhead expenses, return on investment, and profit. Cost can also include what you pay to make your market aware of and understand your product or service.

For example, your price structure should take into account the cost for advertising. According to an article in *Entrepreneur* magazine, advertising costs can be as much as 60% of sales revenue. The article described how Orville Redenbacher popcorn has a higher price than competing products because the company spends more money on advertising to convince customers that their popcorn is better than other brands. This advertising cost is reflected in their price. Tax is another part of product or service cost. About 32% of the cost of bread represents taxes on this product.

Costs come in a multitude of flavors—fixed costs, variable costs, direct costs, indirect costs, purchase costs, ownership costs, marketing costs, sales costs, even the cost of lost contracts. Understanding and defining these costs can be one of the toughest jobs that you'll tackle. Yet, your price can only be as good as the cost information behind it.

The best way to baseline costs is to identify all the tasks associated with each os your shop's service. Each task represents a cost to your business. Some tasks are billable. Others are part of your overhead.

By projecting costs and then developing a historical record of your actual expenses, you can better estimate future work.

Your costs of doing business are partitioned primarily into fixed, variable, direct, indirect, and overhead costs. These terms are related and are often confused. So let's dip our toes in the cost and overhead pond and wade slowly through the shallows.

Fixed Costs

Fixed costs are those expenses that you must pay whether you have little or lots of business. Fixed costs don't vary with the volume of sales. They exists because you're in business.

Even if you work out of your home, there are costs to using rooms, lighting, electricity and furnishings. These can be fixed costs.

And you must pay someone to produce billable services—even if it's you. It doesn't matter if you design and layout Web pages yourself or have another person do the work. Billable work must be performed to generate income. Below is a list of fixed business costs:

> rent
> insurance - business
> insurance - vehicle
> insurance - health/medical
> insurance - dental
> taxes - federal
> taxes - state
> taxes - city
> taxes - county/parish
> taxes - sales
> taxes - property
> taxes - other
> special assessments
> business fees
> business licenses
> loan payment
> depreciation
> lease - equipment
> lease - vehicle
> utilities - basic
> salaries
> parking
> cleaning - office and grounds
> telephone (office) - basic
> telephone (cellular) - basic
> telephone (voice messaging)
> beeper
> alarm system
> on-line service - basic

By listing costs that apply on a spreadsheet, you can track, monitor, analyze and better control these fixed expenses. Do the same for your variable costs.

Variable Costs

Variable costs are those expenses that change with the level of business activity. If you take on more projects, you'll use more paper, toner, electricity, and telephone connect time. The basic part of your utility bill is a fixed cost. But, the additional electricity required for each Web design project is a variable cost.

Thus, some expenses are part fixed, part variable. You should separate these into their fixed and variable components for better cost analysis.

Below is a list of typical variable costs:

>wages (direct labor)
>wages (indirect labor)
>wages (part time help)
>wages (freelance help)
>taxes - payroll
>insurance (workers compensation)
>marketing
>advertising
>commissions
>legal services
>pension fund
>interest expense
>credit card payments
>postage
>office supplies
>telephone (office) - over basic rate
>telephone (cellular) - over basic rate
>telephone (modem line) - over basic rate
>on-line services - over basic rate
>utilities - over basic
>copying
>printing
>sales meetings
>repairs & maintenance
>purchases - hardware
>purchases - software
>purchases - other

travel expense
vehicle maintenance
gas purchases
professional services
entertainment
contributions
subscriptions / dues
other variable costs

By putting your variable costs on the same spreadsheet as you did your fixed costs, you can analyze and clearly see where much of your income is going. Hopefully, you're receiving more income that you are generating expenses.

Direct Costs

Costs can also be partitioned into those associated with a project and those that you must pay anyway, even if you don't have a specific job to charge the expense to. Direct costs include:

- salaries of employees whose efforts can be directly associated with a project (called *"direct labor"*)

- equipment leased or rented to do a job

- materials used on a specific project

- consultants hired to support a project

- job-specific computer and software purchases

- job-specific documentation purchases

Remember, ANYTHING that can be charged directly to a project work order (direct labor, direct materials, etc.) is a direct cost. Commissions or finders fees paid for activities that result in a job can be considered a direct cost. So can the time you spend on the project.

Some shop owners don't consider their own direct labor in calculating project costs. This is wrong. Since most Web service providers are also designers and technicians, everyone working on a project should charge their time to the business and be paid for their efforts.

Indirect Costs and Overhead

Indirect costs are those expenses that can not be directly charged to a specific job or project.

We have indirect expenses that we must pay whether or not we sell a product or service. We often call these our *overhead* costs. Indirect costs can include both fixed and variable costs. They include:

- rent	- utilities	- management salaries
- marketing	- advertising	- secretary/clerk pay
- insurance	- taxes	- vacation expenses
- supplies	- depreciation	- vehicle expense
- maintenance		

Overhead costs don't include designer and technician wages. As you'll learn later, overhead is pro-rated, or partitioned into a cost per hour and then allocated to each service that your business performs.

This is done by calculating your annual overhead costs and then allocating a portion of your overhead costs to the total hours worked during a year.

The total hours worked depends on your staffing and how many hours each person actually worked. One person working 40 hours a week with two weeks paid vacation equals 2,000 hours of work a year. A full year of 40-hour weeks is considered 2080 hours. Overhead is calculated on the hours actually paid (not worked). Thus, if your overhead is $20,800 a year, $10 of your hourly rate must go to pay overhead costs. You could work 2,000 hours and take two weeks paid vacation.

Overhead is calculated on the whole 2,080 hours available.

A Web services business will typically have overhead costs that equal 40-50 percent of the income revenue.

If the more expensive hardware and software in your business are typically used by the higher paid employees, your overhead costs will closely track your labor costs. If everyone uses all the equipment and software, your overhead costs will track the shop's billable labor rate. You'll learn about this later.

Actually, overhead can be expressed as a percentage or as an hourly rate. In shops where pay can be directly associated with the equipment used, overhead is expressed as a percent.

$$\text{overhead (\%)} = \frac{\text{total overhead costs}}{\text{total direct labor costs}}$$

For example, a business with an overhead of $65,000 a year and direct labor cost of $130,000, can claim 50% overhead costs.

Conversely, in shops where there's little difference between the hourly wages for the employees, and everyone works on all the equipment, you can calculate an hourly overhead rate based on the actual costs and hours billed.

$$\text{overhead (hourly rate)} = \frac{\text{total overhead costs}}{\text{total direct labor hours}}$$

A business with a total overhead of $65,000 and 2000 hours of direct labor will have an overhead of $32.50 an hour. This must be incorporated into your billing rates.

Overhead Factor

It's helpful to monitor how much or your revenue applies to paying overhead—especially if you look at it from an hourly basis.

The monthly hours that you bill out can vary based on many factors. For example, a freelance Web page designer working out of a home office will bill about 150 days a year—100 hours a month. The rest of the available time is spent marketing and performing non-earning follow-up. This affects your daily labor rate and the fees that you charge.

A monthly $6,000 overhead expense and a 22 days-a-month billing cycle results in a daily overhead cost of $272.73— $34.09 an hour ($6,000 a month divided by 22 days a month divided by 8 hours a day equals $34.09 an hour).

If you earn $100,000 a year and bill 264 days each year, your daily labor rate is $378.78 [100,000 / (22 days/month x 12 months/year) = $378.78]. This equates to $47.35 hourly income.

Dividing the hourly overhead by your hourly income yields an *overhead factor* of 72% (34.09/47.35 = .72). The overhead factor defines the amount of your hourly labor rate that is allocated to paying for overhead costs.

Obviously, overhead costs can be significant. They can easily eat up more than 70 percent of your gross income. As I said, an overhead of 40-50 percent of your gross income is typical. You must ensure that the labor rate that you establish covers your overhead expenses.

Burden Rate

Larger shops (particularly those that work with government contracts) calculate overhead by combining both direct and indirect costs (total annual expense). Then they convert this overhead into a *burden rate* by subtracting direct labor from the total annual expense and dividing the result by the direct labor expense.

Burden rates can exceed 200%. The burden rate is added to a standard hourly fee to generate a burdened hourly rate. This means that each employee has a portion of overhead allocated to their billable work whenever they bid a job. A Web designer making $15 an hour with an overhead load of 125% (actual costs to do work is $18.75) will have a labor rate of $33.75 (add the $15 wage to the $18.75 overhead cost). This means that any job bids that include that person's support will be at the $33.75 rate. Large companies often use accounting systems that apply the burden rate concept.

General & Administrative (G&A)

Figure 2-3 is a composite drawing showing the various components that comprise total costs. Notice that direct materials, direct labor and shop overhead comprise shop costs. By adding to this a shop's selling expense and *general and administrative (G&A)* costs, a total cost is produced.

Direct material costs	Direct labor costs	Shop overhead costs		
Shop costs			Selling expense	
Total shop and sales costs				G & A costs
Total costs				

Fig. 2-3. The components of total cost.

G&A costs include secretarial support, clerical help, and any cost that you didn't place under direct and indirect labor or manufacturing costs.

Some companies group selling costs with general and administrative costs. They call this composite cost benchmark *selling, general and administrative (SG&A)*. G&A (or SG&A) is a catch-all category that varies from company to company and from industry to industry. You must define what costs are included.

Accountants are curiously silent about what specific costs should or should not be assigned to SG&A. This may change in the future. If every portion of your company's value chain are benchmarked and managed, curtailing SG&A growth can have a significant impact on your bottom line. According to *CFO Magazine*, SG&A "is the soft underbelly of a company's spending."

G&A (or SG&A) is expressed as a percent of total revenue. *Computer Retailer Week* projected CompUSA's SG&A to be just under 11 percent—retail stores usually have SG&A under 20 percent. According to *Computer Reseller News*, Internet and PC management software manufacturer, Quarterdeck Corporation had a G&A of 19.4% in 1996. All of these companies must be cost conscious since many measure profit by the pennies per product.

Web service providers have fewer employees with higher expenses per employee. However, you can use traditional publishing and printing as a rough benchmark. The SG&A for publishing and printing typically runs 30 to 35 percent of revenues.

The point is to compare G&A or SG&A within your own industry. If SG&A comparables for your industry are 30% and your shop comes out at 35%, you certainly can't boast about being lean and mean. Business owners need to watch G&A/SG&A carefully.

Cost of Services Sold

Each time you purchase new equipment or new application software, there are two costs involved—the purchase cost and the ownership cost.

We can negotiate various purchase prices depending on where and how we buy. However, once the purchase is concluded, the *purchase cost* becomes the basis for any tax-related depreciation we must apply. Typically, depreciation applies only to large price purchases.

The *cost of ownership* is different. It includes those expenses related to operating and maintaining the system. It takes time and energy to learn and exploit the power in your hardware and software. With hardware becoming more powerful and software becoming more complex, you cannot assign operating tasks to just anyone. You must first become proficient yourself. Then you must teach those who support you. As processing power is dispersed throughout your shop, the functions and capabilities can quickly become more than one person can handle. You may have to hire experts to perform unfamiliar tasks. This will require management, leadership, and education. Each of these factors has an associated after-purchase cost.

There is a related direct expense that you must understand and control. Hardware and software each have an associated *maintenance cost*.

For hardware, it includes cleaning, diagnostic checkups, and repair actions when necessary. It could include a service agreement for third party support.

Software maintenance can include paying for on-line technical support or the cost to customize a program for your business. An example is an accounting package that needs modifications to incorporate changes to the staff, to add new benefits, or to change the tax and social security structure. A database used for market analysis and customer contacts needs update and cleanup. A spreadsheet needs modification to incorporate new information or to produce a different output. Each action has an associated cost.

Then there are the less-obvious costs—the *hidden costs* of ownership. These include upgrade, trade-in and system availability. We upgrade our hardware and software to keep at the forefront of technology, or to increase our capability as business grows. Sometimes we trade in older equipment for new hardware. And sometimes we wait for advertised hardware or software that never becomes a reality. We call this *"vaporware."* Waiting for opportunity has a cost.

In the past, a growing number of products have been touted, hyped, and promised. But delivery has been woefully late, or nonexistent. Basing a business plan on hardware or software that becomes vaporware has a cost. Don't believe the optimistic schedules of eager marketeers. Plan implementations far enough ahead that you can work out the bugs and operational idiosyncrasies (or implement alternatives) long before you put your new system on line.

Calculating the Cost of Sales & Support

According to compensation surveys, the average cost to make a sales call is just under $100. How can you calculate your own sales call costs? According to Dartnell Company, you can use the following formula:

$$\text{avg cost} = \frac{\text{compensation} + \text{field expenses} + \text{benefits}}{\text{average number of sales calls each year}}$$

Even telephone support calls have a cost. Spending 15 minutes on the telephone with a client can cost $15 to $25. If you don't get paid for this service, you still have to pay your staff. Watch out for clients who nickel and dime you with excessive support and follow-up calls which are not part of a project contract agreement.

Productivity

For smaller shops, overhead is a good way to track costs. But productivity plays a major part in the formula. Using overhead and expected productivity, you can calculate what it cost you to provide each hour of service. Productivity impacts your shop billing rates because your calculated hourly cost must be divided by a productivity percentage to establish your actual budgeted hourly cost for a service function.

Not all employees are as productive, and you yourself will not be as productive each day of the week. So you must monitor productivity carefully.

Besides working on income-producing tasks, you'll also be answering the telephone, sorting mail, making out invoices, performing maintenance, and a myriad of other non-billable tasks.

According to the so-called *"30-60-10 Rule"* for small business, you will spend 30% of your time marketing, 60% of your time actually performing billable work, and 10% of your time handling paperwork and chasing after payments. When you consider the time spent preparing for a job and cleaning up after a job, you will probably bill out less than 50% of the available time.

Productivity is directly affected by the number of employees in your shop. While productivity is usually between 30% and 60%, the productivity in most shops seldom exceeds 40 percent. An article in *Quick Printing* reported that "most shops have an average productivity of 40% to 45%."

A "one-person operation" typically achieves no more than 30% productivity. Two or more people in a shop can achieve 40% at best. And it takes about five employees to reach a productivity level of 50% or more.

Calculating Productivity

You can combine the billable hours generated by each of your employees and use this to calculate the productivity of your shop. Then you can apply this to your hourly costs to determine what you actually need to charge to cover costs and make a profit.

If your shop is 50% productive, you can divide the income needed to cover the costs for each hour of operation by a *productivity factor* (0.50 here) to determine how much you really need to charge for each hour of service just to keep your doors open. For example, if you calculate that your hourly rate should be $15, at 50% productivity, you should actually charge $30 an hour to effectively make $15 for each hour that you work (only half of your time is productive and producing billable work).

If you pay a Web page designer $15 an hour, with $10 an hour overhead, and you want to earn 10% return on your startup investment and 10% in profit, you may decide that you need more than $30 an hour to cover costs and profit. But productivity significantly affects what you actually charge.

Dividing the $30 budgeted cost by the 50% (0.50) productivity factor yields $60 as your hourly shop rate. This is what you must charge to realize the $30 an hour average net income that is actually needed.

A shop billing out at $50 an hour and only 30% productive actually generates $15 an hour income—$600 per person in an average 40-hour week. It's critical that you know the productivity of your shop. Higher productivity enables lower hourly rates (or higher profit margin at the same hourly rates).

There are two ways to determine productivity. First, you can compare the labor billed out by an employee times the total hours worked divided by the hourly rate. This productivity formula is shown below.

$$\text{productivity} = \frac{\text{(labor income) / (hours worked)}}{\text{shop hourly rate}}$$

If one of your people billed $1,000 for labor, and worked 40 hours that week with a shop hourly rate of $50, that person's productivity is 50% [($1,000/40 hrs) / $50/hr = 0.50].

A second way to monitor productivity is to multiply your shop's hourly rate by the number of hours worked and then divide this figure into the labor billed (the income) as shown below.

$$\text{productivity} = \frac{\text{(labor income produced)}}{\text{(shop hourly rate) (hours worked)}}$$

At $50 an hour and a 40 hour week, you have $2,000 possible income. Dividing $2,000 into the $1,000 actually earned yields 0.5 or 50% shop productivity.

Some shop owners skew their productivity percentages by working 12 or more hours each day while calculating their financial numbers based on an 8-hour day. If they work the numbers correctly, some of them could discover that they are actually paying their customers just so they can perform work for them. Productivity is a hidden hazard to profit.

Many owners calculate the productivity for each employee as a basis for pay and promotion decisions. By measuring the productivity of individual employees, you can determine what each person contributes to the total required income. Based on this you can compare the skill level and performance of employees who routinely perform the same tasks.

A basic rule of thumb is that each direct labor person should bring in about 2.5 times their wages. This works most of the time, but a better measurement is to compare the labor income for services rendered by an individual with the actual hours billed at the shop's hourly rate.

For example, assume that a designer worked 40 hours and brought in $600 in labor charges. Your shop rate is $50 an hour. But 40 hours at $50 an hour should have generated $2,000. Dividing $600 actual income by $2,000 possible income yields a productivity of 30%. If another Web designer generated $700 in the same 40 hours, this person's productivity is 35%. Assuming each spent an equal amount of time answering the telephone, filling out forms, and handling other administrative functions, the second designer would be worth more to your shop than the first. The pay that they earn should reflect this. Be willing to pay for performance.

Any measurement of productivity should be balanced with factors that take time and effort away from income-generating tasks. Sometimes non-paying tasks take priority. Resolving a customer problem and improving customer satisfaction should be considered in providing a balance between productivity and adequate customer service.

Measuring Productivity by $/FTE

The gross income of Web service shops varies widely with most shops averaging under $50,000 annually. As new businesses struggle to grow, they evolve through several stages—from startup to mature company. With experience, knowledge, and satisfied customers, the gross revenue of each shop increases. The goal is to consistently achieve higher annual gross income.

But gross income is only one way to measure how your business is performing relative to the competition. There's a better way. One that measures productivity per employee. This comparison barometer is called the *"economic model of business productivity."* It's also a good measure of profitability.

The economic model measures productivity in terms of products or services sold relative to the number of employees in a company. The model is normalized to a 40-hour "full time equivalent" (FTE) worker. By comparing the average revenue generated by your full time equivalent staff with the average revenue per employee for each competitor, you can determine if your company has a productivity advantage or disadvantage.

If your company has six full time employees and earns $300,000 a year, your gross average income per employee is $50,000. This can be expressed as "$50,000 per FTE." As a rough measure, this value can then be compared with the dollars per FTE of each of your competitors. If a competitor is earning $225,000 annually with 3 full time employees, their sales revenue per employee is $75,000. When compared with your $50,000 income per employee, your competitor has a 50 percent productivity advantage over your company (75,000 - 50,000 = 25,000; 25,000/50,000 = 0.5; 0.5 x 100 = 50%). This could cause you to re-engineer your business to improve the productivity of your resources (people, equipment, software, facility layout, etc.) so your dollars of revenue per full time equivalent worker improves, making you more competitive — and more profitable.

We confirmed the $/FTE concept using the results of my company's latest pricing and salary survey of Web service providers. The $/FTE concept works for any industry including desktop publishing and multimedia.

Our survey asked each participant for income data and the number of full time, part time, and free-lance employees. Based on the responses, we calculated an average revenue per FTE for the industry. We also analyzed $/FTE based on business location, types of services offered, equipment used, and so on.

We started by investigating the economic model of productivity for related industries and companies. From revenue and employee data printed in recent issues of *Printing Impressions, Fortune Magazine*, and other publications we realized that productivity varies greatly as shown in Figure 2-4.

COMPANY	$/FTE
Web Tech	$203,019
Kreber Graphics	133,333
Applied Graphic Technologies	129,412
Western Laser Graphics	114,286
Wace USA	105,263
Chroma-Graphics	80,361
PrepSat	84,000
TSI Graphics	83,742
Graphics Express	57,143

Fig. 2-4. Sample economic model values.

Based on business strategy, the marketplace and the expectations of owner-operators in the Web service industry, the revenue per FTE by income category was found to vary from about $30,000 to over $140,000 for each equivalent full time worker. In contrast, hardware giant Hewlett-Packard brought in over $250,000 per employee, and Adobe Systems earned over $300,000 per employee.

The average revenue per employee for all companies in the U.S. is roughly $100,000. During start-up, high development costs with limited income produces a lower $/FTE value. As a company grows, $/FTE increases until the company matures. Then, if it doesn't consistently re-invent itself, $/FTE will decline until the company ceases to exist. Both the Web services and multimedia industries are prime examples of fast growth with low $/FTE. Currently, the average $/FTE of Web service companies is well below $100,000/FTE because of increased costs and associated risks in implementing new technology.

With a $100,000 national average, where do Web service providers stand when it comes to revenue per employee? What is the $/FTE of your company? To find out, develop your own economic model and then gather revenue and employee information on competing companies. Look for comparables. Watch for comments in news articles and business profiles published in this and other trade publications. Listen to industry speakers. Check the library and government labor department for industry norms. Since my company collects business information on all types of desktop services, I analyzed the survey data on Web service that was collected over the past two years.

Most Web service shops started in the last two years. Statistically, their cost basis and earnings vary widely. Since Web service is a new industry, we expected the average revenue per FTE to be below the $100,000 national norm. We weren't surprised. Our survey data yielded fascinating insight into where Web service providers stand as a collection of entrepreneurs.

We found that new shop owners tend to undercharge for most services. Women owner-operators tend to pay themselves less than their male counterparts. They also tend to charge their customers less for the same services. And we found that counter prices tend to increase as each business matures. Each of these factors affect the $/FTE of a company.

In our analysis, we defined 40 hours as a full time work week; 20 hours as part time and 4 hours as freelance. We normalized our survey data to these weekly baselines. Then we gave a full time worker a weight of 1.0 FTE, a part timer 0.5 FTE (20 hrs / 40 hrs = 0.5) and a free-lance worker 0.1 FTE (4 hrs / 40 hrs = 0.1).

This provided a weighted scoring method for comparing businesses. By multiplying the number of full timers by 1, the number of part timers by 0.5 and the number of free-lancers by 0.1, we calculated the total number of FTE employees for each business. A shop earning $500,000 a year with five full time, one part time, and three free-lance employees has an FTE rating of 5.8 (5 x 1.0 + 1 x 0.5 + 3 x 0.1 = 5.8) and a revenue per FTE ($/FTE) of $86,207 (500,000 / 5.8 = 86,207).

If a full time worker represents $10,000 per month in sales and a part time worker represents $7,500 a month working only half time, dividing income by FTE means that the part time worker is actually 50 percent more productive (7,500 / 0.5 = 15,000) than the full time employee (10,000 / 1.0 = 10,000). This assumes that each uses a proportional amount of overhead budget and has the same earning opportunity.

In addition, if a shop owner works 60 hours a week, this represents the 1.5 FTE that should become that person's basis for calculation and comparison. We found that many owners work 60 hours and calculate at forty.

The FTE concept can be useful. We can evaluate revenue per FTE against various factors—overall shop earnings, site design projects completed, scans performed and charged, Web pages billed, etc. In your economic model, it is also useful to know the average $/FTE, the range of $/FTE, and the industry average for each of these parameters.

Most start-up Web service shops will have incomes between $30K and $150K during their first few years in business. The typical $/FTE for this new industry is under $50,000. Any shop that produces more than this revenue per FTE value is more productive than the average shop. In fact, they may want to consider adding staff. Their goal is to achieve $100,000 $/FTE or more.

A shop with less revenue per FTE than the $50,000 norm is less productive. Thus the $/FTE value can be used as a benchmark to evaluate your own business and that of competitors. The finer the granularity in your analysis (e.g., looking only at the statistics of shops earning close to your current revenue), the better the comparison.

In its own way, the $/FTE economic model provides the small shop owner a way to compare productivity and to identify competitive advantage. It also hints at possible problems. Perhaps the lower revenue per FTE suggests that their pricing strategies are out of line with mainline American business. Or it could be just a growing stage phenomenon.

Productivity can be measured. And if it can be measured, it can almost always be improved. Table 2-1 shows a subjective analysis of the revenue that a single dedicated Web designer can produce with a simple rating system for their productivity. The example assumes that you are able to keep this worker fully occupied with jobs during the approximately 2080 hours that they work each year (assuming no holiday or vacation breaks during this first year). Also assume that the hourly rate for Web page design is $50. Thus $50 an hour for 2080 hours yields $104,000 possible annual income for the shop.

Table 2-1. Employee productivity analysis.

$/FTE Actual	Income Possible	Percent Productive
$25,000	$104,000	24%
35,000	104,000	34%
50,000	104,000	48%
70,000	104,000	67%

Based on these numbers, it's obvious that the higher the $/FTE, the more valuable an employee is to your shop. The key is to help each employee become as productive as possible.

Factors That Affect Productivity

Most of us have found ourselves assigning selective tasks to certain people. Consciously, or unconsciously, we've judged the ability and productivity of our staff. When certain individuals work together, they can often realize an increased overall productivity due to the effect of synergy—their joint efforts produce a result greater than what each individual could achieve working alone.

However, several factors can directly affect the productivity of an individual or of a team. Interruptions play a significant role in productivity. So does a "down" day, when people are at the low ebb on their biorhythm curves. A full eight-hour "person day" doesn't mean an eight-hour "productive day."

A significant portion of time is spent re-focusing after unscheduled interruptions. Re-focusing after an interruption can take as long as 20 minutes. And this is for EACH interruption! If you get interrupted six times a day, you could lose two hours of productive time. Interruptions directly affect job schedule and worker performance. However, you can affect how and when interruptive activities are handled. A fully focused worker in a larger shop is typically 70-90% productive. This output is reduced by the number and severity of interruptions.

Four types of interruptions affect productivity—communication interruptions, co-worker interruptions, visual interruptions, and sound interruptions. If you can relieve your people of the need to hear and respond to customer telephone calls and spontaneous questions, their productive day will approach a full person day. A quiet and private working environment is the single, most effective thing you can provide to directly improve productivity.

Associated with these interruption factors is the impact of a request to "expedite" a job. As people are pushed, the risk of error increases. When you measure the actual time spent on a job, you must include the time needed to rework mistakes. You should mark up jobs that a customer wants "expedited." This is where the concept of RUSH charges came from.

A useful way to increase productivity is to track service performance time on projects and then pay bonuses for performance in less time with the same high quality. Notice I said, with the same high quality. You don't want to experience wasted time doing rework.

Budgeting Costs by the Hour

With cost and productivity known and monitored, it's possible to develop an hourly expense for each service that your shop provides. This is a key to flat rate pricing. By knowing what it cost to provide a service, you can determine what you should charge to cover your costs plus make a profit on your efforts. Your expense-for-providing-service factor is called a *budgeted hourly cost* (sometimes called *budgeted hourly rate*).

There is a budgeted hourly cost (BHC) for each function that you do in generating billable work. In this section, I'll show you how to develop a BHC for each job function so you can quickly determine how much money you will earn or can negotiate with on every project that you complete.

The idea goes like this: Identify the functions. Identify the costs associated with each function. Determine the time it takes to perform each function. Determine your productivity factor. Calculate the cost per hour for each function at this productivity factor. Determine the units of work output per hour for each function. Calculate an hourly cost per unit of work output for each function. Then identify all of the functions involved in a project. Identify the work units that each function will require. Multiply the total units by the budgeted hourly costs per work unit for each function. Add the materials and other costs associated with the project. Add the total costs for the project. Multiply the result by the profit percentage you want to make. Multiply the total project costs by the return you want to make on any investment to start the business (if you haven't paid this back yet). Add the costs, the profit and the ROI to produce a price that you can quote. Then check industry pricing references to see what competitors are charging. This yields a price range in which you can bid. The process is shown in Figure 2-5. This method is an ideal way to do flat rate pricing.

Identify Functions
  Calculate Cost per Function
    Establish Time to Perform Each
      Productivity Factor
        Cost per Hour Each Function
        Functions Required in Job
          Units of Work per Hour Each Function
          Units X BHC
            Add Other Costs
              Generate Total Budgeted Cost
            Add Profit
            Add ROI
              Price to Bid
                Compare with Competitors
                Select Price to Quote

Fig. 2-5. Flat rate pricing using the budgeted hourly cost method.

Once you've established a budgeted hourly cost for each task in a job, add up the number of work units required, multiply by the budgeted hourly costs for each activity, add material costs such as disks and special rented software, incorporate intangibles such as job turn-around time, design skill, and competitive advantage, and then can calculate a project cost to which profit and return on investment are added to achieve a final selling price. By partitioning any project into functional tasks and applying a budgeted hourly cost to each task you can bid a flat rate on any job.

For example, producing a Home Page could involve receiving text and images on a disk, converting the files into usable form (file conversion), correcting typographical or grammar mistakes in the text (editing), cleaning up graphics, designing a style sheet for the page (design), importing graphics and text into the electronic page (web page layout), and generating a laser printout (proof) for client review and approval. Then uploading the final design to the client's web site. Each of these operations has an associated budgeted hourly cost.

Once all of your operations are identified — keyboarding, file conversion, typography, scanning,, design, layout, proofing, FTP upload and so on, you specify the labor skills and equipment required for each operation. Consider every resource in your business — people, equipment, software, facility, and investment capital. Here is where careful resource management really comes into play. Who do you assign to perform each task? Which equipment should you use? Which web page design program?

Next, identify the annual costs of these resources as allocated to each operation. These costs will be fixed or variable. Then, determine an hourly overhead cost for the shop. You may decide to use a faster designer or faster computer for the job, but calculate costs based on the slowest worker, or computer system.

Each operation or function is a cost category to be budgeted. You determine the number of chargeable hours that each cost category generates. Then, divide the total annual costs for each function by an estimate of the annual billable hours for that operation to get its budgeted hourly cost. Using these, you can price a job based on the combination of the individual hourly rates for each operation.

The more detailed you make your cost breakdown, the easier it is to define tasks and build budgeted hourly costs. The idea is to have the total shop's operating costs partitioned into chargeable activities. Each function is analyzed and production times are established. These times are converted to costs that you budget or allocate to each task. A job will be comprised of several specific tasks. Each task activity has an associated cost category and a budgeted hourly cost.

Once you have your budgeted hourly cost rates, factor in productivity, return on investment, and markup to generate a "basic" price that you can quote. Then look at your competition's prices. Look at the market to estimate the level of demand for this service. Using all three of these factors, establish hourly billing rates for each functional activity. These are the rates that you publish on your counter price sheets or that you quote.

A recent International Prepress Association survey concluded that the best approach for pricing desktop service is to establish a budgeted hourly rate (cost) for each piece or group of equipment worked on. This allocates (budgets) pricing to the hardware and software used to perform a job. Good time assessments on each type of project can help you apply proper markup and establish good budgeted hourly prices.

As work proceeds, record the average times to perform each task. Use these to update your baseline production times. Don't forget "system start-up" and "modified start-up" (re-start) times. Many shops call this "set up" time. They often charge a flat rate for setting a system up to perform a specific service. This is where many "minimum charge" prices come from.

Incorporate start-up and re-start in your final bill. It can take several minutes for your computer system to initialize, run an application program and open in the job that you will be working. The first effort on a job includes setup time. Once the job format is established, then each time that you go back to the job, you must re-start the system, boot up the application program and open the job that were working on. The total time should incorporate these re-start actions.

With budgeted hourly cost rates, you can factor in productivity, return on investment, profit, expected sales, the marketplace and competitive rates to generate a price basis for each task. Then you can break any job into activities and cost the job by tasks with unique rates for each task. It's best to bid a complete job to avoid having a client "nickel-and-dime" you on specific tasks.

Both fixed and variable costs are used in determining your budgeted hourly cost for a particular service or profit center. If you vary the number of hours each day that the service is provided or the profit center is active, fixed costs can have a major impact on the budgeted hourly cost that you calculate. Essentially this means that the more utilization you have, the lower the effect of fixed expenses on your budgeted hourly cost because you spread the fixed expenses out over more operational hours. Essentially the effect of overhead is spread out.

Likewise an under-utilized function or profit center can have a higher budgeted hourly cost (caused by a higher overhead). This can prevent your shop from being competitive in certain service areas.

Depending on industry or custom production standards, budgeted hourly cost techniques can provide an easy way to quickly price a job. Your billing baseline depends on the type of job and the customer. Many new owner-operators initially apply a fixed hourly rate to every service (shop rate). With experience, some develop a unique hourly rate for each service that they provide. Then they fine tune these hourly rates and establish page, image, or word count baselines for pricing.

The budgeted hourly costs shown in the examples that follow are based on our survey. They are for comparison only. You should develop BHCs that are unique to your own shop and then use your own BHCs in generating flat rate prices to quote.

Calculating Budgeted Hourly Cost

The following example shows how to calculate budgeted hourly costs for a small web service business. The shop operates out of a home office and makes $70,000 a year. It has a single employee, the owner-operator. Twenty percent of the home is used strictly for the business.

The business has been operating for one year. The owner takes two weeks paid vacation (including the national holidays) and works 2,000 hours a year (50 weeks, 40 hours a week). The sources of income for the business can be partitioned into:

Web Site Design	20%	$14,000
Keyboarding	10%	$7,000
Scanning	10%	7,000
Web Page Layout	50%	35,000
Laser Proof Printing	5%	3,000
Uploading Pages	5%	4,000
		$70,000

To perform these functions, the owner purchased a computer, a laser printer and a scanner with word processing, scanning. scan touch-up and Web page layout and editing software. Total investment was

$2,500 for a computer, $1,000 for a flatbed scanner, $1,500 for a laser printer for proofs, $375 for a word processor, $500 for scan touch-up software, $500 for Web site design software and $375 for Web page editing, browser and FTP upload software.

Determining a budgeted hourly cost for each keyboarding, scanning, page layout, proof printing and FTP upload involves identifying fixed and variable costs, and specifying and allocating a baseline production standard to each activity. Table 2-2 shows the fixed and variable costs associated with this business.

Table 2-2. Fixed and variable cost breakdown.

```
FIXED COSTS
Rent (Indirect/Overhead)
    20 sq/ft @ $2.50 per sq ft per month
    = $50/month                                         $600
Basic Utilities (Indirect/Overhead)
    @ 10% of household costs
Telephone-$50/month @ 10% (600/yr x 0.1 = $60/yr)
    Gas-$11/month @ 10% (132/yr x 0.1 = $13/yr)
    Electricity-$30/month @ 10% (360/yr x 0.1 = $36/yr)
    Water-$9/month @ 10% (108/yr x 0.1 = $11/yr)         120
Property Insurance (Indirect/Overhead)
    $300/yr @ 10% = $30/yr                                30
Taxes (Indirect/Overhead) 11%                          7,500
Depreciation (Indirect/Overhead) 20%/yr                1,000
Hardware Not Depreciated (Indirect) 100%               5,000
Software to Run Business (Indirect/Overhead)           1,000
Business Documentation (Indirect/Overhead)               100
Office Cleaning (Indirect/Overhead)                      360
Grounds Keeping (Indirect/Overhead)                       48
Vehicle Insurance (Indirect/Overhead)                  1,200
Vehicle Purchase Loan (Indirect/Overhead)              4,800
                                                      ======
            Total Annual Fixed Cost:                 $20,758
```

Table 2-2. (continued)

VARIABLE COSTS	
Marketing Expenses (Indirect/Overhead) 3%	$6,500
Advertising Expenses (Indirect/Overhead) 3%	5,100
Salary - Owner-Operator (Indirect/Overhead)	15,600
Salary - Owner-Operator Working on Jobs (Direct)	15,600
Wages - Part Time Help (Direct)	1,000
Cost of Goods Sold (Direct)	100
Supplies Used to Do Job (Direct)	100
Fringe Benefits (Indirect)	2,100
Vehicle Operation (Indirect)	500
Total Variable Cost:	$46,600
TOTAL ANNUAL FIXED & VARIABLE COSTS	$67,358

Notice in our example, that this home business made a profit of $2,642 on the $70,000 income—about four percent.

At first blush, you'd think that the owner's salary should be a fixed cost. But many entrepreneurs defer taking a salary while building their business. Even after they're operating well, if the work load decreases during economic declines, independent shop owners usually reduce their own salaries first to keep the business going. Thus the owner-operator's salary is a variable cost.

Based on Table 2-2, let's calculate a budgeted hourly cost for each activity performed by this home office entrepreneur. The steps are to first design the web site, keyboard the text, scan the graphics, layout each web page, print proofs of each page and then upload the page and image files to the client's site. Table 2-3 shows how to budget costs for web site design. Tables 2-4, 2-5, 2-6 and 2-7 show the BHC for keyboarding, scanning, web page layout, laser proof printing, and FTP uploading to the client's site.

Table 2-3. Budgeted hourly cost for site design.

BUDGETED HOURLY COSTS
Web Site Design

INVESTMENT - Cost of computer system used:	$2,500
INVESTMENT: Cost of software used:	500
SPACE needed (square feet):	20
PEOPLE - Percent of time person is involved:	100%
HOURLY PAY: Typical pay $7	
Since this is a one-person business, the owner wants $15 an hour for all work performed, so $15 is used for calculating the budgeted hourly cost.	$15
ANNUAL HOURS (40 hrs/wk, 50 wks)	2,000
TOTAL HOURS PAID (yearly)	2,080
FIXED (NON VARIABLE) COSTS	
Space Rent ($2.50/sq ft, 20 sq ft)	600
Depreciation (computer system 5 yrs @ 20% per year)	500
System Insurance ($4/M of investment)	10
Basic Utilities (20%)	120
Other fixed costs ($)	10
TOTAL FIXED COSTS	$1,240
VARIABLE COSTS	
Wages - Direct Labor ($15/hr @ 2,080 hrs/yr)	31,200
Pension Fund (@ 2% of labor)	624
Employee Health/Medical insurance (@$131/month)	1,572
Payroll Taxes (@11.35% of labor costs)	3,541
Workers Comp Insurance ($3/M of labor costs = 0.3% of labor costs)	94
Task-Related added utility costs	36
Direct Supplies (take as 1% of fixed costs and wage costs)	324
Repairs & Maintenance (@2% of hardware costs)	50
Software upgrades (@10% of investment)	50
Other variable costs	25
TOTAL VARIABLE COSTS	$37,516

(continued on next page)

Table 2-3. BHC site design (continued).

OTHER COSTS	
Other Misc. Costs	
(@10% fixed & variable costs)	3,876
Sales, General & Administrative Costs	
(overhead = 19%)	11,627
TOTAL OTHER COSTS	$15,502
TOTAL ALL COSTS	$54,259
TOTAL HOURLY COSTS	$27.13/hr
BUDGETED COST/HOUR (50% Productive)	$54.26
UNIT OF WORK (2 web pages per hour)	2 pages/hour
COST PER PAGE (50% Productive)	$27.13/web page

Notice in the table that wages are placed under the Variable Cost category (even though they come under Fixed Cost from an annual budget perspective). This is because various employees (with different hourly pay rates) can be assigned to do this task. It really doesn't matter in the end because both fixed and variable costs are totaled to get the final BHC figure. If the owner hires outside help, use the freelance hourly wage to calculate cost factors. BHC is an ideal spreadsheet application.

The "Other Misc Cost" in Table 2-3 and the tables that follow is called a *"margin of safety"* or *MOS*. The arbitrary MOS number is a cushion, a "fudge factor" that is used to compensate for unforeseen costs. In the example, I used 10% of the fixed and variable costs for the MOS. Some owners use 10% of revenue as the MOS. It's included because experienced operators know that you'll always need "just a little more" the next time you calculate budgeted hourly costs.

Table 2-4. Budgeted hourly cost for keyboarding.

BUDGETED HOURLY COSTS
Keyboarding

INVESTMENT - Cost of computer system used:	$2,500
INVESTMENT: Cost of software used:	375
SPACE needed (square feet):	20
PEOPLE - Percent of time person is involved:	100%
HOURLY PAY:	$15
ANNUAL HOURS (40 hrs/wk, 50 wks)	2,000
TOTAL HOURS PAID (yearly)	2,080

FIXED (NON VARIABLE) COSTS

Space Rent ($2.50/sq ft, 20 sq ft)	600
Depreciation (computer system, 5 yrs @ 20% per year)	500
System Insurance ($4/M of investment)	10
Basic Utilities (20%)	120
Other fixed costs ($)	10
TOTAL FIXED COSTS	$1,240

VARIABLE COSTS

Wages - Direct Labor ($15/hr @ 2,080 hrs/yr)	31,200
Pension Fund (@ 2% of labor)	624
Employee Health/Medical insurance (@$131/month)	1,572
Payroll Taxes (@11.35% of labor costs)	3,541
Workers Comp Insurance ($3/M of labor costs = 0.3% of labor costs)	94
Task-Related added utility costs	36
Direct Supplies (take as 1% of fixed costs and wage costs)	324
Repairs & Maintenance (@2% of hardware costs)	50
Software upgrades (@10% of investment)	38
Other variable costs	25
TOTAL VARIABLE COSTS	$37,504

(continued on next page)

Table 2-4. BHC keyboarding (continued)

OTHER COSTS	
Other Misc. Costs	
(@10% fixed & variable costs)	3,874
Sales, General & Administrative Costs	
(overhead = 19%)	11,623
TOTAL OTHER COSTS	$15,497
TOTAL ALL COSTS	$54,241
TOTAL HOURLY COSTS	$27.12/hr
BUDGETED COST/HOUR (50% Productive)	$54.24
UNIT OF WORK OUTPUT PER HOUR:	
50 wpm, 250 char/line, 15k char/hr,	
1500 char/pg ==>	10 pages/hour
COST PER PAGE (50% Productive)	$5.42 per page

Table 2-5. Budgeted hourly cost for scanning.

BUDGETED HOURLY COSTS
Scanning

INVESTMENT - Cost of computer system used:	$5,000
INVESTMENT: Cost of software used:	500
SPACE needed (square feet):	20
PEOPLE - Percent of time person is involved:	100%
HOURLY PAY:	$15
ANNUAL HOURS (40 hrs/wk, 50 wks)	2,000
TOTAL HOURS PAID (yearly)	2,080
FIXED (NON VARIABLE) COSTS	
Space Rent ($2.50/sq ft, 20 sq ft)	600
Depreciation	
(computer system, 5 yrs @ 20% per year)	1,000
System Insurance ($4/M of investment)	20
Basic Utilities (20%)	120

Other fixed costs ($)	10
TOTAL FIXED COSTS	**$1,750**

VARIABLE COSTS

Wages - Direct Labor ($15/hr @ 2,080 hrs/yr)	31,200
Pension Fund (@ 2% of labor)	624
Employee Health/Medical insurance (@$131/month)	1,572
Payroll Taxes (@11.35% of labor costs)	3,541
Workers Comp Insurance ($3/M of labor costs = 0.3% of labor costs)	94
Task-Related added utility costs	36
Direct Supplies (take as 1% of fixed costs and wage costs)	330
Repairs & Maintenance (@2% of hardware costs)	100
Software upgrades (@10% of investment)	50
Other variable costs	25
TOTAL VARIABLE COSTS	**$37,571**

OTHER COSTS

Other Misc. Costs (@10% fixed & variable costs)	3,932
Sales, General & Administrative Costs (overhead = 19%)	11,796
TOTAL OTHER COSTS	**$15,729**
TOTAL ALL COSTS	**$55,050**
TOTAL HOURLY COSTS	$27.53/hr
BUDGETED COST/HOUR (50% Productive)	$55.05

UNIT OF WORK OUTPUT PER HOUR:
5 scan pages (8.5 x 11) per hour   450 sq in per hour

COST PER SQUARE INCH (50% Productive) $0.12/sq in

Table 2-6. BHC for web page layout.

BUDGETED HOURLY COSTS
Web Page Layout

INVESTMENT - Cost of computer system used:	$2,500
INVESTMENT: Cost of software used:	375
SPACE needed (square feet):	20
PEOPLE - Percent of time person is involved:	100%
HOURLY PAY:	$15
ANNUAL HOURS (40 hrs/wk, 50 wks)	2,000
TOTAL HOURS PAID (yearly)	2,080

FIXED (NON VARIABLE) COSTS

Space Rent ($2.50/sq ft, 20 sq ft)	600
Depreciation	
(computer system, 5 yrs @ 20% per year)	500
System Insurance ($4/M of investment)	10
Basic Utilities (20%)	120
Other fixed costs ($)	10
TOTAL FIXED COSTS	$1,240

VARIABLE COSTS

Wages - Direct Labor ($15/hr @ 2,080 hrs/yr)	31,200
Pension Fund (@ 2% of labor)	624
Employee Health/Medical insurance	
(@$131/month)	1,572
Payroll Taxes (@11.35% of labor costs)	3,541
Workers Comp Insurance	
($3/M of labor costs = 0.3% of labor costs)	94
Task-Related added utility costs	36
Direct Supplies	
(take as 1% of fixed costs and wage costs)	324
Repairs & Maintenance (@2% of hardware costs)	50
Software upgrades (@10% of investment)	38
Other variable costs	25
TOTAL VARIABLE COSTS	$37,504

OTHER COSTS

Other Misc. Costs (@10% fixed & variable costs)	3,874

Sales, General & Administrative Costs (overhead = 19%)	11,623
TOTAL OTHER COSTS	<u>15,497</u>
TOTAL ALL COSTS	<u>$54,241</u>
TOTAL HOURLY COSTS	$27.12/hr
BUDGETED COST/HOUR (50% Productive)	$54.24
UNIT OF WORK OUTPUT PER HOUR:	
Can layout 0.9 Web pages per hour	0.9 pages/hour
COST PER PAGE (50% Productive)	$60.27/Web page

Table 2-7. BHC for printing laser proofs.

BUDGETED HOURLY COSTS
Laser Web Page Proof Printing

INVESTMENT - Cost of computer system used:	$3,000
INVESTMENT: Cost of software used:	0
SPACE needed (square feet):	20
PEOPLE - Percent of time person is involved:	100%
HOURLY PAY:	$15
ANNUAL HOURS (40 hrs/wk, 50 wks)	2,000
TOTAL HOURS PAID (yearly)	2,080
FIXED (NON VARIABLE) COSTS	
Space Rent ($2.50/sq ft, 20 sq ft)	600
Depreciation	
(computer system, 5 yrs @ 20% per year)	600
System Insurance ($4/M of investment)	12
Basic Utilities (20%)	120
Other fixed costs ($)	10
TOTAL FIXED COSTS	<u>$1,342</u>
VARIABLE COSTS	
Wages - Direct Labor ($15/hr @ 2,080 hrs/yr)	31,200

Table 2-7. BHC laser proof (continued)

Pension Fund (@ 2% of labor)	624
Employee Health/Medical insurance (@$131/month)	1,572
Payroll Taxes (@11.35% of labor costs)	3,541
Workers Comp Insurance ($3/M of labor costs = 0.3% of labor costs)	94
Task-Related added utility costs	36
Direct Supplies (take as 1% of fixed costs and wage costs)	325
Repairs & Maintenance (@2% of hardware costs)	60
Software upgrades (@10% of investment)	0
Other variable costs	25
TOTAL VARIABLE COSTS	$37,477

OTHER COSTS

Other Misc. Costs (@10% fixed & variable costs)	3,882
Sales, General & Administrative Costs (overhead = 19%)	11,646
TOTAL OTHER COSTS	$15,528
TOTAL ALL COSTS	$54,347
TOTAL HOURLY COSTS	$27.17/hr
BUDGETED COST/HOUR (50% Productive)	$54.35

UNIT OF WORK OUTPUT PER HOUR:
Can print 360 pages per hour   360 pages/hour

COST PER PAGE (50% Productive) $0.15 per page

Table 2-8. Budgeted hourly cost for FTP upload to the client's server site.

BUDGETED HOURLY COSTS
Upload Web Page to Site

INVESTMENT - Cost of computer system used:	$2,500
INVESTMENT: Cost of software used:	375
SPACE needed (square feet):	20
PEOPLE - Percent of time person is involved:	100%
HOURLY PAY:	$15
ANNUAL HOURS (40 hrs/wk, 50 wks)	2,000
TOTAL HOURS PAID (yearly)	2,080

FIXED (NON VARIABLE) COSTS

Space Rent ($2.50/sq ft, 20 sq ft)	600
Depreciation (computer system, 5 yrs @ 20% per year)	500
System Insurance ($4/M of investment)	10
Basic Utilities (20%)	120
Other fixed costs ($)	10
TOTAL FIXED COSTS	$1,240

VARIABLE COSTS

Wages - Direct Labor ($15/hr @ 2,080 hrs/yr)	31,200
Pension Fund (@ 2% of labor)	624
Employee Health/Medical insurance (@$131/month)	1,572
Payroll Taxes (@11.35% of labor costs)	3,541
Workers Comp Insurance ($3/M of labor costs = 0.3% of labor costs)	94
Task-Related added utility costs	36
Direct Supplies (take as 1% of fixed costs and wage costs)	324
Repairs & Maintenance (@2% of hardware costs)	50
Software upgrades (@10% of investment)	38
Other variable costs	25
TOTAL VARIABLE COSTS	$37,504

Table 2-8. BHC FTP upload (continued)

OTHER COSTS
Other Misc. Costs
   (@10% fixed & variable costs)   3,874
Sales, General & Administrative Costs
   (overhead = 19%)   11,623
   TOTAL OTHER COSTS $15,497

TOTAL ALL COSTS $54,241

TOTAL HOURLY COSTS $27.12/hr

BUDGETED COST/HOUR (50% Productive) $54.24

UNIT OF WORK OUTPUT PER HOUR:
   Can FTP upload 12 files per hour   12 files per hour

FTP COST PER FILE (50% Productive) $4.52 per file

The total costs for design, keyboarding, scanning, layout, laser proof printing and FTP uploading of the final files of a single Web page (at 50% productivity and an hourly wage of $15) are shown below.

web page design	$27.13/web page	(2 pgs/ hr)
keyboarding	$5.42/page	(10 pgs/ hr)
scanning	$0.12/sq inch	(5 scans/hr)
web page layout	$60.27/page	(0.9 pgs/ hr)
laser proof printout	$0.15/page	(360 pgs/ hr)
FTP upload to site	$4.52/file	(12 files/hr)

These are budgeted costs. After adding all the cost for the whole project, you add materials costs, profit and return on any initial investment that you may have incurred to start the company. This produces a reference from which to price. The final price is set to what the market will bear. Let me say again. The final price is set to what the market will bear. Charge all you can charge.

Example 1 - Single Home Page Site

Now let's cost out a typical Web services project. The job involves designing a simple Home Page for a client. The client will provide a draft design comprised of text only. No GIF or JPEG images will be included. There will be an e-mail link inserted at the bottom of the Home Page.

Three draft designs will be generated. The client will select the design of choice. Then your company will recommend the Internet Service Provider (ISP) best suited for the location of the client, obtain a domain name for the client, install Netscape on the client's computer and FTP the Home Page up to the client's web site on the ISP server. Table 2-9 describes the project and its associated costs.

Table 2-9. Activities Associated with a Web Home Page project.

PROJECT: Home Page Design & Upload to Site

Direct Project Costs

Related Costs (billed at $50 per hour Shop Rate)

	Hours	Total
- kick-off meeting with a client	0.5	25.00
- corresponding	0.1	5.00
- communicating on the telephone	0.1	5.00
- answering questions by phone	0.2	10.00
- communicating by fax or modem	0.1	5.00
- follow-up meeting 1	0.3	15.00
- follow-up meeting 2	0.3	15.00
- draft design submission meeting	0.3	15.00
- final page design meeting	0.3	15.00
- travel time	0.0	0.00
- scheduling work	0.1	5.00
- recording actions performed	0.1	5.00

Table 2-9. Activities (continued)

- recording times spent on job	0.1	5.00
- invoice client and get paid	0.1	5.00
	TOTAL:	$130.00

The message here is that there IS a COST to each meeting, each phone call and each action taken related to a project. These cost should be incorporated into your project price.

Direct Costs - Creative (Simple)

	Hours	Rate	Total
- conceptual development	0.5	50	25.00
- organizing web page design	0.2	50	10.00
- web page style sheet	0.2	50	10.00
- content generation	0.4	50	20.00
- illustrations and artwork	0.2	50	10.00
- masthead graphic with logo	0.2	50	10.00
		TOTAL:	$65.00

Direct Costs - Production

	Hours	Rate	Total
- system power-up	0.1	50	$5.00
- convert files to useable form	0.0	50	0.00
- convert data for importing/placing	0.0	50	0.00
- job preparation and setup	0.1	50	5.00
- download client draft design	0.0	50	0.00
- keyboard text	0.2	54	10.80
- proofread, edit and spell check	0.1	50	5.00
- typography	0.1	50	5.00
- scan art and photographs	0.0	55	0.00
- image manipulation and retouch	0.0	55	0.00
- implement page design (layout)	0.2	54	10.80
- place text and graphics (layout)	0.0	54	0.00
- place clip art (layout)	0.0	54	0.00
- place CD-ROM photos (layout)	0.0	54	0.00
- HTML editing (layout)	0.2	54	10.80
- link graphics files to Home Page	0.2	54	10.80

- print first draft; review and edit	0.2	50	10.00
- adjust / modify layout	0.2	54	10.00
- print final proof for sign-off	0.2	50	10.00
- put Home Page & link files in dir	0.2	54	10.80
- contact ISP	0.1	50	5.00
- register client's domain name	0.1	50	5.00
- register client's e-mail address	0.1	50	5.00
- installing ISP software	0.2	50	10.00
- upload web pages to ISP server	0.2	54	10.80
- check site with other browsers	0.2	50	10.00
		TOTAL:	$149.80

Cost of Goods & Services Sold

- laser printer paper (4 sheets @ 15¢ each)	0.60
- printer toner (4 pgs, 80% coverage @ 50¢ ea)	2.00
- file conversion software (already have)	0.00
- special typefaces and fonts (already have)	0.00
- photographs (used freeware photos)	0.00
- purchased clip-art / illustrations (already had)	0.00
- outsourcing part of project tasks	0.00
- microfloppy disk (1 disk @ $1 each)	1.00
- telephone charges (5 calls @ 25¢ each)	1.00
- modem connect time (1.5 hrs @ local rate)	0.00
- travel expense (52 miles @ 31¢ per mile)	16.12
- postage (1 priority mailing)	3.00
- facsimile (fax) toner used (two faxes at $1 ea)	2.00
TOTAL:	$25.72

Total Related Costs:	130.00
Total Creative Costs:	65.00
Total Production Costs:	149.80
Total Out-of-Pocket Expenses:	25.72
Shop Overhead Expenses (4.4 hrs @ $22)	96.80

TOTAL PROJECT COST	**$ 467.32**

Usually, indirect and innovative times are billed at an hourly rate. Machine production times are often billed on a per page basis. This example was for a simple design of a Home Page. The problem here is that

$467.32 cost is more than the market price for a typical Home Page and connect support. This suggests that the owner should schedule fewer meetings (perhaps only a kick-off and then fax drafts of the designs). By doing this, the price should come down to around $300, closer to the current market price for a Home Page.

Next, we'll analyze a cost estimate for a complex six-page web site.

Example 2 - Six Page Site Design

Once you develop your own spreadsheet estimator, you'll find yourself using it more and more. Here is another example of how careful specifications can help you partition even complex projects into fully costed and manageable tasks.

PROJECT TITLE: Company XYZ Web Site

Description:
The site will consist of a Home Page with links to five other pages: a page describing the company, a page describing the products and services, a "what's new" page, a question and answer page and a feedback/order page.

Information Required
Characters to be keyboarded
Text characters or # final pages to proofread
Scans (grouped by size and difficulty)
Scans needing retouch
Pages to be designed
Pages for layout (group by complexity)

Specifications
1 Home Page
5 linked web pages

2 colors each page
1 graphic each page
1 banner graphic for Home Page
1800 characters to be keyboarded
4 graphic line art images to scan
2 graphics clip art images to link
1 e-mail address to link

Customer Supplies
1. Concept drawing of each page
2. Hand written text ideas
3. Line art drawings (4) on vellum (to be scanned)
4. Home Page banner design (image file to be placed)

Shop Provides
1. Printed draft of design for proofing (6 web pages)
2. Final design on disk
3. Printed hard copy of final design.
4. Final design uploaded to ISP site

Questions to be Answered
1. Who corrects errors found during preflight?
2. Who holds copyright to final site design?

Actions Required
I. Design the site
  A. Develop Home Page
    1. Place and link custom masthead graphic file
    2. Add menu button links
      a. Text-only links
      b. Custom graphic buttons or image map
    3. Place and link graphic image file
    4. HTML text formatting and Home Page layout

B. Develop Sub Pages
  Company Profile, Products & Services,
  What's New, FAQ, Order Form
  1. HTML text formatting
  2. Web page identification icon graphic
  3. Side-to-side navigation bar
     a. text-only links
     b. custom graphic buttons
     c. HTML text formatting of Industry
        Links page
  4. Design Feedback/Order form
  5. Products/Services menu links
     a. text-only links
     b. custom graphic buttons
C. Link Pages and Images

II. Place information content at client's site
  A. FTP upload pages to server

III. Other Activities
  A. Meetings & Consultations

Activities Required	# Web Pages at Each Difficulty Level		
	75%	100%	125%
Keyboarding	6		
Proofreading	6		
Scanning		4	
Retouch		2	
Design	2	2	2
Layout	2	2	2
Laser Printing	2	2	2
FTP Upload	(all page files)		

Table 2-10 shows the cost estimate for this complex 6-page web site.

Table 2-10. Cost Estimate for Six-Page Site.

Cost & Production Calculations

Activity/Complexity	Output	Cost	Est. Time
Keyboarding			
100%	6 pages @ $5.42/pg	$32.52	0.6 hrs
Proofreading			
75%	6 pages @ $13.50/pg	$81.00	0.5 hrs
Scanning			
100%	4 scans @ $1.00/scn	$4.00	0.8 hrs
Retouch			
100%	2 images @ $15.00/ea	$30.00	1.0 hrs
Design			
75%	2 pages @ $20.35/pg	$40.70	1.5 hrs
100%	2 pages @ $27.13/pg	$54.26	2.0 hrs
125%	2 pages @ $33.91/pg	$67.82	2.5 hrs
Layout & Link Files			
75%	2 pages @ $45.20/pg	$90.40	1.5 hrs
100%	2 pages @ $60.27/pg	$120.54	2.0 hrs
125%	2 pages @ $75.34/pg	$150.68	2.5 hrs
Laser Print Proofs			
75%	2 pages @ $0.11/pg	$0.22	0.8 min
100%	2 pages @ $0.15/pg	$0.30	1.0 min
125%	2 pages @ $0.19/pg	$0.38	1.3 min
FTP Upload to Site			
	6 page files @ $4.52 per file	$27.12	0.5 hrs
	7 image files @ $4.52/file	$31.64	0.6 hrs
	TOTALS:	$731.58	19.10 hrs

TOTAL COST ESTIMATE:	$731.58
TOTAL TIME INVOLVED:	19.1 hours
AVERAGE COST PER HOUR:	$38.30

NOTE: This estimate is for labor only. Materials are charged extra.

The numbers in Table 2-10 aren't what's important. The key is the process. This is one way to generate an estimate on a job. To this estimate, you add profit and return on any investment to get the final target price that you quote. In this case, adding a 10 percent profit (assume your initial investment has been paid back) results in $804.74 that you quote.

How Costs Vary During a Project

There's no question that your cost basis changes during a project. As you use more time on the equipment, your electrical and telephone use increases. You also incur additional costs in paying for part time help. Work pick up and delivery, and trips to buy materials adds to your gas and vehicle expense. Then you'll use more paper, printer toner, or other materials in conjunction with a project. This will increase your project costs. These variable costs should be charged directly to the project.

If you buy new equipment or software upgrades, installation and checkout costs will average 2.5-10% of your total cost. The actual costs depend on system complexity, the hardware and software mix required, and staff involvement. These costs should be amortized over the life of your equipment and be charged to each job proportionately. Be certain to charge the fixed costs associated with work on a particular project directly to that project. The more fixed costs that you can bill to a project, the easier the pain when you evaluate and track your overhead costs.

Summary

This chapter provided a detailed look at cost and how cost is used to establish price. In the next chapter, you'll see how the marketplace affects the prices that you ask.

3
Marketplace and Price

"It seems that everybody in the business world just has to have a Web site these days."

In the Web service business, there doesn't appear to be a limit to the size of your market. Each time we attempt to place bounds on the size of this industry, new opportunities emerge. LANs and WANs expanded to Internet, and now Intranets are the rage. Everyone wants faster communication. Everyone wants to conduct business anytime and everywhere. And many don't know how to work in this new medium.

The Market for Web Services

To be successful in this business, you've got to know your market and the potential for each service that you're contemplating. In this chapter, you'll learn how to analyze the market potential for Web services.

During research on this book, I spent many hours on-line determining the number of companies who have actively established Web sites and are now promoting their wares electronically. This is precisely what you should do. Study the market, estimate demand and then look at competitors. With costs, the market, and your competition understood, you can then develop a strategy and a business model for getting your share of the gold.

Market Analysis

Make a thorough study of the potential in the Web service industry. Look at advertisements, product announcements, corporate annual reports. Are the non-technical companies establishing a Web presence? (Most technical companies know the value of the Internet and are already on-line.)

How many people are buying Web services? How many are located in your immediate area? What's the demographic trend for the future? What's the purchasing power of your market? What prices are customers willing to pay? Who are your potential customers? What businesses are they in? What businesses will still be here in five years?

Recent magazine articles report that Internet commerce is exploding. The big winners are tapping the on-line community to cross-market their sites and increase visits. With low capital requirements, Web-based businesses are springing up everywhere. Not all will succeed. But they want the presence. They smell the money to be made. It's your challenge to find them and help them do just that — make more money. By doing so, you'll gain great profit yourself.

According to Bruce Judson, author of *NetMarketing: How Your Business Can Profit From the Online Revolution*, over 5,000 new commercial sites appear every month. He says that most of these don't have a marketing and promotion plan for their sites. You could be the person who helps these entrepreneurs get their sites noticed and visitors coming back to buy again.

Today, when younger people want information, they don't look in a newspaper. They look on-line. And these young buyers will look for products on-line before they'll look for products in a printed catalog. The future is clear. Generations X, Y, and Z (or whatever you choose to call young up-and-comers) will be buying and selling over the Internet. The speed and convenience of electronic buying and selling will significantly extend the reach of any business entrepreneur. So your market is huge. HUGE! And it's diverse. Just about any type of business is a candidate for on-line commerce. You are the resource that can help them make commerce happen.

Market Type

How you decide to price your Web service often depends on the type of market in which you plan to compete. If there are many Web service providers in your area already, you take a different approach to pricing than you will if you operate in a community in which you are the only business of this type.

Basically, there are four types of markets in which you can operate—monopolistic, oligopolistic, purely competitive, and monopolistic competitive. Don't worry about remembering these terms. I'll simplify their meanings shortly. Just accept that it's important to know the market environment before you decide where and how you want to operate your own business.

In the jargon of economists, a *"monopolistic"* market is one in which there is one seller, many buyers and no price competition. You operate the only shop in your area and you have many customers. The nearest competitor is in the next town so you don't really have a price competitor to deal with. You get to service all the businesses in your own locale.

When you're the "only game in town" you have an ideal situation, but you must still price carefully so you don't tempt buyers to select other alternatives for the service they need (e.g., hire students, or hire support from out of town).

You also don't want another entrepreneur to see value in starting a competitive business in your neighborhood.

Therefore, price your services to cover costs and return good profit without encouraging competition.

A market in which there are few sellers, plenty of buyers and price is based on what competitors do is called *"oligopolistic."* In this market, the high cost to get set up keeps the participants low. So, few people operate this type of business. For those that do, all the competitors offer a similar product, so the pricing strategy depends on not only what the customers prefer, but also on what the competitors do.

If this is your market, reducing your prices will cause your competition to reduce their prices. Raise your prices, and they may or may not raise theirs. If they don't, you may have to retract your price increase just to keep customers.

Now if there are many buyers, many sellers and price is relatively the same among sellers, you are in a *"purely competitive"* market. The service is the same, so you can't charge more than your competitor because a customer knows that the same service is available for a lower price elsewhere in town. This makes both buyer and seller price-takers rather than price-makers.

The inability to offer a different service, means that all of the sellers must price the same. Your only advantage is to be where most of the customers go to shop. Here it's a game of street traffic and exposure.

The only way to get away from a purely competitive market is to offer additional services to make you different. The homogeneous services become essentially lost leaders that are used to attract business to other higher-margin services.

For example, there are thousands of Internet Service Providers, and prices for site hosting are within a narrow range. This has driven many undercapitalized service providers out of business. Those that survive, know that you make your money on differentiation. You make money by providing unique services that people crave. And this puts you into the fourth type of market—monopolistic competitive.

Finally, a market in which there are many buyers, many sellers and yet many different prices, is called *"monopolistic-competitive."* I believe that this is the type of market in which you operate. Here you can succeed and have the most fun. This market is personified by service differentiation. You try for maximum differentiation so you can achieve maximum profit. You offer unique Web site designs, you provide site publicizing and Web marketing consultation. You help generate new content and guide your customers to implement what works in attracting and holding electronic customers. You become different and distinct from your competitor.

The customer determines price so pricing analysis and strategy become important. This is where goodwill, advertising, capability, and all the other aspects of business can have the most affect. For most of us, this is the market in which we want to operate. But how big is this market?

Market Size

If you plan to operate in a small town, and serve only the local businesses, you could find that your market is not large enough to make your shop succeed. Two sales a week at $100 each won't pay the rent and feed the family too. You will have to attract business from other areas by advertising outside the county, state, or your national borders. Every entrepreneur seeks the largest market with the least competition.

We've found that Web service providers can be located anywhere. They operate from large and small communities, and they aren't afraid to seek business from anywhere in the world. During research on this book, we noted a large number of Web service providers operating from remote areas of Canada and in faraway sites such as Australia and Hong Kong.

One colleague that I met operates a Web design and publishing business in Hawaii. She advertises in national publications and on the Internet and draws business from all over the world. Yet she operates from her condo on an island thousands of miles from the mainland.

The whole world is literally an open market for Web service today. It's no problem to design a site for a client that you never meet in person and to upload the files to an ISP that you also have never met in person. On a daily basis, my company shares word processing, page layout, and image files with printers located thousands of miles from our office. The global village is real.

Thus, your market is the whole planet. There are several dozen countries actively supporting Internet commerce and more getting Internet-capable every month. As other countries come on-line, they become ripe orchards for picking profitable financial fruit. They need your services. And they will pay the going rate to get it. Do an Internet search on Web service and look at where new companies are located. It's an eye-opener!

How The Economy Affects Market Size

Fifty years ago, Abraham Maslow developed a hierarchy of needs to describe people and what they perceive as important. A similar hierarchy of needs can be developed based on the economy. Buyers look at a service based on personal need. The level of this need can rise or fall depending on current situations, future plans, current finances, and the economic outlook.

As the economy sours, most people conserve more and reduce spending. They increase bargain shopping, select less expensive solutions, and put off major purchases.

The response of many service providers is to cut prices, extend credit, and offer more for less as they try to stimulate sales. They alter their services to provide lower-cost alternatives. They cut the frills, unbundle the services, and may also offer self-directed Web page generation options.

As the rate of inflation increases, buying power declines and shoppers become even more price sensitive. So businesses stress lower prices and better values. The rate of inflation strongly influences how customers react to price. The economy often determines perceived need.

How Perceived Value Affects Market Size

Your service can command a higher price if it's marketed as different and of premium quality. Purchasing decisions are often driven by the emotional and psychological character of the buyer. After committing to a sale, many buyers use logic to rationalize the wisdom of their decision. They were drawn to your shop by the value that they perceived in your services. Once they buy, you can help by telling them that they made a wise choice. This justifies their decision.

By being considered preeminent in your field, you can successfully charge a "premium price." In this case, your "premium price" is an aggressive advertisement for quality. However, you must deliver on the perception. If you get tainted with bad press, your image and prestige will suffer. So will your sales.

When a customer really likes a job that you did, you can increase your asking price next time and they'll still buy. This added price is the *"WOW"* content. Price is really what a customer is willing to pay.

If customers will pay more, then most retailers charge more. The McDonald's fast food restaurant chain calls this *"value pricing."* They generate a "value menu" as a long term phenomenon rather than simply use it as a tactic to meet competition. McDonald's knows what customers really prefer. They set higher margins on french fries and soft drinks because these are the most common sales that accompany combination meals and sandwich orders.

Likewise, you could set higher rates for CGI and Java programming because these are perceived as more intense and requiring more skills than traditional Home Page design. You can also set higher rates for consulting on Web marketing than you can for site design consulting because the former implies increased profits.

How Esthetics and Location Affect Market Size

There is a distinct difference in how some customers perceive a business that operates out of a garage, out of a "hole-in-the-wall" strip center, or out of a professional business complex.

When a customer comes to you, esthetics and location become important in how you price your products and services. Each of these three locations can be a successful business. But each may cater to a different customer mix. That "mix" depends on where your customers are located.

The advantage that you enjoy is that Web service providers can operate anywhere. They are typically one or two person businesses and operate out of a home. Web service is the fastest growing home business in America. It is also rapidly growing in Canada.

Therefore, decide how you want to target your prospective market. If you only want to service geographically distant customers, then you don't have to worry abut having an outside office. You can operate out of your home office and wear your jeans and sweat shirt to work. If you plan to physically meet with your clients, you can still work out of your home, but you will arrange meetings at the client's location. In every case, you must portray professionalism and expertise. Therefore, select a customer base, learn all you can about them, and market accordingly.

How Government Regulations Affect Market Size

Pricing directly affects both consumers and businesspeople, so local, state, and federal regulations have been implemented to keep customers and competitors from being served unfairly.

Before you start a business, and certainly while you operate your business, you must be aware of the laws and ordinances that affect how you can function. The number of regulations that you must deal with directly affects how many competitors you will have.

Your local Chamber of Commerce and government offices can help you determine the local, state, and federal regulations that you must follow. Each state has its own version of an Unfair Sales Practices Act that limits the mark-ups you can place on certain items. You can charge more, but not less than specified mark-ups allow. These "minimum mark-up" laws still allow sales of old or out-dated products, but they are designed to protect small businesses by forcing discounters to apply at least a minimum mark-up to their products. This lets a small operator remain competitive with a larger operation.

In 1936, the federal government passed the Robinson-Patman Act to prevent price discrimination. This act makes it illegal to charge a lower price to one customer than you charge to another similar customer. You should not induce, give, or receive discriminatory prices. What you charge (or pay) must be consistent for all. For example, you can't give a discount to one party without offering the same discount to everyone else. This helps you when large retailers demand a wholesale discount even though they may purchase in small quantity. Just quote Robinson-Patman.

This Act does enable cooperative advertising and promotions as long as the same opportunities are offered to all customers on proportionally the same terms.

There are two provisions in the Act that may appear discriminatory, but are accepted. The first allows you to charge one customer a lower price if your purpose is to meet the same low price offered by a competitor. Thus, a customer who brings you an ad for the same services offered by a competitor at a lower price can realize a savings if you are willing to lower your price to match the competitor's price. You can meet a competitor's lower price without violating the intent of the Act.

The second provision lets you price a product differently between buyers if you can prove that the difference represents a pass-through of costs saved by selling to one buyer over another (e.g., one buyer is local and doesn't require materials related to the job to be packaged and shipped).

The Federal Trade Commission Act established a watchdog agency to monitor how businesses operate in the United States. Both the Robinson-Patman Act and the Federal Trade Commission Act were designed to protect consumers and small businesses. Congress also passed the Sherman Antitrust Act to deal with price. Only by keeping current on local, state, and federal business legislation can you operate with some assurance that you will avoid legal troubles.

In addition, groups of similar businesses must not organize to set "standard" prices on products and services. The Sherman Antitrust Act, the Clayton Antitrust Act, and the Federal Trade Commission Act all make it illegal for a group of competing businesses to collectively set prices. Each must price independently.

Many shop owners have not learned how laws, ordinances, and regulations can affect their business. Many are operating in gray areas of legality. And some are actually conducting business in violation of law.

If you notice a competitor "operating outside the law," rather than sending "the feds" to catch this person, give the competitor a call and let them know that they may be breaking the law. Most small business owners do not intentionally violate the law. They simply have so much to learn and handle, that unintentional oversights or improper activities occur.

Although ignorance is no excuse, it's still better for all of us to look out for each other, than for us to look out for the law. We should not be in this to drive each other out of business. We should be in this so all of us can win and enjoy our entrepreneurial dreams.

Finally, by completing an objective cost analysis just before you make pricing decisions can give you a valid legal justification for your pricing structure.

Estimating Demand for Your Services

A capability to generate a really nice Web page is useless if no-one knows and no-one cares. Evaluating demand is not as quantifiable as analyzing cost, but demand analysis is critical. Without knowing the demand for your services, you're shooting in the dark, and your business may not survive. Your services may be obsolete and you don't realize it (yet).

A Web design service using only HTML text will fall on its face trying to compete with a shop providing multimedia interactive Web site design with wonderful graphics and navigation buttons that draw the viewer into the site. As Web surfers become more sophisticated, they will expect better designs and faster page loading. It's your challenge to find and develop services that are unique and that potential customers will pay you to develop for them.

The adage for success is simple: Find a need and fill it. Doing it may be less simple. Only by knowing the marketplace and your business can you be sensitive and recognize opportunity. If you can provide a product or service that meets a high demand, your business can grow significantly.

How do you determine market demand for Web services? Most non-technical companies are neophytes in Web site design and implementation. Even while computer magazines continue to suggest that "anyone" can design a Web page and establish a site. Some writers don't adequately warn readers that poor design is still poor design. It takes skill to make design an art.

Then, there are thousands of small companies who want a Web presence, but don't have the slightest idea how to proceed. They have the desire, they have the money, but they don't have a map. They don't (yet) have a technology guide. You can be their guide.

Finally, there are companies who quickly jumped onto the Internet and established Web presence early-on. But they failed to make their sites interesting, failed to keep their sites updated to draw return visits and failed to keep their sites linked to various search engines. These companies are prime targets for your "we'll update and maintain your site" presentation.

For example, few on-line entrepreneurs know that when they sign up for free listings on various search engines, they are listed in these directories at a lower priority below companies that pay for premium listing position. If there are 500,000 companies offering a particular service and a company did the "free listing" thing, their company could be 495,957 down on the directory list. There are things that you can do to help keep a company higher up on a search engine directory list. This represents real value to the client. This knowledge is worth money!

Another fallacy concerns how long a site is listed. Many companies think their site will be listed on search engine directories forever. You notice these sites every day during your Internet searches. They are the sites that cannot be found when you click on their URL in the directory description. They are no longer connected to the search engine directory. We call these *"dead sites."* The sites may still exist, but they are no longer linked to the search engine. These companies are potential cash cows for you. You can help them get and stay listed.

Demand for your services is directly influenced by the customers that you target — their tastes and preferences, their income, the size of this market, and the price and availability that you establish. These demand factors can be represented in a curve that graphically shows the maximum number of customers that you believe will buy your services at a given price. In the demand curve shown in Figure 3-1, the vertical axis is price. The horizontal axis represents quantity of customers of a particular service. The curve shows how changes in price affect changes in the number of customers who demand a particular service.

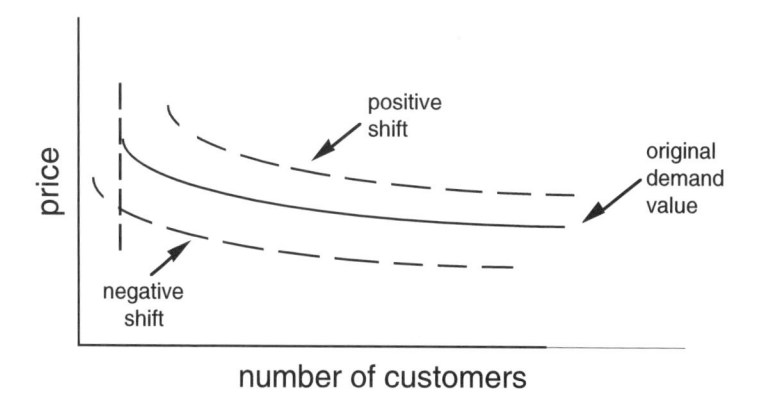

Fig. 3-1. A typical demand curve.

The trick here is to determine the shape and location of the curve on the graph. An increase in the size of the market causes the curve to shift to the right (positive). An increase in competition causes it to shift to the left (negative). An increase in the income level of your customers causes a positive shift to the right—more services are demanded. An introduction of new technology can cause a negative shift of the curve (to the left). An increase in the need for Web design and publishing services will cause a positive shift of the curve (to the right).

Therefore, as you encourage corporate and private users to buy more Web services from you, you can move the demand curve.

Elasticity of Demand

The slope of the demand curve is called its *"elasticity factor."* If customers are swayed primarily by price, the market for a service is price sensitive and demand is said to be *"elastic."* Each time you change price, sales move in the opposite direction. A decrease in price may generate enough additional sales to increase total revenue because demand for this service is elastic. If a change in price has no effect on revenue, the demand curve has *"unitary elasticity"*—price up, total sales constant.

An *"inelastic"* demand means that revenue follows price. A reduction in price actually results in a decrease in revenue. In this case, customers equate lower price with lower value and go elsewhere. Raising the price would actually generate more revenue because of the higher value perceived and higher price received for each service sold.

Figure 3-2 shows the elastic and inelastic demand conditions.

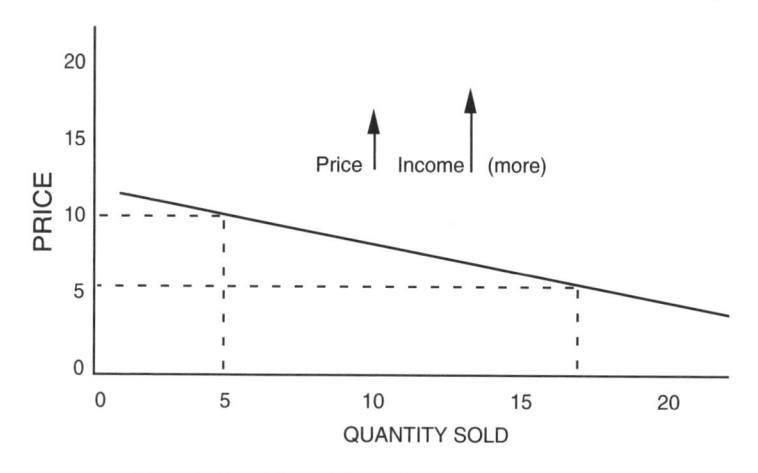

Fig. 3-2a. Elasticity of demand (elastic).

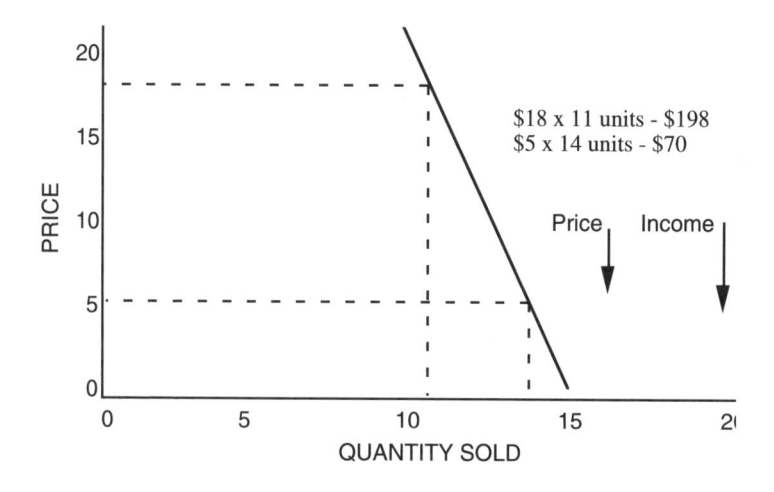

Fig. 3-2b. Elasticity of demand (inelastic).

The shapes of these demand curves vary by service and by time. A particular service with a wide customer-base appeal is more price elastic than one with a limited appeal. The more people who want a service, the more elastic the demand.

Factors that Affect Demand Elasticity

Several factors strongly influence elasticity—the relative importance of a service to the customer's budget, your price, and the availability of alternative services.

As shown in Figure 3-3, there is an ideal price for each service. Below that price, clients begin to feel that the quality is inferior. Above the ideal price, customers feel the value doesn't warrant the higher cost to them.

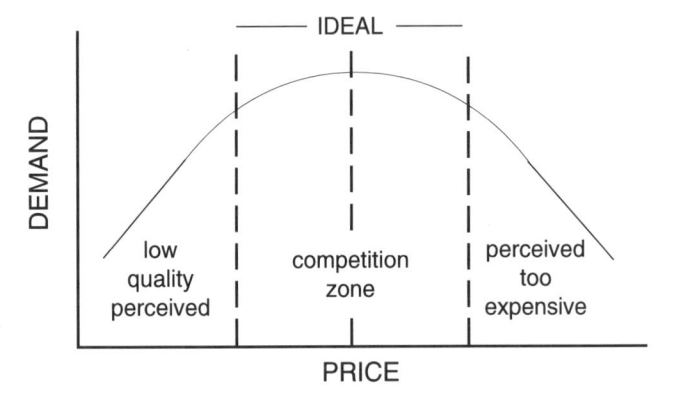

Fig. 3-3. The relation of price to demand.

A high-price job can make a customer price sensitive (demand becomes elastic), but an inexpensive job such as getting a single Home Page designed and uploaded to an ISP server has little impact on a budget, so price sensitivity does not play an important role in the buying decision. This is why there are more promotions for support on larger projects than there are for relatively minor sales such as HTML data conversion, text-only Home Page design, and simple image file linking.

However, the availability of alternatives for Web service does have a significant influence on demand. When there are dozens of shops offering the same services, the customer will shop for the lowest price.

This elasticity makes them price sensitive, and they will have little or no loyalty to you. To retain these clients, you must be price vigilant and offer to re-negotiate if a customer discovers a competitor offering lower fees. However, be cautious that you aren't being duped by the customer. And, also be careful that you don't accept a job at a loss. Know your costs in detail.

The availability of credit will also affect demand. As shown in Figure 3-4, extending the length of time clients have to pay will increase the demand for your services.

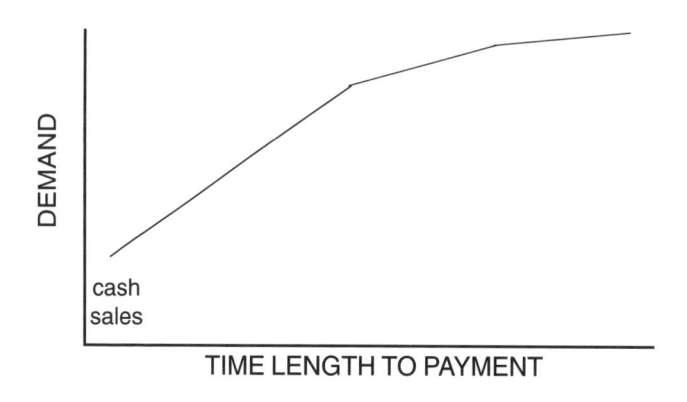

Fig. 3-4. The relationship of credit to demand.

This is a credit society. Everyone wants to have it now and pay for it later. Exploit this for more business.

Finally, there is a direct relationship between discounts and demand. As shown in Figure 3-5, increasing the size of a cash discount will increase the market demand for your services.

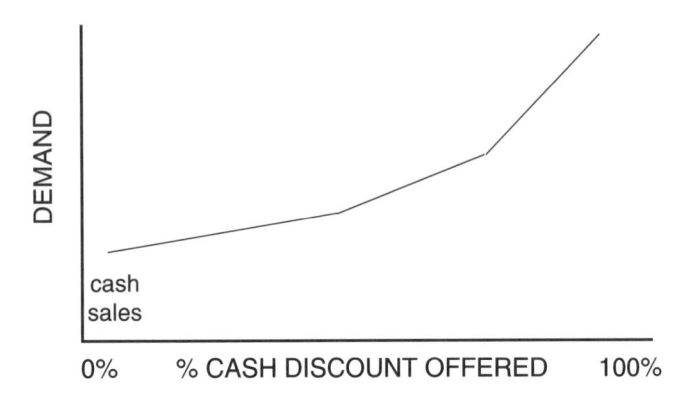

Fig. 3-5. The relationship of discount and demand.

As you'll discover in Chapter 7, this same concept works for coupons and rebates.

How to Evaluate Demand

Elasticity is difficult to forecast, but you can make an intelligent assessment of demand. The key here is to tap every available resource to determine all you can about the shape of the demand curve for those services that you offer.

Typical resources include market analysis, special reports, statistical analysis, market surveys, testing, and experience. Go on-line and access relevant sites. Conduct searches in all the on-line database directories you can. Contact your local libraries to get research support. Work through your local and national business organizations to gather information. Ask your colleagues. Ask your customers. Ask your competitors. Attend business lunches and networking groups. Gather intelligence wherever you are and whenever you can.

Then test your prices for price elasticity of demand using the following formula:

$$\text{price elasticity} = \frac{\text{\% change in number of jobs (demand)}}{\text{\% change in price}}$$

If demand falls 10% after you raise prices 5%, the price elasticity of demand is -2 (minus means an inverse relationship between price and demand — elastic). If the demand for your services falls 3% after raising prices 6%, then you have -0.5 elasticity. As demand becomes less elastic, you know it's getting time to raise prices.

Responding to Elasticity Situations

There are specific things that you can do depending on the demand elasticity situation. If you determine that demand is elastic, make every effort to price your service competitively. If demand changes little as price is varied, change your service to make it more elastic. If revenue decreases as price is increased (inelastic), consider raising your prices to generate more revenue (even with fewer sales). Try to compete based on non-price factors such as staff expertise or job turnaround time.

By carefully monitoring the market, you will soon gain the ability to determine the demand elasticity condition for each service that you offer. Then by consistently monitoring demand, you can quickly react to changes and modify your pricing strategy accordingly.

Doing Your Own Market Research

An article in *Retail Management Letter* described an interesting way to find out what prospective customers think about your prices. Here's how it works (modified for Web service pricing, of course).

Once you have a potential price for a service, make a list of 10 prices in random order. List the price that you think you will charge. Then list prices that are above and below the price that you're thinking of asking.

Now select 100 potential Web service customers at random. Ask each prospect, "If you saw our ad for Web services in a magazine or newspaper, would you buy or not buy our services at these prices?" Have them answer "yes" or "no" for each price on the survey.

Collect and analyze the responses. Often the answers will reveal a price point at which sales will drop off dramatically. They could also show that your service is less price-sensitive than you thought. In this case, price to what the market will bear.

Summary

Knowing you market is critical to business success. By keeping tuned in to what customers are buying, you can recognize and evaluate new opportunities early. You can also become aware when services are no longer profitable. By assessing the demand for each existing and prospective service, you can ensure that your company is there when the customer discovers the need. You can win in the battle to provide Web services.

In the next chapter, you'll learn how to analyze the competition and make intelligent business decisions based on what you learn.

4
Competition and Price

"We've got competition coming, and we've got to slam the door on their fingers."
- director of advertising quoted in trade magazine

Competition can be fierce and it's important for you to know as much about their pricing strategy as possible. This chapter provides ideas, insights and techniques for evaluating and understanding the tactics and motives of your competitors.

The retail world is like a cold war. Competitors pass in the aisles as they check out each other's prices. They smile at one another, knowing that the other party is gathering pricing intelligence to use against them. But they're doing the same to the other party. So it all becomes a trench battle for who has the best price.

Service providers call each other every three months, pretending to be prospective customers. They ask what the other shop's charges and then they use this to update their own prices. It's all a big, yet serious, game.

Analyzing the Competition

As part of your pricing strategy, you need competitor information so you can make intelligent pricing decisions and to decide if offering a particular service is really worth the effort. Sometimes, the profit margin is so low, it's better to let competitors offer a particular service while you focus on other higher profit jobs.

According to an article in *Success Magazine*, "... the critical ingredient of strategy is 'foreknowledge' of what will happen next in the market, among your competitors and in the world." The article goes on to say, "Virtually all the information you need to gain an advantage for your business is not truly secret. It's publicly available, if you know how to look for it."

Collecting Competitor Information

There are many ways to collect information. Some are legal. Some are illegal. This chapter will focus only on legal and ethical intelligence collection methods.

You can read about the competition, visit them, access their Web sites, talk to them, talk to their competitors, talk to non-competing companies, overhear conversations about them at public gatherings and watch them operate. You can also buy the information you need from various research companies. And you can check public records for name filings, recordings and license registrations. These are legal ways to gather information about your competition.

You need a good picture of who your competitors are, where they are located, how big they are, how they market and sell their services, and how much they earn.

Gathering competitive intelligence is time consuming and is expensive. Yet, you need at least some of this information before you make business decisions about services and pricing.

Estimate Number and Location

Take time to look for competitors. Some will be quite visible. Others will be from areas you don't expect. How many Web service providers are there? I went to *INC* magazine's Web site at *www.inc.com* and worked my way over to the virtual consultant reference desk (*www.inc.com/virtualconsult/reference_desk/web-*

development.html) to discover a link to thousands of Internet service providers and Web development companies. When I clicked on ISPs, I was linked to *http://www.thelist.com* where they boast over 5,000 ISPs. You can evaluate ISPs anywhere within the U.S. and Canada or worldwide by country or country code.

This is a fascinating tour. Many of the companies not only list the services provided, but their prices, too. It's interesting to note that these shops advertise internationally. Under "Germany," I found companies who listed prices in U.S. dollars and boasted customers in America (as well as all over Europe). These companies are also your competitors.

I went back to the *INC* reference desk page and linked to various Web development companies that are listed at *www.pair.com/dmd/* (the Developer & Marketing Database maintained by pairNetworks, a Web presence provider). Here I found 210 worldwide entries. The 5,000 plus ISPs at the other site also do Web design, so there could be some overlap of companies listed on both. (I didn't find any.)

But clearly, both these lists include competitors. You need to know who they are and, in particular, which are serving clients near you. Most customers still want to do business with someone in their own home town. This is an advantage. It's also a disadvantage (when you want to reach prospects across the state or country).

Do a search from *www.excite.com, www.yahoo.com, www.webcrawler.com,* and *www.lycos.com*. Look for the sites that advertise Web design and development. I found hundreds of them. These are competitors. They place their ads on-line. I found one Internet Service Provider with over 100 listings in one search engine directory. Every time this company changes anything, they re-submit their site to the search engine directory administrator. This gives them plenty of exposure to customers looking on-line for Web service and support.

I went to *www.desktoppublishing.com* and found a web and desktop publishing forum with a number of infonauts discussing Web page design. Since so much of standard Web page development involves graphics design and page layout, many DTPers are gravitating toward this profit center.

Visit Their Web Sites

What do they look like? How many pages do they have? Do they use banner ads? How do they seem to attract customers? Do they have a newsletter? Do they update their site frequently? Do they offer specials? What markets do they serve?

What links do they have to other sites? Do they include links to pages that they've designed for their customers (a portfolio of their work)? Go to these to see what they've done for their clients. Again, how many pages. How are the pages designed. What page layout software are your competitors using?

You could contact their customers to find out what it cost them to get their sites designed. Ask what they will be charged to update their site? What were they charged to list their sites with various search engines? Are they happy with the service they are getting?

Who Are They?

Read the information at competitor Web sites carefully. Look for biographies on key players. How many employees do they have? What is the background experience of their team? Can you spot any weaknesses in their staffing? How are they organized? Can you find out their reputation in the industry?

Access newsgroup forums and ask about them? Are the responses positive or negative? I remember a recent thread on a Publisher's Marketing Association forum when a member asked about several potential printers for her upcoming book. About a dozen members responded, and it quickly became clear that one of the printing companies had a serious problem with quality and customer service when print jobs did not go as expected. The original inquirer then posted her final decision on the forum indicating that she concluded which printer she would not go with. This left her with two satisfactory options, both of which would work.

The printer with a low customer service reputation probably lost many thousands of dollars in future business, because over 600 publishers are on this forum and read the posted messages every day.

Business people who feel unjustly treated have long memories. See if you can find previous customers who will talk about the competitor that you're evaluating.

You could also access the federal Public Access to Court Electronic Records (PACER) site at *http://www.uscourts.gov/PubAccess.html* to link to a district or bankruptcy court where you can find out if a competitor was involved in litigation. The fee is less than $1 a minute and usually you can get a response in less than a minute. To access PACER, you'll have to register first by calling 800-676-6856.

Then there's always a Lexis-Nexis search. By accessing this database, you can check if any U.S. District Court has records about lawsuits against the competitor. Access to Lexis-Nexis will also cost you some money.

Look at Their Printed Display Ads

Competitors will advertise in local, regional and national trade publications. They'll put display ads in business magazines. Look for them in printed media.

Clip their ads and study them. How large is the ad? Is it 1/4th, 1/6th, or 1/2 of a page? What message is being conveyed? What did they pay to have the ad printed? Ask the publication for a rate card that lists their advertising costs. Do this for all the printed publications that advertise Web services. Watch for advertising by the same company in several different publications.

Try to determine how often they advertise. With the costs, size, frequency and print media known, you can estimate their advertising budget. Then by analyzing the ads, you can determine what services they are pushing.

Read Their Press Releases

The original press release of a competitor can be rich in detail that quite often doesn't get into print. When a press release is sent to a magazine or newspaper reporter, space limitations dictate how much of the release will make it into print.

The original press release can contain information that is not published anywhere else. Competitors often give these out at trade shows. If your competitor has a booth at a local business or computer faire, stop by and pick up all the printed materials that they give out. Besides insight into their market strategy, the press releases can give you the names of the key players in their organization.

By collecting several years of these press releases, you can evaluate their progress (or lack of progress) in areas of the market that you may want to enter.

What Organizations Do They Join?

What professional groups or organizations do they join? You'll find competitors attending professional meetings and joining networking groups. They know that mixing with other professionals and sharing business cards is one of the best ways to find new customers.

Are the Web service providers in your area members of the local Chamber of Commerce? Do they attend networking group meetings? (If not, you should get your company represented before they do show up.)

What Else Do They Do For Publicity?

Some will write articles for local, regional and national publications. They'll do whatever it takes to get their name before the public. You'll see their names in newspapers and expressed on television. They get quoted, they get interviewed. (At least they do if they're smart.) They will do all they can to get their company known by other businesses in the area.

When you see their names mentioned, compliment the writer and then share some insight or information while mentioning that you are also a Web service provider. Get the writer to recognize that your business is a powerful resource, too.

Which Are Your Nearest Competitors?

Identify those whom you consider your nearest competitors, those who seem to be the same size as you and are providing the services that you've targeted. What services do they offer? What is their market position? What can you determine about the area they cover? How do their prices compare with other competitors? How large is their business? Study their techniques. How are they reaching their market (your market)?

The key is to determine what they are doing right and what they are doing wrong. How do they price their services? What "extras" do they offer? Who are they? Where are they? How successful do they seem?

Remember that cutthroat ISPs with rock-bottom prices are dropping like flies in a hot window. By pricing at or below costs, they down-price themselves right out of business. Try to estimate their cost of service? Then determine if their prices are out of line based on what you feel their costs should be.

For years, we've been telling secretarial services and home typing businesses that they charge too little. Unfortunately, many home business entrepreneurs don't have a good handle on what business costs are and how to operate in the black. They set their rates near what they were being paid at another job. And they don't realize that they have expenses that must be covered by the business—payroll tax is just one of these. Charging $8 an hour when their price should be $35 an hour just won't cut it. The executive director of the National Association of Secretarial Services agrees and preaches the same sermon to NASS members.

You can spot the Web service providers who will still be in business next year. They offer plenty of service at reasonable (but not low) rates and give fast turnaround. In our research, we find that the more successful shops have higher prices and offer unique services (with higher profit margin potential).

What About Their Financial Condition?

Take a long, hard look at your competitors. Try to determine their financial condition. Do they produce a financial statement (10-K) that describes how successful they are? (Since most Web service providers are small independents, you'll probably not find a 10-K on them.) It's worth trying to find out.

Can you estimate their profit margin? Assuming that you both have similar costs, can you determine how much they actually make?

By putting all of the monthly costs that you believe they have on a spreadsheet, you can make intelligent assumptions about how profitable they really are. You'll likely conclude that many are barely hanging on.

How Much Are They Charging?

Web service providers often post part of their prices at their sites. Access the site of each competitor. Collect all the prices that you can find. Put these prices in spreadsheets so you can determine the typical and average prices for all of your competitors. We do that in our *Pricing Tables: Web Services* reference.

What's the lowest price you find? What's the highest? What are they charging for site hosting, site development and for site maintenance? What special services do they offer? Can you find out what they charge for special services?

The key is: collect, collect, collect. You want as much pricing information as you can get on each of your competitors. You also need to know the prices charged by Web service providers who may become your competitors as you grow your own business. Knowing what your competitors charge has a major impact on how high (or low) you can set your own prices.

With Results In Hand

Once you've collected information on your competitors are and how they operate, make strategic decisions based on your findings. Should you enter their arena and directly compete? Should you price to match what they charge? This may stabilize prices and avoid costly price wars. But it can stagnate your business. Is a niche market developing that is not being served? Is there some aspect of Web service that few competitors have addressed? Could this be profitable for you?

I'm reminded of the man who operates out of a condo in Oregon. He works three hours a day and earns $90,000 a year. The rest of the time is spent fishing—fishing is great near him. He collects junk mail. Looks for the poor designs. Reworks these mailers and sends them back to the originators under his copyright offering to do work for them. He gets plenty of takers. The same concept could work by looking for poor Web site designs. Redesign the site, then send a hard copy proof to the prospective client. This could be very profitable.

Another entrepreneur puts company product catalogs into on-line databases. She has only five customers, but they pay her over $150,000 a year for her work. She developed the skills and focuses on a unique aspect of Web service. It's working for her.

Decide if you should find and then focus on a niche market. You'll have to set prices to avoid attracting competition? By keeping your prices low, yet profitable, you'll make a reasonable profit without enticing competitors to begin offering these same services. If you can find a niche, and then exploit this while keeping other competitors from finding out, you can earn a handsome income. And have fun doing it!

If you have a unique skill that's in strong demand (or if there's a shortage of businesses like yours), you could maximize your profits by raising prices to "the most the market can bear." Be aware that pricing high could be perceived as "gouging" and "unethical" by customers and business colleagues. Chapter 5 will provide more insight into developing a pricing strategy.

In the end, the customer dictates price. And if a competitor is attracted to your niche, those overcharged customers have memories like an elephant. The trick is to set your prices high enough to keep customers, but not so high that you attract new competitors, or so high that your pricing becomes a legal issue with government or other local businesses. Also, if you charge very high prices over a short term, you risk losing market share to competitors who will offer the same or similar services at lower prices. But if you can be there first, you can and should charge as much as you can, while you can.

Summary

You can successfully research and evaluate competitors. But it takes work. Only you can decide if this task is worth the effort. In the next chapter, you'll discover how to develop your own pricing strategy.

5
Understanding Business Numbers

"You can't control it until you can measure it."

Whatever your reason for operating a Web service business, before you can mine the gold in electronic fields, you'll need to understand the financial concepts that make business work. In this chapter, you'll learn about profit, return on investment, margin and other factors that directly affect business operations.

General Accounting Principles

In the world of business, accounting standards are based on *GAAP (Generally Accepted Accounting Principles)*. These standards are primarily for retail businesses where the principle revenue comes from products, but they can be equally applied to a service business. One of the useful forms used by accounts, (and based on GAAP) defines an income statement to look generally like Figure 5-1 on the following page.

Sales Revenue
Cost of Goods Sold
Gross Margin
Operating Expenses
    Sales & Marketing
    Research & Development
    General & Administrative
        Total Operating Expenses
Operating Income
Other Income
        Total Income Before Taxes (Gross Profit)
Taxes
        Net Income (Net Profit)

Fig. 5-1. Income statement for retail products business.

Sales revenue is pretty self-explanatory. It's what a business earns. However, confusion can occur when you look at *cost of goods sold* and *gross margin*. In a service business, there is little or no cost of goods. Yet, according to GAAP, gross margin is calculated by subtracting cost of goods sold from sales revenue. And gross margin is what trade publications use to measure one company against others in the same industry.

Over half of all businesses in the U.S. are service-oriented. Their principle money-generator is service—labor, the sweat from someone's brow. So when trade publications publish statistics for product-oriented companies, the gross margin numbers are confusing to service providers. *Operating expenses* are similar for both product-oriented and service-oriented companies. So are *other income*, *total income before taxes* (*gross profit*) and the resulting *net income (net profit).* The key point of confusion is where gross margin should be listed on the statement.

The income statement for a service company looks slightly different. Since there is no (or very little) cost of goods sold, gross margin is calculated by subtracting *operating expenses*. And operating expenses become the *cost of services sold*. For example, Figure 5-2 is modeled on a telemarketing service center.

>Sales Revenue
>Other Income
>>Total Gross Income
>
>Operating Expenses (cost of services sold)
>>Hardware & Software Costs
>>Monthly On-Line Charges
>>Wages & Salaries
>>Other Operating Expenses
>>>Total Operating Expenses (total cost of services sold)
>
>Gross Margin (total gross income less total operating expense)
>Other Administrative Expenses (fixed amount)
>>Total Income Before Taxes (gross profit)
>>>(expressed as % of total gross income)
>
>Taxes (% of Gross profit)
>>Total Net Income (Net Profit)
>>>(expressed as % of total gross income)

Fig. 5-2. Income statement for service business

That major difference between Figures 5-1 and 5-2 is that the former lists cost of goods sold and the latter lists cost of services sold. Gross margin is the profitability of a service company's sales effort. It indicates the percent of each service sales dollar remaining to cover fixed and administrative costs.

A research survey found that service department gross margins ranged from 46-67 percent. The gross margin percentage is computed by dividing gross margin by net service revenue and multiplying by one hundred. And another survey found that service gross margins ranged between 26 and 37 percent. Therefore, 26-67% is the range.

Many companies use gross margin to compare service centers, when, in reality, profit after expenses is a much better indicator of how effectively your assets are being used. Some shops focus on cutting operating costs to improve gross margin. Other service center owners feel that the key number to watch is gross profit.

So What Is Profit?

Profit is what you have left over after expenses are taken out. This is not the same as the money that your shop makes and that you put into your pocket. As you saw in Chapter 2, cost is a major factor in your pricing policy.

Maximum profit is the goal. There are two kinds of profit to measure — gross profit and net profit. Look at Figure 5-3.

CyberBucks Web Services

Total Service Sales Revenue	$100,000	100%
Cost of Services Sold (Op Costs)	60,000	60%
Gross Margin	40,000	40%
Sales and Marketing Costs	10,000	10%
General & Administrative	19,000	19%
Total SG&A Expenses	29,000	29%
Income Before Taxes (Gross Profit)	11,000	11%
Taxes (at 40% of gross profit)	4,400	4.4%
Net Income (Net Profit)	6,600	6.6%

Fig. 5-3. Income statement for fictitious company.

Let's analyze this income statement. The company is operated by a single entrepreneur. The owner was able to earn $100,000 for the year. Since the company provides a service, the cost of services sold is the same as the operating expenses. This yields a gross margin of 62%. Then sales, general and administrative expenses are deducted to get a gross profit of $13,000. After paying taxes, $7,800 in profit remains. Not bad considering that the owner was also paid out of the operating costs.

Notice that gross profit is the dollars left over before taxes. Once taxes are deducted, the remainder is your net profit. This is what you use to grow your business.

Net profit helps you survive down business cycles when job opportunities are slow, and you need this reserve to pay the bills. Net profit lets you avoid borrowing from the bank (or your personal savings account) when times get tough.

According to the National Association of Printers and Lithographers, median pre-tax profitability (gross profit) in the printing world is about 4.6 percent. In our Web service example it's 11 percent. In the printing and prepress industries, keeping up with technology takes a huge bite out of profit.

In Web development, the costs of entry are low. Therefore the profit potential is large. In ISP companies, the cost of technology is high, but still not as high as if one had to invest several hundred thousand dollars every couple of years in new prepress and direct-to-plate technology. You have a huge cost advantage in operating a Web service business.

Now let's see what happens if we reduce the cost of services sold in the CyberBucks Web Services company by just five percent. As shown in Figure 5-4, the affect on net profit is dramatic.

CyberBucks Web Services

			% Change
Total Sales Revenue	$100,000	100%	0
Cost of Services Sold	57,000	57%	-5
Gross Margin	43,000	43%	+8
Sales and Marketing Costs	10,000	10%	0
General & Administrative	19,000	19%	0
Total SG&A Expenses	29,000	29%	0
Gross Profit	14,000	15%	+27
Taxes (at 40% of gross profit)	5,600	6%	+27
Net Income (Net Profit)	8,400	9%	+27
			(KEY)

Fig. 5-4. Income statement when cost of goods are reduced just five percent.

It amazing! Reducing your cost of services sold by 5% produces a 27% increase in net profit! This is why closely watching costs is well worth the effort! This mythical company increased net profit from 11% to 27% by causing a small decrease in its cost of providing services. This added profit can make a significant difference when business downturns occur.

Typically, shop owners will strive for a net profit of 5-10% of total sales income. This profit goal should be added to your budgeted hourly costs to arrive at the right prices to charge. In every transaction, incorporate profit and market expectations before settling on a final price.

When you analyze the cost factors associated with your shop, you'll probably find that your labor and direct expenses make up 50-60% of the total costs. Marketing will be another 10-20% of the costs.

Chapter 5 - Understanding Business Numbers   101

Nonmarketing costs will chew up 10-20 percent. Each time one of these cost factors increase, you must take some action to reduce another cost factor to maintain your desired profit percentage. Everything you do to reduce your cost of service adds that much more to your bottom line.

As improved technology comes along, new business opportunity doors are opened while other services are no longer viable options. Most shop owners carefully look at each service and decide which generate the most income for them.

What many don't understand is that in this business environment, too many service providers are chasing sales dollars when they should be chasing profit dollars. It's often the case that one $5,000 job will generate much more profit than a different $5,000 job because the other job has a much higher budgeted hourly cost. It therefore becomes a strategic decision which services to offer.

Service providers are generally smaller than retail companies. Your profit margins (in percent) are higher than the retail store, even though your gross revenue is less. In your case, you also have higher salary costs due to the technical skills required. The key is properly covering all of your costs in the prices that you charge.

The only way you can increase your profit margin is to lower your percentage of costs-to-revenue. A business with the largest market share should also have the lowest cost. Both material and labor costs are directly proportional to market share.

Trading short-term profit (through lower prices) to gain market share may be a good long-term strategy if your material costs decrease as sales volume increases. If not, be careful of quick profits with long term losses.

Return on Investment (ROI)

Not many shop owners take time to think about or calculate the amount of money that they've invested (poured) into starting their business. But if you borrowed money to buy computer equipment or software, you would surely pay interest on the loan. The same holds true if you were to "loan" money to a business—your business. You deserve at least the same interest earnings on your loan. This is called "*return on investment*" or simply *ROI*. If you put money into your business, but don't consider it a loan that earns interest, you're cheating yourself.

Even a modest return of 4% on your investment will just keep up with inflation. You should calculate the ROI "cost of seed money" to capitalize your business, and include ROI as a repayment cost factor when you establish your prices and service rates. Pay yourself back for the loan. You deserve it.

There are a number of ways to calculate ROI. The formula that accountants choose depends on if they are generating numbers for the stockholders or for upper management.

I prefer the "keep it simple" principle where return on investment is the "bang you get for the buck you spend." ROI is the financial gain that you realize from the money that you put into your business. Here's a formula that is simple to understand and use.

$$ROI = \frac{\text{net profit}}{\text{investment}}$$

If you put $10,000 up front to start your business, you deserve a return on these dollars just as if you had invested this money in mutual funds or another security. Today, you should be able to safely earn 2-10% on your money. By diverting money from one investment into another (your business), you should expect some return for this action. You get this by factoring a percent ROI into your hourly rate calculations.

Based on your monetary investment, decide on an acceptable return for the risk that you take operating a business. Then prorate and integrate this return directly into your shop's hourly rates and per page prices.

For a $10,000 investment, and a return of 10% over a 2080-hour working year, you should allocate about 48¢ to each hour that is billed out. You add the 48¢ to your budgeted hourly rate so each hour of billable work generates a return on the initial investment.

Calculating ROI on Marketing & Sales

Your marketing and sales efforts add cost to a business. Yet, you can evaluate each sales call for its return on the investment. This evaluation process helps you focus on generating cost-effective sales. It works like this:

First, establish a target return on a sales call —say 200-300 percent. Then. calculate your total expense for the call and rank-order all of your sales opportunities for their return on the marketing and sales investment. If a projected return doesn't exceed your threshold, don't go after this account. Figure 5-5 shows how to calculate sales call ROI.

Sales time (3 hours @ $50/hr)	$150
Proposal time (3 hrs @ $60/hr)	180
Telephone calls (1 hr @ 25¢/min)	15
Mailings (2 @ $3 ea)	6
Travel (60 mi @ 31¢/mile)	19
Misc (10% of sales time)	15
Total Sales Expenses	385
Value of sales call	$2,500
Profit Margin (40%)	1,000
Sales call ROI	260%

Fig. 5-5. Calculating your sales call ROI.

three-hour sales call followed up by three hours preparing a proposal, an hour of telephone calls, several mailings, travel and other time expenditures puts your sales call total expense (in this example) at $385. If the potential revenue from getting the job is $2,500 with a profit of $1,000, your sales call return on the investment is 260 percent. This means that if a sales call doesn't result in $2,500 in business, you may be wasting your time and overhead budget.

The idea is to evaluate the potential of each prospect from the perspective of what you hope to get for the energy and shop resources expended. Be realistic in assessing the possibility of actually getting their business. By looking at all of your opportunities in the light of potential return, you are able to focus on what matters — a service job that will be paid, and not a sales activity event to check off on a goals list.

The primary benefits of analyzing the ROI of sales calls is to force you to evaluate every sales lead from a cost and benefit standpoint before you invest sales resources into going after the prospect. In a short time, you'll find that you only focus on the best opportunities and avoid those with mediocre potential.

Return on Assets (ROA)

If you were to use $10,000 to purchase equipment and software, the return that you expect from this investment becomes a return on assets.

In the world of financial analysis, people often use subjective decisions to make objective conclusions. They assume a given result and then base dollar investment numbers on the assumption. Although this seems silly, sometimes it's the best shot we can make at evaluating a particular business strategy. The concept of *return on assets (ROA)* is such a case. ROA is a useful measure of profitability and efficiency. In fact, it's sometimes called the *"productivity ratio."*

Chapter 5 - Understanding Business Numbers 105

Your shop's ROA is like return on investment—an investment made after you start your business. You want to be paid for your purchasing decisions. You want to realize a percentage of monetary gain for an investment in something tangible like computer equipment or better software. In this case, the ROA approach is to anticipate a revenue gain from a certain purchase of hardware or software. Here's how ROA is calculated:

$$\text{purchase cost, C} = \frac{ER}{1 + r}$$

where ER is expected revenue, and r is the expected rate of return (a percentage expressed as a decimal).

$$\text{cost of equip/software} = \frac{\text{expected revenue}}{1 + \text{expected rate of return}}$$

Since, we're calculating expected revenue, we rearrange the formula to calculate ER given a known cost and a desired rate of return.

ER = C (1 + r)

If we spend $10,000 for a new computer with all the latest and greatest features, and we want to get a return on this hardware investment of at least 20%, we drop these numbers into our formula and solve for what we must earn to achieve this return. (A spreadsheet works great for this.)

ER = 10,000 (1 + r) = 10,000 (1 + 0.2)

ER = $12,000

Thus, we must earn $12,000 to realize the 20% return that we feel is necessary to cost-justify the purchase. If we purchase on an installment pay plan, we can use the annual costs (including interest) and still calculate the ER for a 20% return.

If your shop rate is $60 an hour, you'd need an additional 200 billable hours over the next 12 months to cover this added $12,000 expense. Will making the new purchase give you the ability to do this?

Conversely, we can anticipate an income from making an asset purchase and then calculate the expected rate of return on this business decision. Again we rearrange the formula. Replace r, the expected rate of return, with ROA, the return on assets.

$$C = \frac{ER}{1 + ROA}$$

$$C(1 + ROA) = ER$$

$$1 + ROA = \frac{ER}{C}$$

$$ROA = \frac{ER}{C} - 1$$

Suppose you are considering the purchase of a new color scanner to use in generating Web page images. The purchase price is $1,600. You feel that you can sell $2,000 worth of scans in a year. What is your ROA?

$$ROA = \frac{2,000}{1,600} - 1$$

return on assets, ROA = 0.25 (25%)

Expressed as a percent, our ROA is 25 percent. By making purchase decisions based on an expected ROA, we can optimize our asset investments. Remember that we are assuming how much additional annual revenue we'll earn using this new scanner.

Keep in mind that technology and customer needs can change rapidly. To stay current, you should base your calculations on a two-year replacement life. This means that you should plan to buy new equipment every two years. It also means that you must be able to resell the old equipment for enough (residual value) that you can make the replacement purchase while realizing a return on the initial investment. Some owners try to build their business so they can run two shifts each day. This gives them a better chance of increasing the return on their hardware and software resources.

Markup

In the markup pricing, the sales price is established by adding a predetermined percentage to the cost of a product. This amount can be a percentage of the wholesale price, or a percentage of the cost. The total markup represents operating expenses, overhead and profit.

Mark-ups differ based on the product, competition, turnover, and sales risk. However, many businesses use a "standard" markup for each product category. Department stores typically mark up clothing 40-60 percent. Staple food items such as bread and milk are marked up by 10-23 percent. Snack foods receive a 27-47 percent markup, and so on. In reality, there's a markup at each stage in the development of a product—in the manufacturing stage, during distribution, and final sale. The net result is a product or service that has been marked up several hundred percent over its initial raw material cost as it passes through each stage in the manufacturing-to-customer process.

If a product cost $10 from a wholesale supplier, a business owner will add a portion of overhead costs (rent, utilities, insurance, salaries, etc.) and profit to this base cost to arrive at a selling price. To get this selling price, divide the wholesale cost by one minus the percent overhead plus percent profit (both expressed in decimal) as shown in the formula below.

$$\text{selling price} = \frac{\text{wholesale cost}}{1 - (\text{overhead} + \text{profit})}$$

Thus, if overhead represents 25% of your costs and you want a 10% profit, you would mark up a $10 product by 53.8% to achieve a selling price of $15.38.

$$\text{selling price} = \frac{10}{1 - (.25 + .10)}$$

$$= \frac{10}{1 - 0.35}$$

$$= \frac{10}{0.65}$$

selling price = $15.38

To get the percentage of markup, apply the formula:

$$\% \text{ markup} = \frac{\text{selling price} - \text{wholesale cost}}{\text{wholesale cost}} \times 100$$

$$= \frac{15.38 - 10.00}{10.00} \times 100$$

$$= \frac{5.38}{10} \times 100$$

percent markup = 0.538 x 100 = 53.8%

The concept for marking up a product is the same for marking up a service Web service providers determine their total costs and then mark up these costs by some percentage to arrive at a price to charge. Even if you outsource some of your work, you'll mark up what you're charged to get the price that you'll pass on to your client.

Markup and Gross Profit Margin

Suppose you did a job whose direct costs were $8,000. You marked up the job's cost by 50 percent ($4,000), and charged the client $12,000 for the work. The $4,000 markup divided by the $12,000 total job price yields a 33% gross profit margin.

$8,000 direct job cost + $4,000 (50% markup) = $12,000

$$\frac{\$12{,}000 \text{ job}}{\$4{,}000 \text{ markup}} = 33\% \text{ gross profit margin}$$

Therefore, a 50% markup is equivalent to earning a 33% gross profit margin on the job.

Break-Even Analysis

One of the best ways to understand the relationship between cost, sales and profit is by performing break-even analysis. This business technique helps you identify the point at which cost equals income. It is the sales volume or quantity point where your costs are covered and profit begins.

There are two ways to find break-even—by comparing total sales volume with costs or by comparing total service items (units) produced and sold with cost. In both methods, you must understand all of the expenses associated with your business. Part of your costs are fixed and don't change with the volume of sales made. Other costs vary with the job—hourly wages, the costs of raw materials and additional utility expenses to produce the services that you sell. To make a profit, you must pay both your fixed and variable expenses. The residual income left over goes toward profit and return-on-investment (if you loaned money to your company).

The challenge is to find the point at which your costs are covered and profit can begin to accrue. This is your break-even point. You can analyze break-even on a grand scale (looking at your total business sales and costs) or on a service-by-service basis.

Whether you choose a sales volume method or total units sold method of break-even analysis, your first step is to determine your fixed and variable expenses.

Break-Even (Sales Volume Method)

This technique relates income to cost. First determine your total fixed costs. This becomes a reference baseline for break-even analysis. Next, calculate your total variable costs. Divide the total variable costs by the total number of sales to get an average variable cost per sale. You can also determine your average dollar-per-sale by dividing the total revenue by the total

Chapter 5 - Understanding Business Numbers

number of sales. Dividing the average variable-cost-per-sale by the average dollar-income-per-sale, you can find the percentage of variable costs in each transaction.

For example, an average variable cost of $90 and an average selling price of $140 yields 64.3% variable cost percentage. Each time you earn one dollar, 64 cents goes to pay for your variable costs and your business keeps about 36 cents. But this is not profit. Not yet. You need to apply this money to pay your fixed costs before you get to count your profit.

$$\text{avg variable cost per sale} = \frac{\text{total variable costs}}{\text{total number of sales}}$$

$$\text{avg dollars per sale} = \frac{\text{total revenue}}{\text{total number of sales}}$$

$$\text{variable cost percentage} = \frac{\text{avg variable cost per sale}}{\text{avg \$ per sale}}$$

To determine how much sales volume you'll need before you get to keep the 36 cents earned on each dollar of sale, you must find the break-even point.

Express the percent as a decimal and subtract it from one (1 - 0.643 = 0.357, the 36¢ extra on each sale). Then divide this result into your total fixed costs. If your fixed costs are $36,000 annually, you will need $100,840 in sales income before all of your fixed and variable costs are covered (1-.643 = 0.357 and 36,000/0.357 = $100,840). This is your break-even. All sales above this point become profit for your company. On the following page are the steps to follow.

$$\text{break-even point, B-E} = \frac{\text{total fixed costs}}{1 - \frac{\text{(avg vble unit cost)}}{\text{(avg unit selling price)}}}$$

$$\text{B-E} = \frac{36{,}000}{1 - (9/14)} = \frac{\$36{,}000}{0.357} = \$100{,}840$$

If you assume that changes in sales volume don't affect your average selling price, that your fixed costs remain constant, and that your variable costs change in direct proportion to sales, you can plot costs versus sales volume as shown in Figure 5-6.

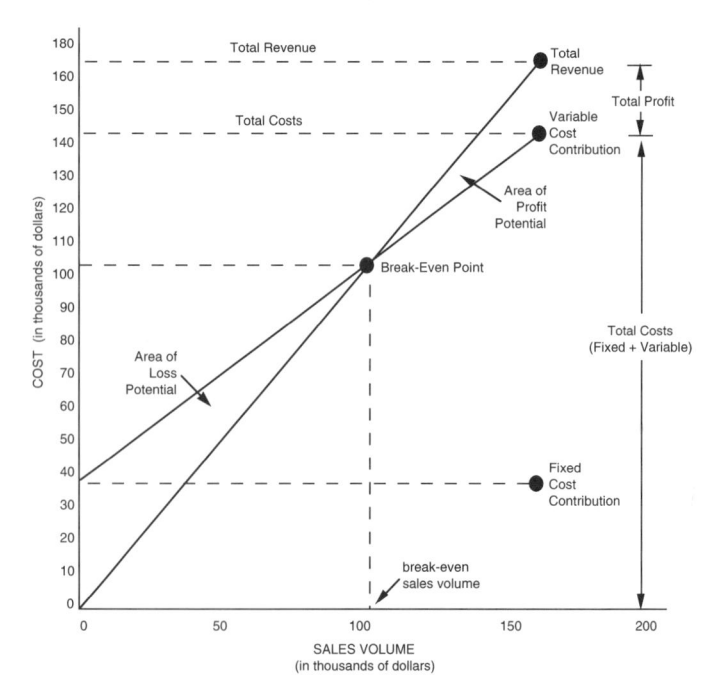

Fig. 5-6. Break-Even chart based on total sales volume analysis.

In this case, the horizontal axis represents the volume of sales. The vertical axis represents dollars in costs and revenue. Break-even occurs at $103,000 in sales.

Break-Even (Sales Quantity Method)

Another way to do break-even analysis is to determine how many sales are needed before costs are covered and profit can accrue. There are three things that you need for this calculation: the unit price of the service you're selling, and your fixed and variable costs. With these three, you can calculate break even using the following formula:

$$\text{B-E quantity} = \frac{\text{total fixed costs}}{(\text{unit sales price}) - (\text{variable cost})}$$

If you charge $2,000 for designing a six-page Web site, your fixed monthly costs are running $6,000, and variable costs are 40% of your sales revenue ($800). Plugging the numbers into the formula, you get

$$\text{B-E quantity} = \frac{6000}{2000 - 800}$$

B-E quantity = 5 jobs sold

You must average five sales each month (earn $10,000) to break even and begin making a profit. If you do less than this, you are working at a loss.

You can also find your break-even quantity by determining the margin of contribution made by the average sale. The *contribution margin* is the difference between the average price per sale and the average variable cost per sale.

contribution margin = avg price per sale
                               - avg variable cost per sale

Dividing the total fixed cost by the contribution margin yields a break-even quantity.

$$\text{B-E quantity} = \frac{\text{total fixed costs}}{\text{contribution margin}}$$

Using the same numbers as in the previous example, you see that an average sale of $2,000, less an average variable cost of $800, yields a contribution margin of $1,200. Dividing our total fixed cost of $6,000 by the $1,200 contribution margin, we get 5 units of service sold. This means that we must sell 5 Web jobs at an average price of $2,000 each to cover our fixed and variable costs.

$$\text{B-E quantity} = \frac{\$6,000}{\$1,200} = 5 \text{ units}$$

To get break-even in dollars, multiply the break-even point in units by the price of each unit. This will check the arithmetic of the first method (5 x $2,000 = $10,000). You must sell $10,000 worth of Web development service each month to break even.

By using the same assumptions as we did for the total sales volume method, you can plot revenue versus units of sale to show graphically when break-even occurs (Figure 5-7).

The money made on each sale is applied first toward paying fixed costs, then toward paying variable costs, and finally toward profit. If we lower our average service price, we contribute less toward paying for fixed and variable costs and there will be less remaining

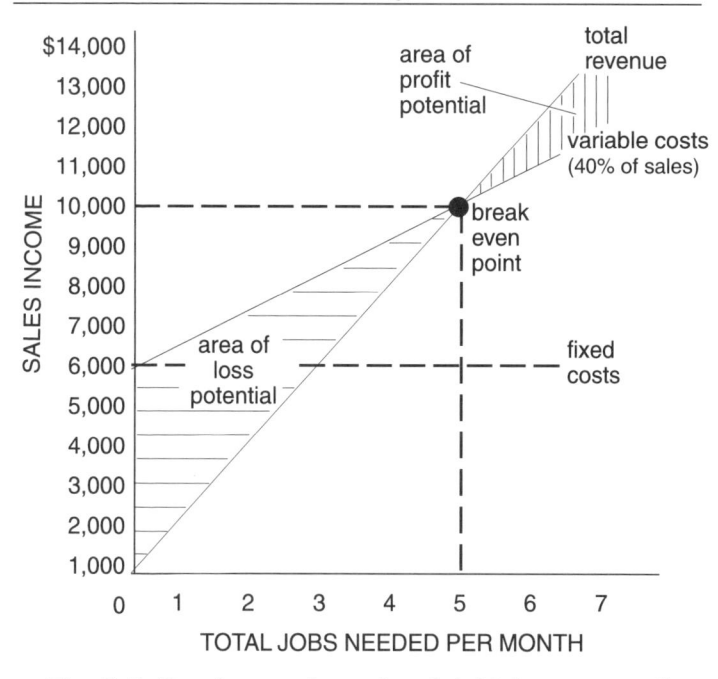

Fig. 5-7. Break-even based on total jobs per month.

for profit. This also means that we push the break-even point on the graph further out to the right.

You can perform break-even analysis for each type of service and see what you'd have to earn on each (if it were the only service you provided). This can be an eye-opener. For one thing, you'll see which services are the best for you to offer and which you should drop.

Typically, the smallest 20% of the orders account for less than 5% of your sales income. It may not be worth making these sales. There's a point at which fixed costs exceed income and you should decline the sale.

The break-even chart shows you graphically why some sales just don't make financial sense. A pallet of low quantity service sales may generate revenue that is consistently below your fixed costs with a small variable cost added. This suggests that you should decline these jobs, or add a surcharge (charge a higher price) for low dollar sales. This is why many shops have a sliding price scale with a minimum charge for specific services. A lower price is charged for volume jobs.

The ideal way to perform break-even analysis is to develop a model using a computer spreadsheet. This lets you dynamically change the variables and determine new break-even points based on different selling prices and costs. It's particularly helpful when you begin changing the price on different service products.

Break-even analysis can help you decide the viability of a prospective new service. It can show you when it's too costly to produce and sell at a selected price.

If you don't think that you can make $10,000 each month, you have four choices: 1) accept the loss and continue to build business volume, 2) raise your Web development price, 3) lower your price and hope to generate more volume, or 4) aggressively cut your fixed and variable costs.

It may not be possible to increase your income by raising your prices. Competition may hold prices too low to make this service worth selling. Your costs can also vary. And it may not be possible to lower prices because there just isn't enough business coming in. These are tactical decisions (covered in Chapter 7).

Finding Break-Even on Advertising

Of course you'll advertise at your Web site. But what if you are considering placing an ad in a local newspaper or trade magazine. There's a way to calculate break-even on your ad. Most people would take the average sales amount and divide it into the cost for the ad.

Let's assume that your typical (or average) service job is $250, and you think it would be a good idea to advertise in *Web Services* (a hypothetical magazine for the public). It costs $1,200 to run a 1/6 page ad. Working the numbers, you get:

$$\text{B-E quantity} = \frac{\text{display ad costs}}{\text{average unit sales amount}}$$

$$= \frac{1{,}200}{250} = 4.8 \ (5 \text{ sales})$$

You conclude that you only need five sales from the ad to pay its costs. But this doesn't consider doing the work. You still have to budget for labor, G&A and any return on your investment before any profit can be made. This changes the picture significantly.

Suppose you have a 5:1 cost of services sold to price ratio. It costs $80 to do the work and you charge $250 for it. And assume that your G&A runs 19% and that you want a 10% return on your initial business startup investment. Now let's analyze the numbers correctly.

Typical Job Price		$250.00
Cost of service	$80.00	
G&A (19%)	47.50	
ROI (10%)	25.00	
Total Costs:	$152.50	
Allowable cost per order:		$97.50

By dividing the $97.50 allowable cost per order into the $1,200 cost for the ad, you'll discover that you need 13 sales (round 12.31 up to nearest whole number) just to pay for this ad.

$$\text{B-E quantity} = \frac{1200}{97.50} = 12.31 \ (13 \text{ sales})$$

Rather than five jobs, you actually need 13 sales. After 13 jobs are done, you start making a profit.

What if you could do the job faster? Suppose that you upgraded your hardware and software. If the cost of service sold could be reduced to $60 this would reduce the total costs to $132.50 and the allowable cost per order to $117.50. This would result in a break-even quantity requirement of only 11 (10.21) sales. A 25% reduction in costs resulted in a need for 17% fewer sales. When you work the numbers all the way, you'll discover that reducing costs allows the savings to drop right through to the gross profit line. A nice reality.

Break-even analysis isn't perfect. It doesn't consider discounting, customer demand (elasticity) and the actions of competitors. Nevertheless, it can help you quickly see the impact of various pricing strategies. It's one of the tools that you have for managing your business. By knowing the break-even point, you can determine which products or services to offer. It helps you decide if making an unprofitable sale to gain a long term customer is really worth the sacrifice. And it helps you highlight excessive fixed overhead expenses such as rent, leased equipment, and staff.

To succeed in this business, you must consider every analytical tool that might help you make better pricing decisions. Break-even analysis is a useful tool for Web service providers. Another is margin analysis.

Margin Analysis

In *margin analysis*, you evaluate the cost and expected income associated with producing and selling more of a particular service. It focuses on profit maximization rather than break even. Here you associate the cost of taking on just "one more" project (called "*marginal cost*") with the associated added income (called "*marginal revenue*") that you can earn.

Chapter 5 - Understanding Business Numbers   119

As shown in Figure 5-8, a *margin curve* can be constructed that shows the relationship between price, quantity, cost, revenue and demand. As more units of service are sold, the average cost decreases, pulling the marginal cost down. The marginal revenue also declines because the most recent sale becomes a comparatively smaller portion of the total income.

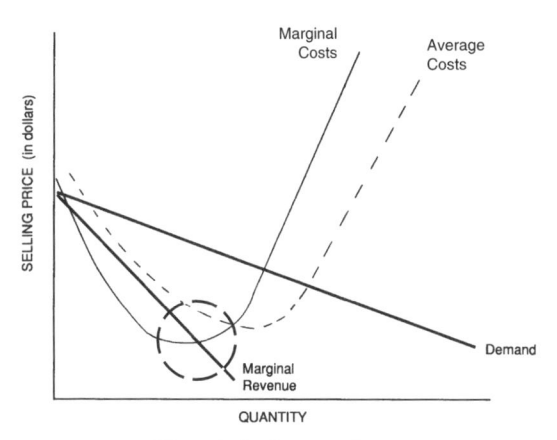

Fig. 5-8. A margin curve.

A some point, you must expand your facilities and increase your equipment and staff so you can handle additional business. This added expense makes the marginal cost and average cost curves bend upward. The key is that maximum profit is realized at the point where marginal cost exactly equals marginal revenue.

If you focus on the area where marginal costs and marginal revenue intersect on the margin curve, you can identify a point where more business won't generate additional revenue for the company. Take a look at Figure 5-9 on the next page.

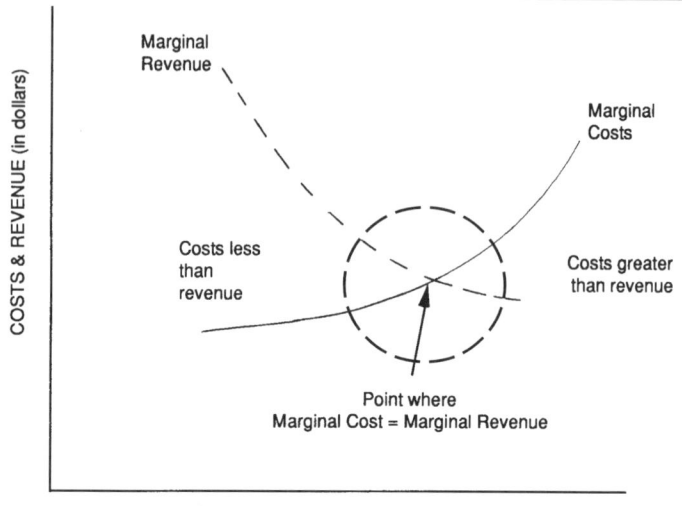

Fig. 5-9. A margin curve showing the relationship between marginal costs and marginal revenue.

The idea is to find the margin crossover points for each service that you offer and then strive to hold sales of each service unit at the point where marginal revenue exactly equals marginal cost.

Finding Optimum Order Size Using Margin Analysis

An interesting technique for determining if marginal orders are really worthwhile is to find your optimal order size. This requires knowing your cost per job and your gross profit margin. The process works like this:

First, find the spread of your job orders by sales dollar size. Some will be less than $250. Others will be between $250 and $1,000, others $1,000 to $5,000, etc..

Second, for each spread category, determine the total number of sales, the total sales dollar value, the percent these sales are of the total sales, and the average sales dollar per order.

Third, find your gross margin. Subtract the total cost of services sold (all categories combined) from total sales (all categories combined) to get a shop gross margin. The cost of services sold will represent the total costs to produce the services that you sell. This includes direct labor charged to the jobs. By dividing the gross margin by the total sales, and multiplying by 100, you can calculate percent gross margin.

Fourth, determine your *distribution costs*. These costs include order handling, billing, and salaries for everyone involved in fulfilling the order (but not directly involved in producing the order). A customer calls in. Someone handles the call, takes the order, places the order, adds the order to the job queue, receives the report of job completion, packages the disk files produced during the job for delivery to the client, delivers the disks, bills the customer, and processes the payment. The moneys expended to do these things become your distribution costs.

Fifth, determine your *average distribution cost per order*. Divide the distribution costs incurred over a year by the number of orders handled. Some orders will be large and some small, but this estimate provides a fair assessment of what it costs to fill each order.

Finally, calculate your *break-even order size*. Divide the distribution costs per order by the percent gross margin to find the order size needed to break even on the sale. If it costs $14 to handle an order and your gross margin is 35%, you need an average order size of $40 (14 /0.35 = 40) just to match your costs—to break even. On a $36 order, you can expect to earn $12.60. But if it cost $14 just to handle the order, and you only earn $12.60, you would be losing money by accepting the order. However, if you got a $250 order to design a Home Page, the cost to process and distribute the order is still $14, but your expected gross margin is $87.50.

So after you subtract the $14 processing cost, you have $73.50 as a contribution to overhead and profit.

Break-even and margin analysis provide a valuable picture of your business and help you develop an optimum pricing strategy. Cost analysis gives you a clear picture of the margin possible, but your competitors' price lists and what your customers will pay for your service still influence the prices that you can charge. A good market-driven strategy considers both the internal cost issues and the external customer and competitor marketplace in setting price.

Improve Profit With Margin Analysis

Seek those services that yield the highest margin. High margins help make up for those jobs that just don't end up very profitable. Try for a 50% gross margin.

For comparison, here are the gross margins in other industries and companies:

book selling industry	40-50%
computer manufacturers	15-35%
software manufacturers	54-65%

Do you know your own shop's gross margin? You should.

Summary

Now that you know how to deal with the financial numbers that will determine if you'll make a profit in your venture, you're ready for Chapter 6, where you'll learn how to develop a pricing strategy for maximizing your profit potential.

6
Pricing Strategies

"This is not a 'let's-wing-it' operation."

Pricing is one of the most challenging issues that you deal with in operating your business. It's part of your strategy. In your business plan, you established your goals and objectives. This chapter will help you establish a pricing strategy. It will also explain creative pricing techniques currently being used by service providers around the world. And you'll learn when and how to raise (or lower) prices while continuing to expand your business.

Developing A Strategy

Pricing decisions are often the result of hunch, gut feel, intuition, or "let's charge that price, too" reactions. These are often "shooting in the dark" actions. Pricing decisions should be made from a position of knowledge and understanding. Figure 6-1 shows the process for developing a profitable pricing strategy.

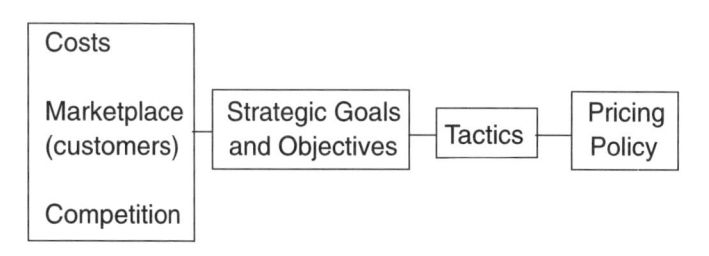

Fig. 6-1. Creating a profitable pricing strategy.

Once you understand costs, the potential of your market, and your competition, you can develop a strategy and implement tactics to price for profit.

In the marketplace, each prospective customer has a need that requires intelligent response to price, quality, and schedule. You add value by the way that you handle these factors. If you can offer the greatest value in at least one of these three areas, you should get your share of the available business. If you offer the best in two or more of these factors, you should get more than your share of jobs.

There are two distinctly different types of customers that you must deal with in pricing your products and services—the *commodity customer* and the *solutions customer*. The commodity customer wants to buy at the lowest cost and neither wants nor desires hand-holding.

COMMODITY CUSTOMER	SOLUTIONS CUSTOMER
lowest price only	answers first then price

Fig. 6-2. The two types of customers that you'll deal with in your business.

The solutions customer wants the best price but also wants a source for answers when operations become too complex and confusing. Many businesses sell basic products or service without technical backup. There are others who thrive on the premise that the customer needs information and therefore place customer service and support paramount in their strategic decisions.

Today, most customers seem motivated only by price. They'll quickly take their business elsewhere when problems arise or your quoted price exceeds their threshold. Although little customer loyalty exists (or business-to-customer loyalty, for that matter), the customer's expectations and attitudes still lag whatever business loyalty that may exist.

Yet, contrary to what you may now feel, a business that is solutions-oriented will likely be more profitable than one that is commodity-oriented. Technology and information transfer are becoming too complex for simple solutions. The company that can gently guide a customer through a project will likely earn respect and more business. For customers only interested in price and output, you can establish a special rate structure for them (differential or tiered pricing). Or, you can let them seek out and purchase from the "canned-product" discount price shops.

To develop your strategy, you must think like your customer. This means that you've truly got to know your client. What first attracts them to a business such as yours? Price? Quality? Response time?

If it's price, then you must be competitive. I didn't say charge the lowest price in the area. Nor did I say be the most expensive (although there's much to be said for being among the higher priced companies). The key is to provide sufficient perceived—as well as real—value to warrant the prices that you charge.

A pricing strategy that encourages a higher number of sales in an elastic market can produce stronger profits. If you adopt a pricing strategy based on maintaining a high margin, you may find your customers moving to another competitor. This causes some shops to focus on unique and special services. With something distinct to offer, your margins are higher, and the number of competitors is reduced. The personal computer industry once enjoyed this position, but high margins brought in more competitors until price cutting erupted. Today, the PC is simply a hardware commodity. The profit margins of PC manufacturers have shrunk to very low numbers.

A similar thing is occurring in Web site hosting. Some ISP businesses have reduced their prices to a point that, although their volume is high, their margin is so low, profit is minimum. These shops use site hosting as a "loss leader" while pushing other (value added) Web services to recoup and maintain a healthy profit margin.

One school of thought suggests that shops bundle services to minimize the complexity that the customer must endure, offering a "total" solution to any job. Some service providers prefer that they not get involved in the difficult stages of Web site development until they learn the ropes. As they gain experience, they gradually add services until they can handle front-to-end design, implementation and maintenance. In the end, everything that you can do to help a client through this process provides more value to them and more income to your business. A total package deal is enticing to new Web clients.

In addition, larger companies prefer a "bundled" approach. Small business clients, who can do some of the work themselves, will likely opt for the unbundled approach and purchase only those services that they can't provide themselves. They are reluctant to pay for services that they don't need or think they can do themselves. Often they do a part of the project only to later discover that they should have used your service on these things, too. This makes them a return client and a cash cow for follow-on business.

Talk to any customer, and they'll say that quality is very important. Yet, when push comes to shove, many customers are willing to accept lower quality to get a better price or response time. It's up to you to find what quality they will accept. Then produce to their standard.

To many business people, your fast response is key. They are typically rushed on most projects and appreciate a support organization that can work evenings and weekends (if necessary) to get out a job that is well done and meets their harried schedule. Some Web service shops find that over 60% of their business involves rush jobs. The question is: Are these shops charging a premium for expediting a project ahead of others in the job queue?

Selecting Which Services to Offer

Most service providers determine a cost, apply a markup and set price. I suggest that you take a different approach and evaluate whether a service is a good profit generator before you add it to your marketing brochure or flyer.

Take one service that you are considering. Determine your budgeted hourly cost to provide that service. Then look at what other service providers are charging. This is how the customers value that service. Based on this selling price, calculate how much is left (after covering costs) for profit and return on investment. If the answer is: Not much! Then carefully re-evaluate the service. Can you reduce costs in some way so you increase the profit and ROI numbers? Perhaps you could outsource this service at a lower cost basis and thereby improve the profit and return potential.

If you are building brand name, you may want to enter the market with your prices set to those of your competitors and gradually secure a price premium and improved profit margin by consistently reducing your cost of services sold. By letting the customer dictate the price, you are establishing a good initial price level from which you can build future growth (assuming you can address cost issues such as output per hour, hardware and software expenses, and labor costs).

Defining Your Business Objective

Clearly understand why you are in business. Is your goal to build a retirement nest egg? Is it to build a large, thriving business to turn over to your kids? Is it to just have fun in life? Is it to earn all the money that you can by a certain age? Is it to return good service to a country that has served you so well? Are you adopting previous skills to a new business environment? Are you seeking financial independence from a stressful job in a large company? Or are you simply taking control over your own life and destiny? Whatever the reason, you need to recognize and accept why you are operating this Web service business.

Next, you must decide the real nature of your business. Is your business to provide solutions? It is to provide time for others to do different things? Are you offering a profit opportunity for your customers? Are you selling Web site development and design, or are you selling worry-free on-line commerce?

Consider the "Gillette safety razor" strategy. Gillette made his profit by selling blades, not by selling razors. He sold his razors at a loss so he could really sell the patented blades at a comfortable mark-up. What the customer wanted was simply a lower cost shave. Gillette sold a way to get a one penny shave—substantially less than going to a barber at the time.

Xerox adopted the Gillette razor pricing strategy and developed a huge market by selling copies of documents, not by selling a copying machine. There could be a Gillette razor in your business too.

From your analysis, develop a mission statement that explains why you are operating as a Web services provider. Take time to describe what kind of company you are and where you intend to go. Chart your course.

With this statement clearly in mind, gather your staff (which may be just you), and begin an analysis process leading to goals and objectives. Look at your products and services. Are you providing the right products and services to the right markets in the right time frame? What about competitors? What products and services are they offering? What is their market position? What can you determine about the area they cover, the prices they charge, and the extent of their business? Can you spot any weaknesses in their strategy?

Based on this assessment, establish short term and long term goals for your business. Decide where you plan to go, what you plan to do, and where you plan to be three years from now. Do you want to improve efficiency? Quality? Market share? All of your full time staff should be involved in this process.

The goals that you establish form the basis for your marketing plan—your road map for operations. A key to surviving a competitive market is good planning followed by good plan execution.

After looking long range, take a shorter view and answer the same questions for the near term. What do you want to accomplish each year between now and three years from now? This defines your tactical plan.

Based on the strategic (long term) plan and your tactical (short term) plan, carefully establish business objectives. These objectives should be specifically expressed and be not only achievable, but measurable. Each objective should have a set completion date and a person assigned to be responsible.

With objectives clearly defined, develop a pricing strategy that represents a framework in which your pricing objectives can be translated into pricing tactics. These tactics become the specific decisions or actions that you'll follow to carry out your formula for success.

Once you've defined the goals and objectives for your business, communicate these to your staff. It is from these goals and objectives that you establish specific tasks for each of your employees.

As you implement your plan, monitor the daily operations and periodically measure quantitatively how you and your team are doing in meeting these objectives. (Chapter 8 describes what to measure.) When an objective has been met, tell your staff. Then reward everyone for their part in making success happen.

If your goals become unrealistic, change the formula, change the ground rules, or (if necessary) change the players. It's important to accept change in your formula. Change will occur. And only by being willing to revise your goals and objectives can you keep moving along on your path of success.

Many business owners are followers. They price their goods and services based on what competitors charge. But what happens when all Web service shops are doing the same thing? There is no leader, just price confusion. You need a logical way to determine what your prices ought to be. Then you can decide what you want them to be. At least you'll know the difference. And you will feel comfortable that you are pricing for profit, not for paucity (scarceness, or meager income).

Pricing Strategies to Consider

There's pricing, and then there's pricing. In this section I'll share some of the creative ways that other shop owners are pricing their products and services. Some of these are similar. Some are based on cost. Others are based on competition. And others are based on desire and wishful thinking.

As shown in Figure 6-3, there are basically four strategic pricing orientations—cost-oriented, shop-oriented, competitor-oriented, and market-oriented.

In the following paragraphs, I'll describe strategies based on each orientation, and I'll provide graphical examples where appropriate.

COST-ORIENTED PRICING	COMPETITOR-ORIENTED PRICING
Markup	Match Them
Cost-Plus	One-Half
Cost-Volume	3X Pricing
Targeted-Profit	Straddle
Targeted Return	Head-On
SHOP-ORIENTED PRICING	**MARKET-ORIENTED PRICING**
Floor-Price Plus	New Service
% Capacity Plus	Leadership
Net Revenue	In "Zone"
Single Price	Loss-Leader
Desired Pay Plus	Customer Set
Only With Commas	Customary
Price by Expertise	Subjective
	Tiered
	Penny Pricing
	Composite

Figure 6-3. The orientations of pricing strategy.

Cost-Oriented Pricing

Here, prices are set after calculating all your costs. This becomes the baseline from which to start. The strategy is to cover your costs, then generate some level of revenue above this point.

Cost-oriented pricing includes markup pricing, cost-plus pricing, cost-volume pricing, targeted profit pricing, targeted return-on-sales pricing, and targeted return-on-investment pricing.

Markup Pricing

In markup pricing, you set your rates by adding a predetermined percentage to the wholesale price or the cost of a product or service. As shown in Figure 6-4, the total markup represents overhead expenses and profit.

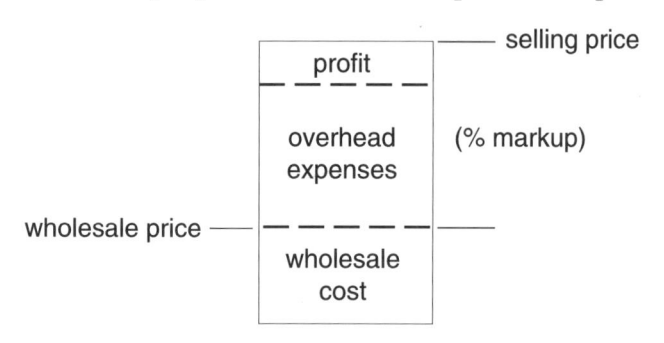

Fig. 6-4. Markup pricing.

Markups differ based on the type of service, your competition, turnover, and the sales risk. Many businesses adopt a "standard" mark-up for each product category. Clothing is typically marked up by 40 to 60 percent. Staple food items such as bread and milk are marked up by 10 to 23 percent. Snack foods are marked up 27 to 47 percent, and so on.

In reality, there's a markup at each stage in the development of a product—manufacturing, distribution, and final sales. The net result is a product that has been marked up several hundred percent over its initial raw material cost as it passes through each stage in the manufacturing-to-customer process. I once read that 31% of the cost of bread represents taxes that the customer eventually pays at the grocery counter.

If a product cost $10 from a wholesale supplier, a business owner will add a portion of overhead costs (rent, utilities, insurance, salaries, etc.) and profit to this base cost to arrive at a selling price. To get any selling price using this technique, divide the wholesale cost by one, minus the percent overhead plus percent profit (both expressed in decimal) as shown below.

$$\text{selling price} = \frac{\text{wholesale cost}}{1 - (\text{overhead} + \text{profit})}$$

Thus, if overhead represents 25% of your costs and you want a 10% profit, you would mark up a $10 product by 53.8% to achieve a selling price of $15.38.

$$\text{selling price} = \frac{10}{1 - (.25 + .10)}$$

$$= \frac{10}{1 - 0.35} = \frac{10}{0.65}$$

selling price = $15.38

Then, to get percent markup, apply the formula:

$$\% \text{ markup} = \frac{\text{selling price} - \text{wholesale cost}}{\text{wholesale cost}} \times 100$$

$$= \frac{15.38 - 10.00}{10.00} \times 100$$

$$= \frac{5.38}{10} \times 100$$

% markup = 0.538 x 100

= 53.8%

There are several variations of markup pricing— a calculated markup for each product or service, a standard markup on all products, and a markup based on some accepted reference. By basing your price on covering total costs, including overhead, with a predetermined markup for profit you are implementing *full cost pricing*.

If your price covers the variable costs of doing business with a predetermined mark-up for profit but not all of your overhead, you are applying *incremental cost pricing*. This method assumes that your mark-up will cover overhead and provide a fair profit. It is only effective for those skilled in pricing.

The formula below can be used to calculate price using cost plus mark-up. Price is equal to direct materials times markup plus estimated time multiplied by your hourly rate.

price = (dir matls x markup) + (est. time x hourly rate)
      = (total production costs) x (mark-up)

In the *calculated markup* approach, each product and service is analyzed to determine its associated costs. Then a markup is applied to each product or service based on demand, perceived value, and similar factors. Markup or cost-based pricing is often used on time and materials contracts.

In *standard markup* pricing, a shop owner partitions the products and services into specific categories. Each category is assigned a "standard" markup. The appropriate markup is then applied to each element in a category.

Retail stores have different possible markups for each type of product (driven by competitor prices or industry-standard markup percentages).

In the service industry, one form of standard markup is to allocate a basic rate to each cost center and then to use these rates and the productive hours available to estimate and price a job. This approach is called *"budgeted hourly cost pricing."*

There are two versions of the *accepted reference markup* approach to pricing. The first approach is to establish base prices for all products and services by analyzing the actual operating costs and then adding an appropriate markup to each service. The final "standard" prices are then printed on a "list prices" sheet. This retail price list is shown to customers. Some shops call this a *"counter price sheet."*

The second approach is to purchase a book of industry standard billing rates for the services that you offer. This book is then consulted each time a job estimate is required. You assume that the rates listed already include markup. Our *Pricing Tables: Desktop Services* and *Pricing Tables: Web Services* books are industry standard references for billing rates.

Except for competitive bid situations, markup pricing is probably not appropriate because it doesn't maximize profit when the possibility exists that the market will bear higher prices. In addition, a cost basis for service is often difficult to determine. Nevertheless, markup pricing is considered the fairest pricing method for both buyer and seller. It's the norm in the retail world.

Cost-Plus Pricing

In *cost-plus pricing*, the customer pays for the cost of developing a product plus some percentage or fixed amount above cost. It's similar to markup pricing except there is no fixed markup. For example, a customer brings a complex project to you. There are elements in the project whose costs are uncertain. Instead of trying to "guess" your costs, you offer to do the job for your costs plus a percentage.

This is a good strategy when a customer wants services that you don't normally provide, but that they want you to oversee. Subcontract the job and provide the client with a copy of the actual invoice from the subcontractor. On the invoice, add a percentage to the charge for administrating the job.

The percentage in cost-plus pricing varies from 10% to over 40% depending on the tasks, the location, and the business.

Here's how to use cost-plus to come up with a shop hourly rate. Suppose you have two employees, you and one other person. Collectively, your team is 50% productive at best. You can bill out your work 25% of the time, and your employee is billed out 75% of the time. This means that in a 40-hour week, your shop averages 20 hours of billable work for each person. With two weeks paid vacation, this comes out to 1,000 hours a year per person. Your prices must be set so the annual sales revenue makes up for both two-week vacations.

Adding up the annual fixed and variable expenses, you estimate $120,000 for the year ($10,000 each month). At 50% productivity, you must collectively earn the $10,000 in only 173 billable hours (173 hours available each month, two people working at 50% productivity means 346 hours available, but 173 worked). This comes out to $57.80 an hour to cover costs. Then you add a flat 25% premium to your total costs and price your services at $72.25 an hour.

Another cost-plus method starts with job cost. To this, you add 70%, disregarding any discount. This becomes your selling price—simple to calculate and simple to apply.

Cost-Volume Pricing

In *cost-volume pricing*, a cost-volume curve such as that shown in Figure 6-5 is generated to equate the volume of sales income to production and overhead costs. It shows graphically that, as you increase sales, the net unit service costs decrease. A percentage of the cost of sales will expense out as overhead, so as volume increases, the cost of services sold (per unit of service) actually decreases. This suggests that if you lower your sales price, more people should buy, and the added volume should further increase your profit.

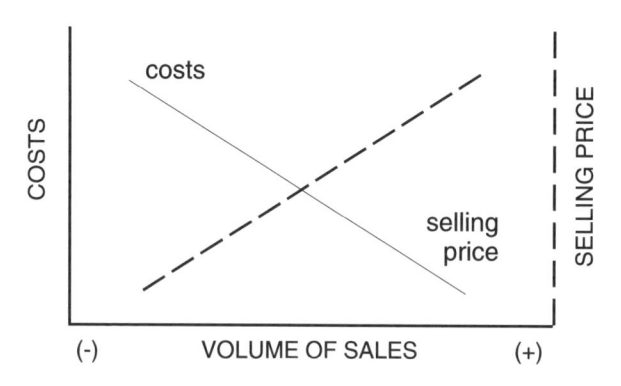

Fig 6-5. A typical cost-volume curve.

Some people call this approach "doing yourself in." It's risky because it presumes that your competition will sit still while you manipulate prices in the marketplace. This approach is based on your having an accurate assessment of the customer base and of your competition. And it assumes that you clearly understand your costs on a service-by-service basis.

The cost-volume approach is often a trap, because as you lower your price, the competition usually lowers theirs in response. You effectively become a price leader on the way down toward insolvency. The inherent risks are simply too great for most shop owners to attempt.

Targeted Profit Pricing

In the *targeted profit pricing* strategy, you set a specific annual profit target. Next, you determine your fixed and variable costs. Then you estimate how many units of a product or service you can sell and how sensitive demand is to price. Next, you set a target profit value and decide what price you can charge (Figure 6-6).

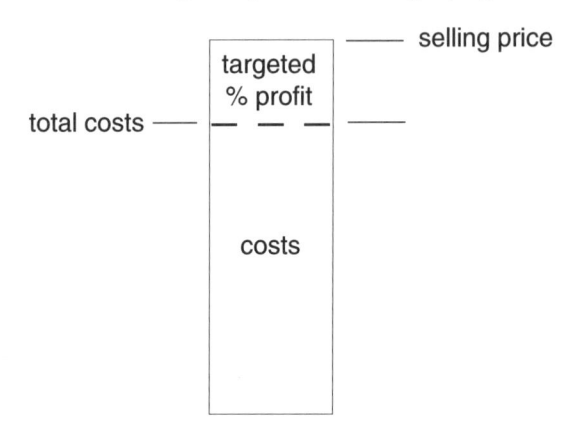

Fig 6-6. Targeted profit pricing.

Since profit equals revenue less costs, we can use the following formula to derive a price.

targeted profit = total revenue - total cost

where

total revenue = (price) x (quantity)

and

total cost = fixed cost - (variable costs x quantity)

Therefore,

profit = (price)(qty) - [fixed cost - (variable costs x qty)]

Solving for price, we get:

$$\text{price} = \frac{\text{profit} + \text{fixed cost} + (\text{variable costs} \times \text{quantity})}{\text{quantity}}$$

This simplistic formula assumes that the price you select will not change the quantity of sales realized from the quantity estimated. It also doesn't account for the investment needed to achieve the sales volume (cost of services sold).

By knowing your cost of services, the revenue you want and the profit you want to earn, you can back into this formula and determine the best quantity and the best selling price to use by changing the variables in your "what if" cost/price breakdown spreadsheet.

Targeted Return-on-Sales Pricing

Similar to targeted profit, the *targeted return-on-sales* strategy focuses on pricing so you get minimum or higher return on each sale (Fig. 6-7). You use the same fixed and variable costs as you did for the targeted profit pricing method, with the same quantity of sales.

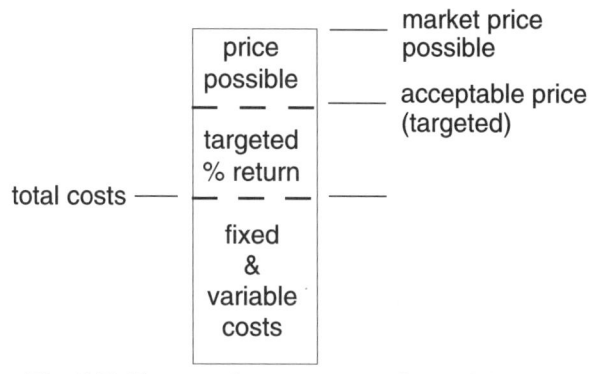

Fig 6-7. Targeted return-on-sales pricing.

In this method, you use the formula:

$$\text{targeted return} = \frac{\text{targeted profit}}{\text{total revenue}}$$

$$= \frac{\text{price} \times \text{qty} - [\text{fixed cost} + (\text{vble costs} \times \text{qty})]}{\text{price} \times \text{quantity}}$$

Solving for price we get:

$$\text{price} = \frac{-\text{fixed cost} - (\text{variable costs} \times \text{quantity})}{\text{quantity} (\text{targeted return} - 1)}$$

The result has negative values in the top and bottom of the formula. These cancel out, resulting in a positive price value.

Targeted Return-on-Investment Pricing

In *targeted return-on-investment pricing* you assume that you can obtain at least as good a return on the money that you invested in a business as you can by investing in financial securities (Fig. 6-8).

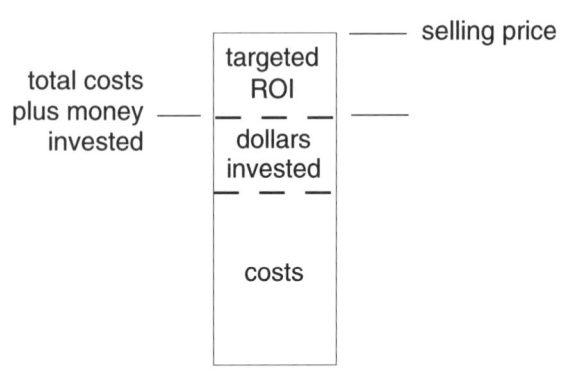

Fig 6-8. Targeted return-on-sales pricing.

If you feel that you can get a 10% return by investing in stocks, bonds, mutual funds, etc., then you can develop a business model that relates price, quantity, unit variable costs, fixed costs, overhead, taxes, etc. to yield the same 10% return on investment for a number of variable business options.

In this method, you select a profit and then work backwards to determine what price will cover your expenses and still yield your desired return.

This is a sophisticated version of cost-plus pricing. The profit-oriented pricing methods described are ideally suited for computer spreadsheet analysis.

Shop-Oriented Pricing

In a *shop-oriented pricing* strategy, your primary focus is on your own shop and what you want to charge.

Shop-oriented pricing includes floor price plus, percent capacity plus margin, net revenue inventory sell-off, single price any customer, desired pay plus, and only pricing with commas accepted.

Floor Price Plus Some

In a *floor price plus some* strategy, you determine the minimum price at which you are willing to sell a service. This becomes the floor price. Then establish a target sales price. (See Figure 6-9 on the next page.)

Any sale that is less than the floor price will result in a loss. So by clearly defining your "must-sell-at" and "want-to-sell-at" levels, you can determine how each sale impacts the profitability of your shop. This lets you sell at different price levels and still have a feel for profit per sale. You can accept lower margins on some sales and higher margins on those sales in which you enjoy a market niche.

The trick is to avoid tying up valuable resources on jobs that contribute little to your bottom line. Evaluate

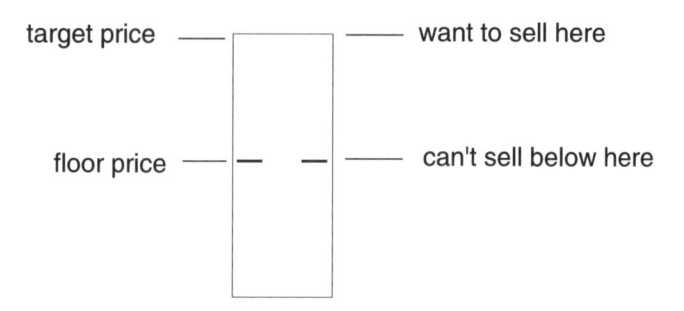

```
target price ──┐   ┌── want to sell here
               │   │
               │   │
floor price ───┤─ ─├── can't sell below here
               │   │
               │   │
               └───┘
```

Fig 6-9. Floor price plus pricing.

each sale relative to available shop capacity and where the income falls in your floor/target price range.

Percent Capacity Plus Margin

In *percent capacity plus margin* pricing, you calculate your standard costs as if your shop is operating at 70% capacity (70% productive). Then you add a specific "margin" equal to your standard costs to arrive at a price (Fig. 6-10).

```
                          ┌──────────┐── selling price
                          │ targeted │
                          │ % margin │
          total costs ────┤─ ─  ─ ─ ─├──
                          │          │
                          │  costs   │
                          │   at     │
                          │  70%     │
                          │ capacity │
                          │          │
                          └──────────┘
```

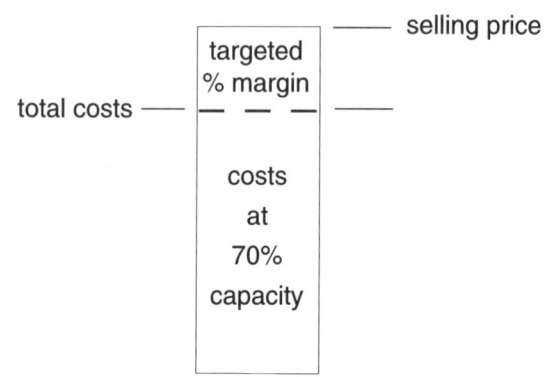

Fig 6-10. Percent capacity plus pricing

If you calculate your budgeted hourly costs at 70% to be $43 for a particular service, and you want 40% margin, set your price at $60.20 per hour.

Net Revenue, Inventory Sell Off

Also called *"net revenue marginal analysis"*, *"net revenue, inventory sell off"* is used to determine when the last item in an inventory lot has been sold. It lets you reduce the selling price for remaining inventory so you can eliminate dated inventory.

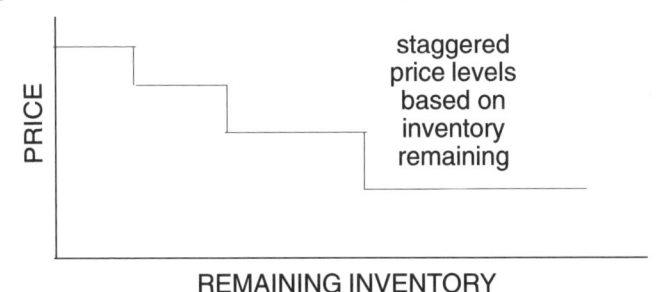

Fig 6-11. Net revenue, inventory sell off pricing.

This technique is used for retail products such as disks of clip art, toner cartridges, etc. It can also be used to meet aggressive sales tactics by your competition.

Single Price, Any Customer Pricing

In *single price, any customer* pricing, you apply a fixed price to every customer. No customer gets special treatment. The high-end corporate customer pays the same fee as the non-profit, low-budget customer.

An example is a manufacturer who charges resellers 50% of the *suggested retail price (SRP)*, whether they buy one or a 100 units. It's one price, any customer, any quantity. This makes bookkeeping really simple.

Desired Pay Plus

In a *desired pay plus* pricing strategy, you increase your desired hourly wage by some multiple. Canadian desktop service provider, Don McCahill, uses a "two-times" (2X) rule to establish his fee. He takes what he wants to earn and then doubles this figure to come up with an hourly rate to charge (Fig. 6-12).

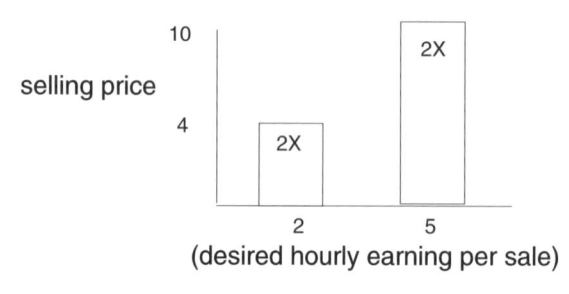

```
          10                           ┌─────┐
                                       │ 2X  │
selling price                          │     │
           4         ┌─────┐           │     │
                     │ 2X  │           │     │
                     │     │           │     │
                     └─────┘           └─────┘
                        2                 5
              (desired hourly earning per sale)
```

Fig 6-12. "2x" pricing.

To make $35 an hour after expenses, he'll mark up his service rates to $70 an hour.

If you currently earn $50,000 a year, you're making about $24 an hour. Some Web service providers apply a 2.5X multiplier to determine their hourly shop rate. To net $24 an hour, they charge $60 an hour (24 x 2.5). This rule of thumb lets them earn what they desire while covering overhead, fringes, administration, and marketing.

With a good handle on your overhead and capital investment, you can adopt a lower (say 2.1) multiplier. This reduces your fee basis to $50 an hour and still lets you net about $24 an hour after expenses.

Only Pricing With Commas Accepted

In *only pricing with commas*, you restrict your jobs to those that earn higher dollars as shown in Figure 6-13.

A recent article in *Home Office Computing* described how a technical writing and desktop service business successfully adopted a pricing strategy that focuses only on high price jobs. According to the article, if a job does not price out to over $1,000 (has a comma in the number), the job is declined or passed to another shop.

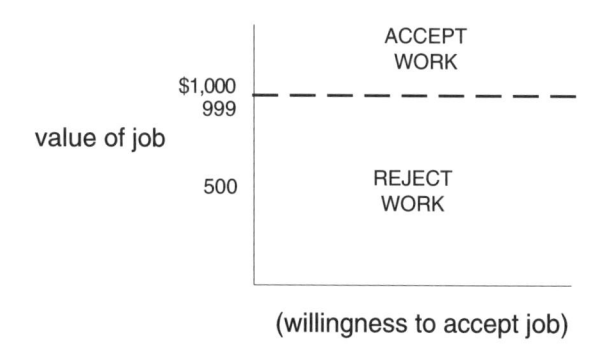

Fig 6-13. Only commas pricing.

The strategy here is that jobs with small income potential don't leave room for negotiation. They also do not provide the profit potential that a bigger project can. The idea is to pursue the big dollars and leave the scraps and business job tailings to the low price shops.

Pricing by Expertise

In *pricing by expertise*, you base your rates on the expertise of you and your staff. *Newbies* (new business entrepreneurs) typically charge a lower rate than more experienced designers. As your expertise grows, so should your billing rates (Fig. 6-14).

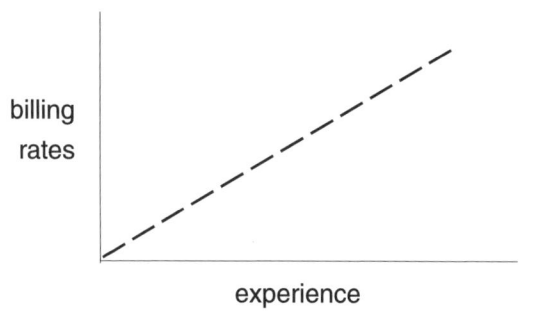

Fig 6-14. Pricing by expertise.

For example, a newbie could charge $30 an hour. A talented and educated designer could charge $50 an hour. And an experienced designer could charge $75 to $150 an hour. Your sample portfolio should show this.

Some Web service providers charge much more. It depends on the customer and on the type of service. According to *WebWEEK*, 85% of the top design firms only accept jobs with price tags higher than $30,000. The article said that GE's web site was done for just under $6 million. Most service providers are happy if they earn $100 an hour and get at least $600 for each Web site design project.

Competitor-Oriented Pricing

In a *competitor-oriented pricing* strategy, your primary concern is what competitors are currently charging.

Competitor-oriented pricing includes matching the competition, competing head-on, "one-half" pricing, "3X better, 3X below" pricing, and straddle pricing.

Match the Competition Pricing

In *match the competition* pricing, you base your rates on what the competition is charging. It doesn't require analysis to determine the best prices for a profit objective. And it assumes that your competition is being successful by charging the prices that they advertise.

There's a risk in assuming that your competition knows what they're doing. They could be selling at a loss or below acceptable profit levels without your knowing it. If all the competitors match each other, everyone can lose money together. Some say "misery loves company," but this is taking the adage too far.

"One-Half" Pricing

"One half" pricing is a simple way to set rates. Here you adopt a modest pricing strategy in which you find out what the most expensive competitor charges and then cut these rates in half. (Figure 6-15)

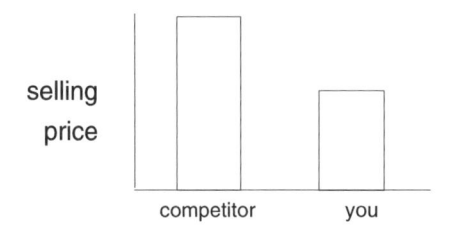

Fig 6-15. "One-half" pricing.

This pricing strategy can work in systems integration environments where the markup is extremely high. But this strategy has high risk for the Web service provider. The simple pricing solution may actually be no solution. In fact, it may convert all of your products and services into price loss leaders.

"3X Better, 3X Below" Pricing

The *3X better, 3X below* pricing model is for a new kid on the block who wants to challenge an entrenched competitor. Many prospective customers will wonder if you'll succeed and question why they should switch service providers. They also question how your products and services will support their own operation better than their current supplier.

Don Jones, president of four successful startups, was interviewed in *Success Magazine* regarding his formula for taking on large, entrenched market leaders.

He feels that you first need a product or service that's unique. Then you need better resources and a significantly better product offering if you want to go after the business of an entrenched competitor. Jones says that you must provide products or services that are at least three times as good as the market leader.

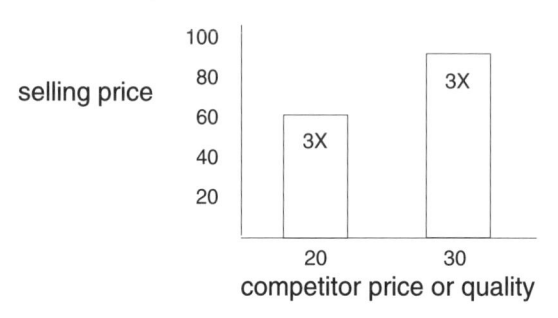

```
100 |
           |
 80 |           ┌────┐
selling price  |           │ 3X │
 60 |           │    │
           ┌────┐    │    │
 40 |      │ 3X │    │    │
           │    │    │    │
 20 |      │    │    │    │
           │    │    │    │
           └────┴────┴────┘
              20        30
         competitor price or quality
```

Fig 6-16. "3X" pricing.

This means that you must analyze your competition and understand what qualities the market leader has that customers appreciate most. What makes these customers take their business to that competitor?

In this strategy, you address product and price. You can take the leadership position by developing a service "goodness factor" that's at least three times better. Then set your prices at one-third what the largest competitor charges. This can be difficult, if not impossible. But Jones infers that he did this successfully four times.

Straddle Pricing

Straddle pricing is a strategy for rewarding return customers. Here you publish price rates that are higher than your competitors, but once a prospect becomes a customer, they receive a discount card (or number) that they can use against future purchases. It lets them get the same service for less than what competitors charge. In essence, you set your prices above and below what competitors are charging. Then you show your new customers know how to play the game.

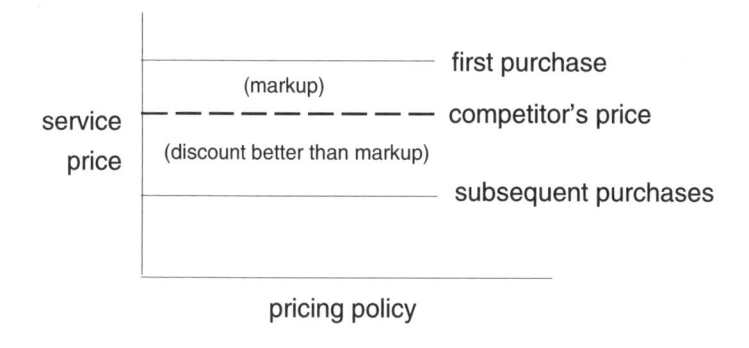

Fig 6-17. Straddle pricing.

The new customer subsidizes the return customer knowing full well that on their next job, they too, will receive a better price.

Competing Head-On With Lowest Price

Typically, a shop owner will find out what a competitor is charging and then charge 5-10% less. But sometimes, you decide to go all out and *compete head-on with lowest prices*. This is dangerous for a small shop. You are competing head-on with price merchants who may have deep pockets and can afford to undercut you on price. Yet it can work.

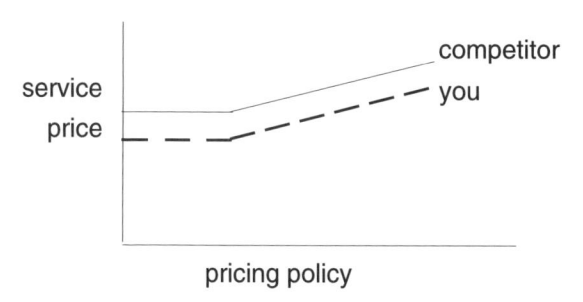

Fig 6-18. Competing head-on.

If you want to be the lowest price in town, offer few, if any frills, operate at low margin, and strive to make your money on volume.

The key is to set low, no-frill prices and then be consistent. Don't confuse people. Competing on price means that this strategy drives every other business decision that you make. Cost controls everything.

Cut your overhead to rock bottom. Pay cash so you can get another 3-5% shaved off the price for anything that you buy. And hire freelancers so you avoid the extra payroll and employee benefit costs. The lower your fixed costs, the higher your potential margin.

Competing head-on with low prices is tricky, but not impossible. But you can't get fancy. And you must stay totally committed to this marketing strategy.

Market-Oriented Pricing

In a *market-oriented pricing* strategy, your primary concern is with what your competitors are charging.

Market-oriented pricing covers new services, leadership, pricing in the zone, loss-leaders, target price set by customer, accepted-as-customary, subjective, tiered, penny pricing, and composite pricing.

New Service Pricing

When introducing a *new service*, consider a strategy that sets a relatively high price during the initial stages of the life of the service. This is called *"skimming."*

Skimming makes good sense when the demand for your service is uncertain, you've invested a lot of money in developing the capability, there isn't any known competition, or when the service will likely grow slowly.

Chapter 6 - Pricing Strategies 151

Fig 6-19. New service pricing.

If you want to build market share rapidly, consider *penetration pricing* where you set relatively low prices during the initial stages of offering the service.

Leadership Pricing

A price leader is a company that is able to make a change in their pricing based on cost and demand conditions without starting a competitive price war. In *leadership pricing* you can make a rate change announcement and others will follow (not undercut) the new price. Consider the airlines. When American announces a price change, other airlines quickly fall into line with similar prices.

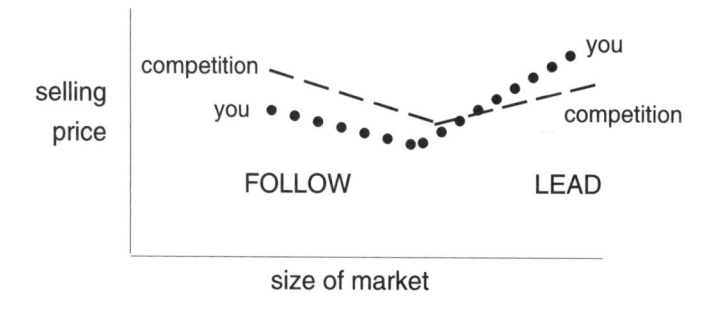

Fig 6-20. Leadership pricing.

If you intend to become a price leader, your business must develop and possess certain characteristics. Your shop must service a large share of the market. You must be committed to a particular product or service line and have a large service capacity. You'll also need the newest, most cost-effective equipment and support software. And you'll need a tight distribution system that can get price change information out quickly.

Be sensitive to the price and profit moves of your industry. Know pricing strategies intimately and have a sense of timing to correctly know when price changes are necessary. Good marketing research can help you forecast market response. You must maintain good customer relations and gain a reputation for providing superior customer service. With effective project management controls in place (and operational), and clearly understanding the legal issues surrounding pricing decisions, you can position yourself to be a price leader.

Operating as a price leader is perfectly legal as long as you don't conspire with another firm in making your pricing decisions. A price leader sets rates independently of the competition, although the prices that competitors charge are certainly considered during strategic analysis.

Pricing in the "Zone"

This strategy recognizes that you don't have to set your prices exactly in a theoretical bulls eye for customers to buy. If your pricing is in the "zone" you should get your share of available business.

Web service is not a commodity, and the level of service differs from shop to shop. This is why our Web service pricing survey discovered a wide range of rates. Shops are offering different design packages, different response times, and different performance levels. Even the ISPs have established budget, standard and premium levels of site hosting and maintenance.

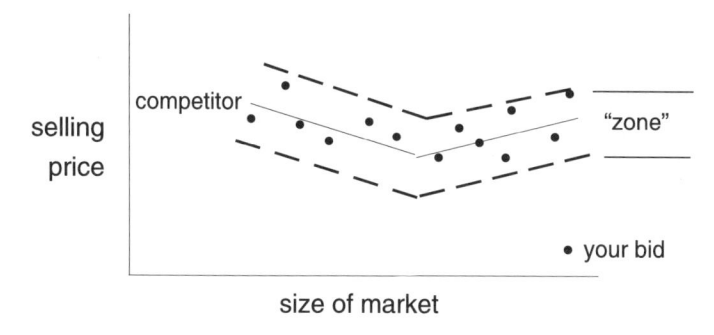

Fig 6-21. Pricing in the "zone."

The key is that they differentiate their service. Then they set prices to hit within an acceptable area—*pricing in the "zone."* They don't try to hit a hypothetical bullseye! They partition their price levels for a three-times difference between the lowest and highest price.

According to *Service & Support World*, there is usually a 25% difference between one level of service and the next. And the "strike zone" service price is within 6-25% of that charged by competitors. Therefore, you should still get a job, even if your prices are 10% higher. So, target your price to come in within the zone. That should be good enough.

Since the price strike zone for a service typically ranges two to three times between bottom and top, just getting within a narrow range of your competitor prices will let you successfully compete. The zone is then established by reasonable differences between similar services. Within a zone, prices can be 10-25% apart.

Thus, sell a customer on the value of your solution. If competitor prices come in farther apart (outside the zone), they must be bidding a different level of service. In this case, the one who matches the customer's needs best will win the job.

With strike zone pricing, your customers don't have to like your price. They just have to tolerate it.

Loss-Leader Pricing

In *loss-leader pricing*, a product or service is sold at break-even, or just below cost to attract customers to your business so you can then sell them on other (high margin) products and services.

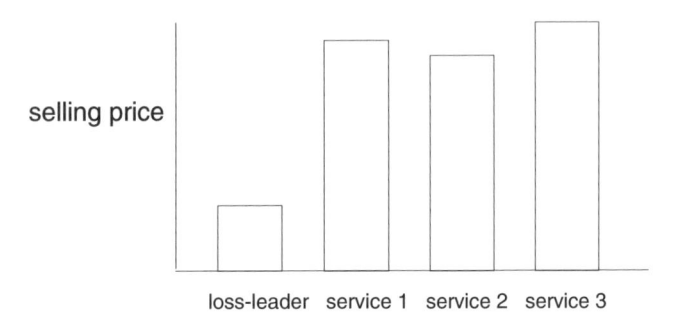

Fig 6-22. Loss-leader pricing.

Your goal is not to increase sales of the "no-profit" service, but to attract sales of services that generate high profit. Averaging out the package sale, you hope to realize good profit on each transaction.

In a retail store, magazines are not very profitable (20% gross margin), but magazine purchases often accompany purchases of candy and drinks, which have higher margins. Thus, the magazines are basically loss-leaders used to help sell more snacks and soft drinks.

Customer-Set Target Pricing

In *customer-set target pricing*, the client tells you what they are willing to pay for your service. Then you evaluate whether you want to work for this. Car salesmen are masters at this game. There's a window sticker price, but you want to pay less. So, they ask you what you will pay for that wonderful vehicle. You give them a price and then they use this as a baseline from which to nickel-and-dime you higher.

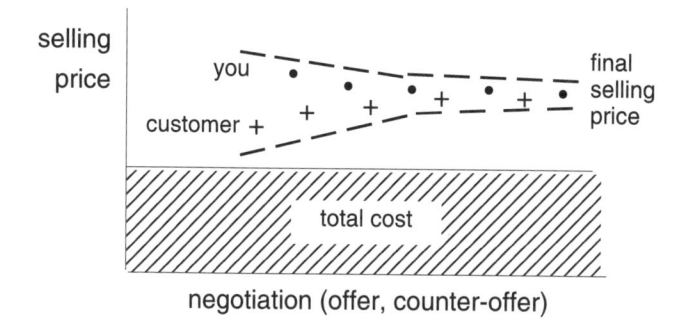

Fig 6-23. Customer-set target pricing.

As a Web service provider, you give the prospect your posted price and then ask them what they are comfortable paying for the job they described. Be certain to partition the job into all of its meaningful tasks so the prospect understands clearly what is being provided and what to expect in the end.

Accepted-As-Customary Pricing

In *accepted-as-customary* pricing, the customer is pre-conditioned to pay a "standard" fee for certain products or services. For years, you could sell black and white copies for 10¢ each. But, raising your price to 15¢ would exceed the accepted price threshold of customers and they would shop elsewhere. When paperback books were priced at $3.95 each, and printing costs increased, a publisher would change the quality of the paper, or the quality of the binding to lower manufacturing costs so they could hold the $3.95 price constant for the buying public. The $3.95 was the accepted price, and most publishers felt this was a threshold over which buyers would not budge. Today, paperback books are selling for $5.95 and $6.95. Readers are still buying.

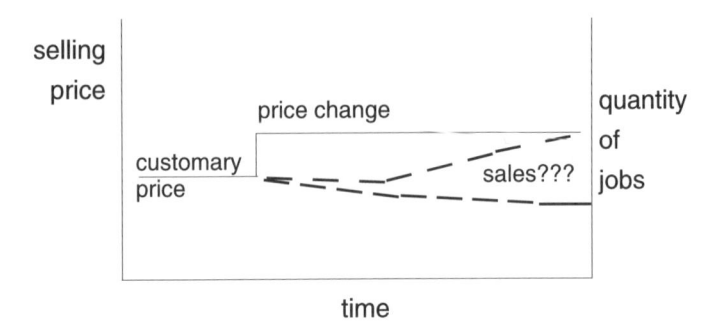

Fig 6-24. Customary price strategy.

However, bucking the accepted standard price can be risky. A lower price can cause customers to think they're getting poor quality. Raise prices too much and customers think you're too expensive. Competitor pricing and market expectations drive your pricing decisions. A similar strategy is "going-rate" pricing.

Subjective Pricing

Subjective pricing is another market-oriented strategy. After years in the business, an owner gets a "feel" for what a price should be. Using this subjective feeling, the owner can price products and services at, below, or above this benchmark.

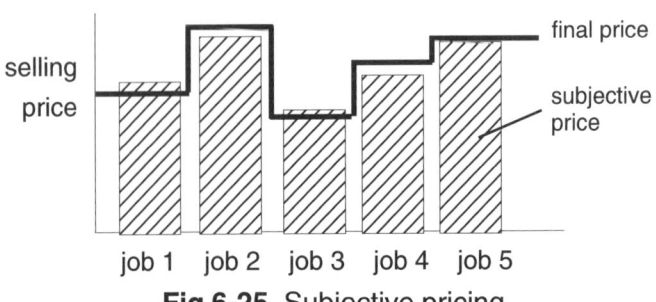

Fig 6-25. Subjective pricing.

Businesses that target their products and services for a specific market will price accordingly. To sell to the high-end corporate customer, price your products and services to meet the expectations of this market. You base your prices on market research and your opinion of what is acceptable.

Tiered Pricing

If you unbundled your services, tweaked your rates, tried discounting and still margins continue to shrink, try *tiered pricing*.

Here you establish different levels of service and give each its own set of prices. Tiered pricing is based on the fact that 10% of buyers are price shoppers. The rest dislike high prices but will tolerate them to get more perceived value. Value is in the eye of the buyer.

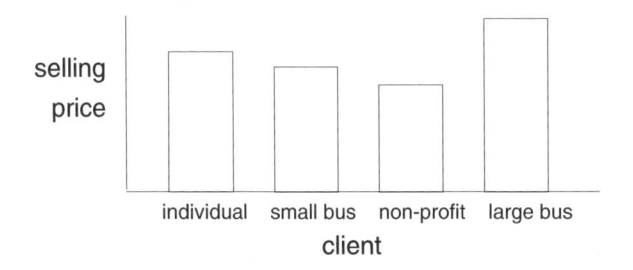

Fig 6-26. Tiered pricing.

This means that you can often bill large companies more for products and services than you can the smaller price-sensitive business clients.

A variable pricing strategy applies different prices to different customers. The high-end corporate client is charged a premium price, while a non-profit business, or home-office entrepreneur is charged a much lower fee. There is a risk here for price discrimination, so be sure to work costs and margins carefully.

Research indicates that large companies are often less fazed by higher fees than smaller companies. The large organizations are more concerned with your continued availability (survival) and quality of service than they are with what you charge. They take longer to get signed up to your products and services, but they don't haggle over "nickels and dimes." Therefore, the larger they are, the better your chance of increasing your fees on everything you offer. These customers appreciate the quality and value your shop has to offer and are willing to pay more for your support.

Many shops find that larger accounts provide a strong boost to their net profit. However, you must factor in the additional effort required to realize the sale. The after-sale support can also increase significantly.

Often, large accounts will pay a consulting fee up front, but your cost-of-sale can also be larger because they may insist on a lengthy multi-page proposal before any contract is signed and billable work can begin. One technique is to charge prospective clients for generating a proposal. If they then sign a contract with you, credit the proposal cost to your job price. Then, if they were just shopping for competing bids, you still get paid.

There's also the specter of discounting. It never really goes away-even with large companies. If they make a volume buy, they will likely expect a discount.

This means that pricing for larger accounts takes as much analysis as it does for average accounts. You can't just pull a price out of thin air because your prospect is a large company. The corporate buyer is usually quite sophisticated, and they talk to others in the business.

One form of tiered pricing is to unbundle all of your services so you can sell each individually. Let the client pick and choose the level of service that they want. This maximizes your ability to offer something for everyone.

When you consider tiering your services, carefully establish the size and scope for each pricing level.

Some shops partition their services into equal pricing levels—say 10% pricing packages. Each level of service and support includes a defined level of hand holding and support. For example, you could have one price for generating a "standard" Home Page. No alterations or other design changes can be made without incurring "extra" charges. They get no design consulting or suggestions for improvement. The input from the customer is simply converted into a Web page based on a fixed format template.

For those who want a dialogue with the page designer, and who want to optimize their site, another tier of prices kicks in. This means that those with the most experience can get a job done for the least cost. It also means that you will be paid for the work you actually do. This minimizes the "giving" without "receiving" that is so prevalent in service shops today.

Penny Pricing
Adding Cents Makes Sense

The cents numbers appended to advertised prices is an area where profit can be made with little or no added cost. This *penny pricing* is a good strategy to adopt.

Advertising scanning at $5.36 an image probably won't generate any more sales than you would get by advertising it at $5.95, but the higher price can add 59¢ of pure profit to each sale. Natural price points occur in business. By using these points you can increase price without changing a customer's perception of worth.

Price points can influence the buying patterns of the public. Mathematically, they represent discontinuities in a price elasticity demand curve. You can sell much more at $5.95 than you can at $6.05, but not much more at $5.85 than you can at $5.95. Six dollars is the point of discontinuity. Customers consider the 10¢ difference between $5.95 and $6.05 a major hurdle but hardly notice the difference between $5.85 and $5.95. Yet $5.95 represents 10¢ more in direct profit. Making 10¢ more on high volume sales can add up fast. Supermarkets make a business by working with pennies of profit.

Natural price point discontinuities are more frequent at lower rates. These are where abrupt shifts in demand (price elasticity) occur. Knowing where these points occur can significantly affect your bottom line.

Eric Mitchell, publisher of *The Pricing Advisor* offers good advice on how you should use price points in your business strategy. He partitions product pricing into categories—less than $1, $1 to $10, $10 to $100, and more than $100. Each price category should be handled differently. The ends of each price range represent discontinuity points.

Mitchell suggests that you can effectively add to your profit by pricing products less than a dollar at a value ending with nine — 39¢, 79¢, 99¢ etc. When most customers see a product priced at "less than a dollar," they notice the tens digit value, but not the cents digit value. It's exactly what happens when you buy gasoline. The price may be $1.40 and nine tenths per gallon. We only notice $1.40 per gallon.

Therefore, rather than pricing your product at 96¢, make it 99¢ and your customer won't care. The extra 3¢ in income passes directly to your gross profit line.

Mitchell further suggests that you avoid ending prices with 1s, 2s, or 4s (e.g., 21¢, 42¢, 64¢), although ending in 5 is acceptable (e.g., 95¢). Just remember, you're trying to focus on profit. The more you can get for your product without changing the perception of value for cost, the better your profit picture.

For products priced between $1 and $10, Mitchell suggests ending the price with the digit 5 or 9 (e.g., $1.15, $1.39, etc.). Avoid using any other digit. A price of $2.75 is equally as attractive as $2.79. Yet, by adding a few cents here, a few cents there, you generate more profit—significant if you're handling thousands of characters of HTML data or graphic images each week.

SELLING PRICE	TACTIC	EXAMPLE
<$1	price by 9s	39¢
$1 - !10	price by 5s or 9s	$1.55 / $7.29
$10 - $100	price by 25s or dollars	$24.25 / $99
$100 +	dollars, no cents	$125 / $750

Fig 6-27. Penny pricing.

When the price exceeds $10, use increments of 25¢ or round off to a whole dollar value without cents (e.g., $11.50, $12.75, $24.25, $37, etc.). Between $10 and $100, he suggests that you avoid using .99 (e.g., $11.99, $24.99, etc.). He feels that endings of .25, .50, and .75 are preferable because they suggest fair pricing. Thus we see $11.50, $12.75 and $96.75.

Above $100, Mitchell suggests that you stick with whole dollar amounts and never display the $.00 ending. A price of $110.00 looks much larger than a price of $110. It's all in the way we as customers view price.

This strategy is currently used pricing trade and paperback books. In 1985, publishers priced their books using a .95 point level to distinguish them from other consumer goods. This has changed. The decimal point prices have been raised from .95 to .99. Some publishers round off to the next highest dollar point. Hardcover books are sold with prices rounded off to the nearest dollar or the .50 price point. No consumer resistance to this new pricing strategy has been reported.

Many other products are being introduced with prices that end with .99 rather than .95. Mass market prices are rapidly being converted to the .99 point.

Since most Web service providers bill in round numbers, you may be missing a lot of added revenue. There's no client pain, and the extra profit is free.

Composite Pricing

You can also combine pricing methods to produce your own *composite pricing* policy. For example, you can have one set of prices for established services and another set of prices for new services. You can price for flexibility in a particular market niche, bundle your services, price for leadership, or price for market share.

Each pricing policy has different goals, objectives, assumptions, and requirements. Each also has its own deficiencies. The optimum way to set your rates is to develop a composite that includes the best things from each pricing strategy.

Use industry standard rates. Consider the pricing policy of competitors. Analyze your own business. Determine the time it takes you to perform certain tasks. Place a value on skills and experience. Then, wrap all this into a custom pricing package that works for you.

When your draft price list is complete, adjust and fine tune the basis for each price to create your final rates. By developing a custom pricing structure, you can quickly and accurately estimate jobs without spending a lot of time re-constructing their cost basis. Composite pricing lets you bid jobs with full confidence knowing that your desired profit is integrated into each price quote. A computer spreadsheet program can be used to develop "what if" models that you can adjust to find the optimum pricing and selling strategies for each product and service.

Smart Strategies

A good pricing strategy is a major part of your battle to gain market share and increase bottom line profit. But you must still deal with the insistent telephone price-shopper. And you must build and maintain your company image in any economic climate.

If your prices are higher than the competition, you'll have to demonstrate enough value to cause prospects to select your shop over others. A key factor in this is the *economic value* of your service. There is a *reference value* price that every client feels comfortable paying.

You can raise this acceptance bar by adding more value than your competitor offers. We call this the *differentiation value*. The reference value to the client and the differentiation value you offer make up the economic value that the customer feels. It's the maximum price that a smart shopper will pay.

Some clients will ask you to justify the cost-benefit of your prices against pricing by competitors. If you can't do this, you'd better re-think your pricing strategy. Or you re-look at the target market that you've selected.

Your goal is maximum sustainable profit. To get this, you'll need "street smart" guerrilla tactics. Here are some helpful tips.

Analyzing Your Customers by Profit

Most of us categorize customers based on sales volume. But, there's much more to customer analysis.

Customers generally fall into one of two categories. Some are price-sensitive (cheap). Others are quality-sensitive (upscale). You must determine which type of client you support.

Prioritize your customers by recency, frequency, and value. How recent has it been since they bought your services. How many times have they given you business (frequency). And how much was each job worth (value).

New accounts won't generate additional profit until they become return customers. It's the return customers who give you the most profit margin. You invested in advertising and marketing to win new customers. Now try to keep them and get them to hire you again. Clients who return are best because each dollar of service revenue cost less to generate. You've already sold them on the quality and level of your services. Advertising and marketing to get these clients has already been done. You'd like 60-70% of your sales revenue to come from these type of customers.

Late 19th century economist, Vilfredo Pareto, concluded that a large percentage of results come from a small percentage of sources. His theory became the *Pareto Principle*, also known as the *"80/20 rule."* This principle is part of the Total Quality Management (TQM) programs used today. It can work for you.

According to the Pareto, 80% of your revenue comes from only 20% of your customers. Focus your energy on these customers. By charting recency, frequency and value, you will see who are the best customers. Then make careful business decisions about the other, less profitable customers.

If customers ask you to provide new services, you're entering an area where you have little experience and you must deal with learning curve. This can significantly affect your cost of services. You must charge more to cover this reality.

A better approach is to pick those clients whose long term needs match your core competencies. By selling only to those who need the service skills that you have, you earn maximum profit with minimum stress.

As you analyze your customer base, note how much profit each client generates. You could discover that small customers are more profitable than larger clients. In fact, the small jobs could be subsidizing the larger contracts. This is why many shops avoid school and government markets. Hard negotiations and extended payments can make these markets tough and stressful.

Make extra effort to develop a good relationship with customers who place quality service as their top priority. These are the customers who will bring repeat business. They will also be excellent referrals for long term business growth. To the contrary, price-sensitive customers still want quality service. But they often demand much more than they are willing to pay for.

Also consider resource utilization and spreading the source of your sales income. It may be better to have 100 customers producing $500 each than five customers generating $10,000 each. Most of us prefer to spread our sales income over as many sources as possible to smooth business cycles and to operate shop resources at capacity. In this way, the loss of one major account won't put part of your staff out of work.

One business owner that I spoke with carefully read our desktop publishing pricing guide. Based on it, he developed a vertical marketing and pricing strategy that he implemented shortly after completing the book. He later telephoned me to tell me that he had gone off into a new vertical market. He had won seven contracts. One was a huge contract. It was earning him thousands of dollars in net profit each month. He had never before had so much profit available. Since this one contract dwarfed the other six, I strongly urged him to get more of the smaller contracts so he didn't have so much of his income depending on one source of work. The last time I heard from him, he had hired an accountant and was earning over $40,000 in net profit every month. I was elated for him, but worried that he was operating at great risk if most of his eggs were in one basket. If the large revenue generator suddenly experienced hard times and delays or cancels the contract, the service provider is left holding an empty bag of jobs.

In Web service shops, the ideal revenue spread is 50% contract customers and 50% new, single-project customers. An article in *INC* magazine explained that you can avoid the "too-few-clients" syndrome by trying for a ratio of 60% short-term business clients to 40% long-term contracts.

Whatever business targets you select, the long-term contracts can keep the cash flowing while short-term jobs can provide the marketing room you also need.

Measuring Market Share

Here's a way to track your customer base to determine if you are gaining or losing market share.

On your spreadsheet, track the number of customers you have each month with the income that they collectively generate. Then generate a monthly chart showing total customers and total revenue by month.

With this you can make sound business decisions about your customer base. The key is that you'll have a clear picture of your business success in the market.

If your chart shows more customers each month, you are gaining market share. If the number of customers is declining, but the sales revenue is increasing, you know that you are focusing on the most profitable segment of the market. And this is good. You are increasing your share of available market revenue.

If the number of total customers and the total revenue are both declining, this could be signaling an overall slow-down in the economy, a seasonal slowdown such as "the dog days of summer" when many projects slow down because of moves and vacations, or an aggressive competitor. Slow-downs are good times to consider special sales promotions and catch-up training for you and your staff. They are also good times for you to take a "re-charge" break, and go on vacation, too.

Quoting a Price Over the Telephone

You'll always have telephone shoppers who want to know what you'll charge to design and upload to their site a "simple" page or form. For them, you'll need quick access to your counter price sheet.

Telephone shoppers are price shoppers. They're searching for the lowest price for a job. They could be competitors. They may be actual shoppers. To them, quality comes second. But price is king..

When they call, get as much information on the job as you can. Put bounds on the amount of effort you'll need to apply. Then, be prepared to respond quickly in quoting a "ball park" price for the job. Not being willing or able to quote an approximate price can signal a potential "rip off" or suggest that you're unsure of your own abilities and resources. Be certain they understand that your price is "ball park" only.

Dealing With Price Fishing

For most newbies, the way you get sample prices is to call competitors, pretend to be potential customers and ask what the soon-to-be competitor charges. This can be nerve-wracking for the caller since it's an insincere act and this causes stress. It can also be a major frustration for the honest service provider with little time to spare.

Proposal requests that come in by e-mail are another example of price fishing. You can tell when you're being "hit" by a fishing request for bid. There are many more questions about procedures than their are statements specifying the scope of a job.

There's no gain in answering requests for proposals that go nowhere. Often these come from competitors who are using the anonymity of the Internet to root out pricing information. No-one wants to waste precious billable time answering fishing calls. Some shop owners would probably share their rates outright if the caller or e-mail poster would just be up front—especially if it the response causes others to keep their rates up and not undercut.

Related to this are the prospective clients who e-mail "rapid fire proposal" requests simultaneously to several dozen Web design shops. They are seeking the lowest price they can get. Often they use the responses as ammunition in negotiating with the shop they really want to have do the work. The professional shop can't afford to waste time responding to prospects who are planning to jump to the "cheapie" design firm anyway.

One useful tactic that I've seen used is for the shop to offer to generate a proposal for a client, including brainstorming and site consulting—for a fee. They typically charge two hours of consulting time. Then they tell the prospect that if they select their Web service company for the job, they will credit this cost to the full price of the project. This deters "lookie-loos" and keeps the relationship professional. It also enables clients who just want to know the scope of a job to get expert advice for minimal cost.

Quoting a Completion Time

Once your prospect has decided to buy, they will expect almost immediate response. These clients can be quite demanding, and fast turnaround can be a major issue with them. Evaluate your work load and how fast it takes you to provide each service. Then decide what a fair completion time should be and set a price for the standard time to complete.

Rather than guessing in the dark, analyze your work and then focus on turning around a job quickly and at the best price possible. If anyone wants output faster, apply a rush rate multiplier to the final price.

Charge them extra for the impact their priority placement has on the other jobs in process. If you advertise that you can complete a "standard" Web design project in 48 hours and a client wants it done in 24 hours, you should charge a RUSH RATE that is some percentage over the standard rate — a 100% premium is typical for doing a job in half the time. Thus if your standard price is $130 for a simple Home Page and you are asked to complete the design in half time, you should charge the client $260. This can be a lucrative way to earn much more profit with little added cost.

Donating Services

Occasionally shop owners donate time and services to charitable or religious organizations. There is a risk to being generous when people get professional services at little or no cost. Some people develop a perception that the value of your time and service equals the price they pay. Some can also expect the same rapid response that you give to your "paying" customers.

Another risk is present when you do something without charge for one group and other groups show up expecting similar free support.

You can easily spread the word about your business by doing volunteer work in community groups. But often, when you later try to charge for new or repeat services, many turn away because they want your professional services at no cost and are not interested in paying for your support (even when the project is outside the interests of the nonprofit group).

Therefore, limit what you contribute freely, and make it very clear from the outset that you are donating your time for services that you normally charge a customer. Explain that you are in business to earn a living, and you cannot provide free services without detracting from your income. If people balk, ask them if they would ask an attorney or doctor for free advice. You'd be amazed. Some people wouldn't dream of asking a lawyer or doctor for advice, but see nothing wrong with asking you. However, by just asking the question, you help to educate them that you are a professional and are not there as a free commodity.

Some service providers submit an invoice with each completed job, specifying what the work should cost. At the bottom of the invoice, they mark "Complimentary" or "No Charge to Non-Profit Organization."

But every job has a cost, and at the least, you should be reimbursed for the cost of materials.

Adding Loss Leader Jobs

Don't accept unprofitable business just to get more exposure in the market place. You need profit, not exposure. If you take a job at a loss, you dedicate valuable resources that would be better used supporting a profit-making job.

There are better ways to reach the market.

Adding Products and Services

Advertising and marketing companies are rapidly adopting and offering Web development services. These companies are competitors to independent Web service owner-operators. Desktop publishers are also offering Web services to their customers.

On average, Home Page design is priced at $60 an hour. Most service shops charge a lower price for each additional page of output produced and for each additional graphic image that is linked to the site.

Web service and support is becoming a lucrative sideline business. Chapter 1 described some typical prices for site development and design. (Our *Pricing Tables: Web Services* reference lists the typical and average prices for every aspect of Web services including site consulting, page design and site management.)

Another way to add service is to rent your hardware and software for use by customers who want to do their own Web design. You can establish an hourly system rental price by developing a profile of an average page design job. What equipment and software are required? How many hours are spent performing layout and design? How many pages are in a typical Web development and design job? How many proof pages are typically printed out on a laser printer?

When you rent your hardware and software, bill more for the labor intensive activities than you do for those that consume machine time because some users will expend more time using the hardware and software than others. As always, base your final price on costs, desired profit and what the market will bear.

Check the products and services sold by other Web development shops and peruse trade magazine articles for ideas on new services that you could offer.

Don't Give Away the Store

I say again. Don't give away the store! In this book, you have the information necessary to get paid what you're worth. All that's needed is for you to build the courage to ask the prices that you deserve to earn.

One of the startling findings of our surveys, and of the hundreds of interviews that we've conducted, is that many service providers simply don't value their own skills high enough to command the salaries that they should earn. For the past six years our pricing surveys have shown that, statistically, women pay themselves over 20% LESS than their male counterparts—even when they own and operate the business!

You CAN (and SHOULD) charge fees that are more in line with the education, skills, and experience that you have. But then, YOU must believe this statement before you will earn what you deserve.

As one Web designer put it, "…providing a creative service and giving it away for a few measly bucks is not very smart to say the least." Providing a service at a low price can hurt the entire profession.

Rather than giving free scanning and clip art use to customers who buy design support, unbundle these services and establish a price for each. Then charge for these "freebies." You bought the hardware and software to generate income. You should receive a return on each business investment.

If you want to do a project just to learn or fine-tune your own skills, call it what it is. Don't call it service and charge a lower price. If you want to learn how to design and incorporate a five second animation on a Web page, do it off-line, on your own time. Don't link learning to service. Learn first, then sell the service.

Rather than giving unlimited hand-holding and free answers to clients, recognize that information has value. Consider a consulting fee with a minimum charge based on 10 minute increments of time. Not only will you make money for what you know, but you'll also reduce the repeated requests for free advice. This alone will give you more time and energy for making money.

How to Break Out Top Profits

Thousands of small shops are struggling to stay afloat. When recessions occur, their margins sink and competition gets tougher. Recessions hit everyone hard. Yet, some shops not only consistently hold their own, they realize profit margins of 30 and 40 percent! Why? How? What do they know that many others don't?

Interestingly, what they know works best, both in good times and in bad, is to focus on the basics—the so-called "core competencies." This means that they apply common sense to their business practices. They develop close customer relationships. They form partnerships with their customers, their vendors, and even their competitors, and they offer flexible products and services. But more important, they understand that they are in business to make money. They charge for their time and the use of their equipment and materials.

These people succeed regardless of what niche they are in, regardless of their size or location. They generate six figure incomes operating independently out of a shop-barn on the plains of Kansas or out of an 820 square foot condo in a congested metropolitan area.

Meanwhile, other shops offer products and services based solely on what they think competitors charge. They lose money on their service because they underestimate the time and energy required. They fail to use the business expertise and contact sources already present in their suppliers. And they leave hundreds of dollars on the table each time they negotiate a job.

High-margin shops implement good business practices. They charge separately for each service, or they bundle all the tasks into a composite job with a keen eye toward break-even and maximum profit. The successful shops offer different packages, hourly rates, and support services to their customer base. When the economy slows, they don't change their service. They just change how it's packaged. They make pay schedules and contracts flexible and work to ease the cash flow problems of their customers.

Other highly successful shops achieve a 30-40% margin by staying within a small business niche, adding performance, and carefully watching their checking account. They regularly talk themselves out of taking on certain jobs if the work will spread them too thin. They won't promise the quality or schedules that they can't deliver. Whenever possible, they overdeliver on each job. Thus, they keep customers coming back.

Some hire part time professionals and work hard to develop a cadre of experts who have the broad overall knowledge and business skills needed. By forming partnerships with their customers, their vendors, and other shops, they keep their own personnel costs down and maximize their individual profit potential.

The consistent advice from high-profit shop owners is to be a business person first and then work to make your customers successful. View profit, return on investment, and margins as more important than having the latest equipment and the newest version of software.

Instead of getting caught up in the new technology frenzy surrounding Web development, get caught up in business planning and sound implementation. Become business and profit oriented. Everything else follows.

Successful shop owners suggest that you work to reduce your fixed costs. Carefully forecast cash flow; find better ways to manage your variable costs, and take the time to do a better job defining the market.

Focus on the kind of business that you want to be, and then gear all of your time and energy toward that goal. Yet, be sensitive to change. Know your limits, and don't be afraid to adapt as conditions change. Recognize that your business is constantly evolving. You just can't afford to remain static. To do so will cause your shop to be left behind in the electronic dust of competition.

Instead of pricing at the market, high margin people set prices using cost plus techniques, price just under what the market seems willing to bear, and build in plenty of profit. Rather than chasing volume, these shops control growth. They walk away from deals that don't offer the profit they want. They are convinced that they can't make up lost profit through volume sales.

They also cultivate customer relationships like horticulturists cultivate fine roses. They learn their customer's needs and maintain an attitude that the customer is always right. They work hard to learn the business issues of potential customers. The more they know, the more value they offer to their customer base. Their goal is to help their customer make more money. By doing so, they increase their own profit margins.

These entrepreneurs realize that once they get a client, they can substantially increase profit by getting repeat business. Once the marketing and advertising has brought in the business, all repeat jobs generate residual income with lower costs and higher net profit.

Rather than taking a short term view of business, they look and plan long term. They are willing to invest money now so they can earn more later.

They also go out of their way to find and build new relationships. For example, one shop reworks poorly designed Web pages that they find on the Net. They correct the warts and moles and then send a copyrighted re-designed page proof to the company that originally established the site, offering to re-work the whole site for them. This shop doesn't make money on the re-design of a single page, but it often gets substantial follow-on jobs. Their strategy is simple. Give more value than the customer expects. View each customer as a 20-year client. Expect follow-on jobs, and consistently serve as a team player. There strategy works.

Pricing Assumptions by Competitors

If your pricing information is based on bad, or too little information, you could make pricing decisions on data that may be grossly in error.

If your competitors are reacting to each other's pricing moves, they may follow each other down to consistent losses. Don't mirror the competition. Do your own analysis; develop your own desired prices. Then compare your numbers with the competition to see how they vary. Closely evaluate prices that differ widely from the price that your competition charges. Modify as necessary until you achieve a price list based on sound cost analysis and savvy market research.

Countering Cutthroat Prices

All too often, competitors arrive who declare an all-out war on other service providers by undercutting all prices. It seems as though every man, woman and child on the planet are jumping onto the Web design bandwagon. Shop owners complain that "propeller heads" and "network jockeys" are giving cheap service, and customers are getting poor work and paying next to nothing for it. They say that all too many are giving away their work at unbelievably low prices. This is seriously devaluing skills that professionals have spent years developing. One Web service provider exclaimed, "Welcome to the next great shakeout in advertising."

Nathan Morton writes in *Computer Reseller News*: "We are today in a 'take no prisoners' phase of weeding out the weak, the mundane, the imitators and the opportunist from the marketplace. We are going through maturation and the purification that comes from soul searching and a heavy dose of cutthroat competition for market share both occurring at the same time. We are pushing, thinking, shoving, cutting, focusing, listening, and inventing like we have never done before."

As Jim Kidwell, writing in *Printing Impressions* put it, many businesses are crying, "The competition is killing us. They're absolutely giving printing away."

Morton and Kidwell are describing realities in the technological revolution that is pushing the business envelope, today. Their descriptions apply equally well to Web services. We are in the beginning stage of an Information Age revolution that is forever changing the way we live and work. And there's price wars and pain as this new world is formed.

Price wars erode the value of the work of true desktop professionals. With hundreds of people from all walks of life starting service businesses, Web design and development has become one of the fastest growing home businesses, today. It's much like the phenomenon that occurred 10 years ago when desktop publishing exploded onto the business scene. Just look at the growing number of display ads and on-line listings for ISPs and Web developers.

The problem is that many of these entrepreneurs are not experienced at operating and managing a business. When they sink both feet into Web service, they often sink in a quicksand of business mistakes.

Since we started conducting national surveys on desktop service pricing, we've noted wide price ranges for almost every service. We expected this broad range to decrease as the industry matured and professionals became more experienced in the true costs of doing desktop publishing design and layout. This has finally started to happen. But, in its place, we now see the same phenomenon occurring with Web services.

Most Web developers have the skills to provide good service. And there are some who have only basic skills and experience. But there are individuals in both of these groups who don't have a clue how to run a business. They have the skills. They don't have the business acumen and experience to survive and prosper. One major deficiency is the skill to set good prices.

The relatively low entrance fee to starting a Web service business means that almost anyone can hang out a shingle and claim to be a Web service provider. This is a phenomenal growth industry. Small, independent shops are finding that they can run circles around the "big guys" and provide the same or better service at less cost and in shorter time frames—as long as they have the required skills. Many do and many are.

Another reason for the phenomenal growth of this industry is that Web service providers can operate anywhere. Many work out of home offices. Unfortunately, many of these entrepreneurs don't understand their true operating costs. Whether a shop is working out of a home office, a business park office, or a storefront, rent and insurance still apply. This means that prices must be based on a sound business basis—one that covers all the known costs. Novice shop owners seldom have the big picture before they start. They also open shop without knowing the true value of their skills. Hence they price way out of line with reality.

Since these novices don't have a handle on their personal value, their shop's often just break even or actually operate below their true costs. They look at their competitors to determine what to charge. Then they set their prices to match others who are already "in the business."

Some intentionally undercut all competitors. These cutthroat artists set prices far below current service providers with the intent of driving everyone else out of the business arena. It's a matter of who has the deeper pockets to survive the price war.

This puts tremendous pressure on successful shop owners who correctly perceive these cutthroat service providers as sharks — willing to do any job at any price. The result is a reduction in the average price for Web development work. It can also be a reduction in the quality of acceptable jobs.

Often these shops underbid everyone and walk away with a dollar drain hole that actually takes money out of their business as they perform work. Yet the job has still slipped through the fingers of the price- and cost-conscious Web service professional. To compete, the business savvy retaliate by lowering their prices. They stress service to the point that they often give away valuable information.

Jim Latham of Ink Spot Printing Services described the printing industry as is in a "lamentable state of competition." He may as well have been describing Web services. "We seem to add value, but we don't charge for it," he says. To be a Web service professional requires a tremendous investment in gaining technical knowledge and skills. Why then do some shops spend so much time telling customers how jobs are done? This information represents trade secrets for the Web services profession.

As clients and customers are educated on the design process, including the hardware and software used to produce quality work, these people listen and learn. Sometimes they become your competitors. Often they learn enough to brow-beat you into price concessions. By intellectual indiscretion, some owners place all service providers in the customer's vise and then help these "customers" turn down the screws, jeopardizing everyone's business survival.

By not setting and holding firm on fair prices, these shops cheapen a proud and noble art, pulling all Web service providers into the same tragedy. Those that go along with the crowd and lower their own prices lead each other into Chapter 11 bankruptcy.

Discount buyers know how to sniff out and exploit weakness within the ranks. They suck financial energy out of a price cutthroater until that shop sinks into oblivion. Then these "leeches" move on to the next unsuspecting cutthroater and begin the process all over.

As prices fall, many Web services will become commodities. This is happening today with the Internet Service Providers. The price of site hosting has dropped dramatically in the past two years. This puts ISP hosting at risk of being just another loss leader.

So how do we counter cutthroat pricing? Jeff Hayzlett, former owner of several printing shops and now a public relations expert, suggests that we jostle lowballers by inundating them with jobs.

According to Hayzlett, "If a competitor bids well below cost, I'd sell [subcontract to] them as many jobs as possible. That increases my profit margin since they're doing the job for less money than I can."

Hayzlett feels that subcontracting more business to low-price competitors eventually crushes them in their own losses. Sometimes by being awarded a Web design project, a shop can lose thousands of dollars just by doing the job. Thus, passing work to those who consistently sell below costs eventually sinks them. Hayzlett suggests that you become their worst nightmare.

According to *The Pricing Advisor* newsletter, the way to fight a price war is by cutting your own prices down to near that of your competitor and waiting for the competitor to realize their true costs and losses. Then gradually raise prices on a few services to signal that "It's time for a truce in this price war."

Others look within their own businesses and address wasted time and re-designs. They identify these as costs that stifle their competitive edge. Then they wage war against these expenses to improve their budgeted hourly costs so they can lower price and compete better.

I feel that the best way out of this "price-only" situation is to build more value in the customer's eyes. As cutthroat prices produce razor-thin margins, keep a tight lid on your costs and specialize. As a business banker once shared: "Stick to the basics. Stick to what you do well, and the money will follow." She was right. By keeping your focus on a specialized service (or a specialized industry) you heighten your efficiency and increase your ability to respond positively to price pressures. Become known as the best there is in your area of expertise. Then price accordingly.

Don't get discouraged. As Web service providers come and go, rays of brilliant sunlight will shine on your business (and your bank account). Focus on value and keep costs constantly in mind. Then price for whatever the market will bear. Don't become known as the "cheapest price in town." Become known as the "highest quality shop in town."

Beating the Competition

A recent article in *VARBusiness* described how to pitch solutions to the right person in a prospective client's company. Often an service provider is beat out by a competitor even when the shop's proposal was the best solution. A competitor came in offering a watered-down solution at a lower price and won the job.

The problem was that the shop owner failed to network with the right people in the client's company. This person didn't communicate ideas and solutions with everyone in the decision-making and order-generating processes. Nor did the shop owner solicit feedback from everyone involved. A contact management program can help you make sure you don't leave anyone out of this marketing loop.

It's critical to know not only the person asking for your proposal, but everyone else who is involved in making the final purchasing decision. You must find out who these people are and make sure that you communicate the value of your solution to them.

Therefore, learn how your prospect evaluates and buys the services that you offer. Then communicate and sell your solution to all the right people. Each company has an unpublished organization chart of who the real decision makers are and who can be counted on to support (or sabotage) a submitted proposal. We call this the "hidden wiring diagram" of an organization.

To reach the right people, be visible. Be supportive. And be aggressive. You want the job. They want the solution. Keep yourself in their court and you'll likely keep competitors out of it.

The "10 Plus 10" Strategy

Paul Eldrenkamp, founder of home-remodeling company, Byggmeister Associates, was interviewed by *INC* magazine regarding his very successful business strategy. He described how operating on cash flow and using customer deposits on projects to pay off past jobs is a bad way to run your business.

Early in his career, he approached his business by asking how much income he needed to meet the next payroll. Then he bid prices to meet this. His time estimates were off, his overhead was at best a guess, and his profit factor was wrong. He confessed that he didn't clearly understand margin and markup.

Now he focuses on profit and uses a "10 plus 10" approach to his business. He operates his business so 10% of his sales cover his compensation and 10% becomes net profit. To do this, he needs a gross margin of 30% or more. He developed a database of standard times for all his tasks and uses this to minimize the difference between estimated and actual production costs. He carefully tracks jobs in progress and flags overruns before his margins evaporate.

Rather than charging for a Ford and delivering a Cadillac, he delivers only what was agreed. To get the 30% margin he needs for his "10 plus 10" objective, he builds relationships, develops mutual trust, under-promises and over-delivers. Throughout a project, he will manage expectations, so his clients feel good about the experience. His "10 plus 10" formula is working.

Summary

A chapter on strategy is a book unto itself. However, strategy is only made good when implemented in a professional environment. In Chapter 7, you'll learn successful tactics to use in winning the war for profits.

7
Pricing Tactics

"The only acceptable profit is maximum profit."

Price is where the rubber meets the road. Price is where you make it or fail in business. This chapter deals with the tactical actions that you take to maximize this year's profit and return on investment.

Charging by the Page, Hour, etc.

Web service providers often struggle with the basis for billing out work. You'd like to charge by the hour, but your clients really like the page rate. So, do you charge by the page, by the hour, by the content?

It turns out that some tasks are charged by the page, some by the hour, some by the MB of file size, some by the square inch or resolution, and others by the project. Certain projects are more suited for one charging basis than others depending of the characteristics of the work. The question is, which tasks favor what type of billing?

On small, one or two page projects, most Web service providers should price by the page. Establish a "standard" page and then set a price for the first and succeeding pages.

For example, you could price a single Home Page at $280 including a masthead graphic, up to two photos or graphic images, up to 200 words of text, an e-mail link, three links to other sites and one hour of free updates. The second page could be priced at $140. And you could tack on another $35 for site publicity to 10 Web search engines. You can build a price sheet that reflects prices and services for single page sites up to major sites with 20 or more Web pages.

Just don't fall into the trap of giving a client a flat page price without limiting the number of characters, words, images and links on the page. One disappointed Web designer quoted a Home Page price and then got the "world's longest pages" to place on the Page.

Actually, for large projects, it's usually better to quote a flat rate price. The customer wants to know the total cost so they can budget for the complete job. They can't do this if you bid an hourly rate. This means that you must carefully spec the job and calculate your budgeted hourly costs so you can make a good estimate of the time involved. Be certain to factor in extra to cover unforeseen costs.

By bidding a flat rate, your client won't nit-pick. If the job is completed faster, the client will be happy, and you'll realize even more profit than you expected.

A problem can occur when a client makes multiple changes after a project has begun. If you know that a client always changes the draft of a design, do the first draft quickly. This will avoid wasted time and enable you to estimate project time better.

One good way to handle this is to keep a daily record of the time spent on various projects and in doing specific tasks. Our *Desktop Production Standards* book and software enables a Web service provider to develop accurate time standards and budgeted hourly costs for any task.

By generating budgeted hourly costs, you can set prices by the unit or by the hourly rate. For example, scanning is typically charged by the scan. But scanning is not as cut and dry as some may think. There's size, resolution, and retouch issues to consider.

Likewise, page layout can be charged at a fixed rate based on a specific "standard" template design and then at the hourly rate for anything beyond the "standard" design package. Any additions to the design such as adding images, banners, navigation buttons and the like should be charged by the unit. For example, additional GIF or JPEG images could cost the client $10 each.

A final consideration involves "porting" a design over from a brochure or other document. Here you should charge a different rate per page than if you were to design each page from scratch—such as $150 for a custom Home Page and $50 for each simpler second-layer page.

If there are repetitive actions used in the project, such as converting 50 TIFF files and optimizing them for the Web, you can set a special rate for these. This gets into what you are willing to negotiate away on a job.

Incorporating "Other Charges"

Service providers can leave money on the negotiating table by not considering every task that is provided during the completion of a job. For example, there's a cost in preparing a bid. There's a cost in meeting with a prospect. And there's a cost in incorporating "simple" changes to a design after it was uploaded to the ISP server. There's a cost in expediting and completing a job sooner than normally scheduled. There is also a cost in providing free local pick-up and delivery, in mailing a disk file to a client, and in letting a client delay paying a bill. Finally, there's a cost in dealing with demanding clients. We call this the *"hassle factor."* Some clients are difficult to work with. Since time is one of your biggest expenses, an unpleasant client can result in more work on a project than normally experienced.

You should be paid for every action taken on behalf of your client. Or, at least you should understand what you are giving away that could be charged to a client.

Therefore, do your homework. Break out EACH task and service. Identify a budgeted cost for each function.

And, whenever you can, incorporate these costs in your price. The customer may "always be right." But the customer should also pay their own way.

One way to keep the customer focused on giving you clear specs up front and to avoid making unnecessary changes is to explain to your client that a single change at the rough design stage will cost $5 to implement. Making a change at the finished layout stage will cost $50, and making a change to a completed site can cost $500 to incorporate. Just tell them this rough rule of thumb and they'll think twice about waffling on the final design. This also helps them understand that the earlier in a project they implement change, the lower their final bill.

Tactical Pricing Actions

Armed with market intelligence, and both break-even and margin analysis, you can select tactical actions to reach or exceed the strategic pricing objectives that you established earlier.

For example, if part of your objective is to achieve a 20% return-on-investment, you could implement tactical actions that identify price levels that yield this desired return. A strategic pricing objective of surviving an economic downturn could mean that you set prices at a level that will keep business coming in while allowing your shop to scrape by with enough income to cover costs. Avoiding competition could include tactical actions that set prices to discourage competition.

Overcoming Pricing Problems

There are three primary problems with the way that many Web developers price products and services. First, they under-rate the real value of their products and services. They don't realize how much they freely give away. Second they don't understand how a prospect perceives Web service. A perception of quality should command a higher price. The trick is to find a niche where your products and services are acceptable and considered valuable.

A third problem occurs when owners assume that all Web services are alike. If you have a unique product or service, price it to what the market will bear—especially if you've invested time and money into its development.

Price It Right the First Time

Pricing is one of the most important tasks you perform. You should evaluate demand, determine all your costs, and then decide what profit is acceptable. These are not trivial issues. Actions by your competitors, the government, and technology all affect how you operate.

The success of your pricing also depends on the perception of the customer. This is based on what other options are available to your customer and the benefit they perceive in purchasing from you rather than a competitor. Customers have a feeling for what a price should be. This becomes their basis for acceptance. They also have a threshold above which they simply won't buy. Above this point, they will accept lower quality or choose another option.

Your business earns a reputation as it grows. This image has much to do with what a customer expects to pay. If your shop is perceived as providing good, high quality service, your prices can be higher. If your company is perceived as a discount job shop, your prices should reflect this too. You must decide the image that you want to create. Then you must work hard to develop and maintain this image.

Some retail department stores are considered expensive price leaders. Others are perceived as low-cost, low-price outlets. (How many times have your heard the term "K-Mart Blue Light Special?") Yet, in reality, the low-price store doesn't always have a lower product price than a high-price store. It's the perception that draws a certain type of customer to each store.

Sometimes, a higher price stimulates demand because a customer perceives added value. On other occasions, the same product sold at a lower price can also stimulate sales demand. Pricing is an art. There are too many fickle variables to make it a science. Yet we use as much science as possible to make the art of pricing easier to comprehend and apply.

Some shops incorporate flexibility in their list prices so they can hold occasional sales. They add 15-25% to their "standard" prices, then lower the "retail" price by some percent while shouting "SALE" in their ads.

Real estate people recommend adding about 10% to the desired selling price of a house so you can negotiate down and arrive at a final price that seems a win for both buyer and seller.

Urgency also affects your pricing formula. If you have a product or service that comes into strong demand, apply the *"WOW" formula* and increase your prices to meet what the market will bear. Be careful not to set prices so high that this entices competitors to challenge your sales success. Pricing takes skill, patience, and luck.

You must price for profit. This means consistently evaluating the success of your strategy and readjusting your pricing as necessary. By taking the time to price right, you create the opportunity to profit more.

Pricing is a Policy

Much of pricing is done by the "seat of the pants." An acquaintance recently confessed, "I'm swamped with business designing Home Pages for $50 a pop, but I just can't seem to make any money at it." Of course not! This person didn't do a cost analysis and integrate a value for her own time and experience into her price formula. Intuitive and reactionary pricing decisions are dinosaurs in today's dynamic fast-paced world.

The same factors that you consider in arriving at a price for products—costs, perceived value, market segment, and marketing objectives also apply to pricing services. By systematically addressing each issue, you can clarify your own business goals and objectives and select a pricing strategy that best fits your situation. Only through logical, sound, and consistent business decisions can you establish profitable prices.

The top factors that determine your price are the competition that you face and the price your customers are willing to pay. Price is therefore strongly influenced by external forces, not just your own expenses. Your customers don't care what it cost you to provide service. They care only what you charge them, the quality of your work, and how soon you can deliver.

This means that you'll have a tough up-hill struggle raising prices unless you develop a perceived difference in the mind's eye of your customers. If you can't, or you're the new kid on the block, you must adopt a "community standard" pricing policy. This is essentially a "going rate" pricing format. It pays less attention to your costs or to marketplace demand and more to the prices that your competitors are charging.

Pricing in a Competitive Market

Pricing can be both a challenge and a headache. Price drives everything in business. It's usually considered the main tool to gain new business. Pricing strategies are often centered on reactive formulas such as scurrying to match a competitor's price change.

There is a better way—combine cost-based pricing, competition-oriented pricing, and demand-pricing in one composite price. Adding a desired margin to a cost basis to come up with a price is *"cost-based"* pricing. This is an easy way to establish price.

When you set your prices 10-15% lower than your competitors to lure price-sensitive buyers into your fold, you are *"competition-oriented"* pricing. This method accepts a lower margin. But what do you do when competitors have already set prices for minimum margin? You could sell yourself right out of business.

Basing your strategy on competitive pricing can work in the short run. But it can also generate a downward spiral that causes competitors to match each other's lower price on the way down and out. And this can cause buyers to perceive your product or service as just another commodity.

The idea is to make pricing a pro-active event and not a defensive activity. Countless pricing formulas are theoretically possible. The problem with formulas is that they may not address hidden costs. They may also ignore the psychological component of how a price will look from a customer's perspective. And formulas often don't consider the pricing reaction by competitors.

Suppose you want to be known as a high volume service-oriented shop. So you price your services 15% less than the leading Web site developer in the area.

The price leader retaliates by selectively discounting its services to meet your lower price. This causes you to lose (not gain) business opportunities.

You realize that you can't develop a lasting competitive advantage by price alone. So you decide to move away from a strategy based only on price. You decide that designing Web sites for real estate companies is where you belong. You develop a marketing strategy based on premier support these types of businesses.

Building on your expertise, you offer experienced support, fast response time, and quality output. Your prices reflect the premier concept. You develop a promotional strategy consistent with your business focus. Sales build, and your shop thrives.

In another scenario, you decide to provide service to city, county, state, and federal government customers in your area. You know that laws make government buyers very price sensitive, so you develop a low-price strategy based on service cost. However, you discover that low price by itself won't guarantee sales and long term success. Your service product must be packaged so it exactly meets government specifications. It should provide nothing more, nor anything less. You redesign your service offering so it can be delivered at minimum cost in the exact form the buyer expects. You restructure your business to be profitable based on this service package. You down play promotion and focus on getting on every qualified bidders list you can. You ignore the public market and limit your activity to government organizations. Your business grows.

A flash of insight later, you imagine yourself a service provider with expertise in a unique field or in producing a unique Web page look. You have a particular expertise in working with animation and color, so you invest in the equipment and software to provide this service. Then you focus your promotion on those companies who advertise in bright colors and vivid graphics. You build a capability to handle any type and form of color images and to produce any type and form of animation. You build a reputation for having every support tool available related to this work. By becoming the dominant provider of rich colors and animation, you develop a business that is almost insensitive to price. You set prices based on perceived value. But you don't set your prices so high that others are tempted to enter your market niche. While providing high quality service, you set your prices moderately higher than your known competitors.

You conclude that market-driven pricing is the best way to go. Rather than basing your price solely on historical production standards, experience, and on reference tables of standard costs, you decide to integrate all of these into a strategy unique to your market.

The amorphous mass of intelligence data that you gather begins to suggest a pricing strategy. You test the strategy against your estimated costs to see if the margins are acceptable for quoting a particular job. If the margins are too low, you pass on the job. Or, if you decide you still want the contract, you work even harder to improve the efficiency of your operation. You consider better equipment, better working techniques, and reduced overhead expenses. Combining cost and market-driven pricing fosters more efficient operation.

In the preceding scenarios, the consistent theme is that a pricing strategy is based on a marketing plan that is consistent with your business objectives. Just as a marketing plan shouldn't be established in a vacuum, your pricing strategy should have input from all aspects of the business. And it should reflect the goals and strategies of your company.

Once a marketing plan and a pricing strategy have been developed, build a system to implement these business decisions. Establish procedures for pricing new products and services, and for modifying existing prices as market conditions change.

Pricing actions are governed by state and federal laws. Besides the restrictions on collusion and price fixing, you must be concerned about perceived price discrimination. Competitive pricing is a key part of your business plan, but it should not conflict with law.

Reducing Your Prices

Cutting prices can behazardous to wealth. Reducing price can increase sales, but it can also encourage competitors to jump in and start a price war. If you advertise service at one price and then cut your rate, past customers may suspect that they've been gouged.

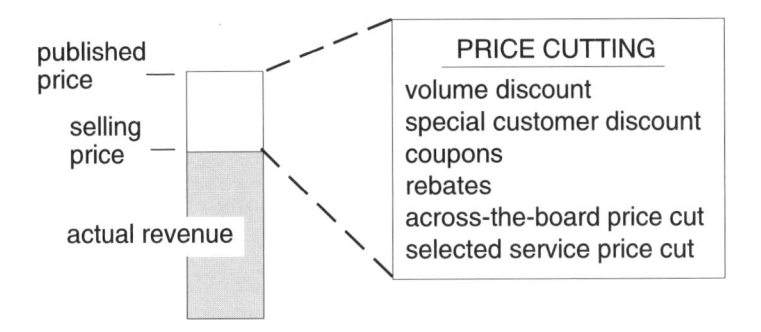

```
published                    PRICE CUTTING
price                    volume discount
  selling                special customer discount
  price                  coupons
                         rebates
                         across-the-board price cut
actual revenue           selected service price cut
```

Fig 7-1. Various forms of price cutting.

Value, not price, convinces a buyer. Customers want quality, but at a cheap price. This forces you to walk a "value-quality-efficiency" tightrope. Pricing requires special skills and a mindset that knows the customer.

IBM and Compaq drastically cut PC prices in the recession of 1991. Normally, during a sluggish economy, price cuts stir increased sales. However, these cuts were not enough to stimulate demand. Sales remained flat, and conservative buyers purchased clone computers, believing that clones offered a better deal (perception). As sales stagnated, these two computer giants suffered huge revenue losses.

Setting your price below costs just to "build or regain market share" may be foolhardy. You'll attract "garage sale" bargain hunters, but when you must later raise your prices to make a profit, you may not find new customers willing to paying the higher price. Everybody loses except the low-price bargain buyers.

If your business provides more than "mail order" service, don't target "customers" who aren't willing to pay for solutions and quality work. Let them go. Focus on buyers who appreciate value and are willing to pay for understanding, empathy, and solution performance.

Price cutting can increase sales and be effective during promotions and markdown sales. It can also reinforce your company's position in the industry. But approach pricing carefully and keep profit in the formula. A shop with excess unused resources typically considers price cutting to increase capacity. This occurs openly, or is disguised as discounting. It can be risky.

"Across the board" price-cutting is not wise. In this approach, the published prices are reduced by a fixed percentage. The owner uses guesswork rather than surgically-precise cost analysis to re-define each price.

Cost analysis is not a discretionary activity. It's critical. You must know every cost for each service. Poor cost analysis can cause pricing errors. This can drive your shop into liquidation or bankruptcy.

Never reduce prices across the board. When you do cut prices, cut them carefully, cut them selectively, and know the affect each action will have on break-even. Some services sell well without special offers; others must be at lower prices to attract customers. A smart approach may be to offer price-off coupons, rebates, or discounts on selected services.

Coupons

One day as I walked down the main street in Lahaina, Hawaii and was passing a certain gift shop, a salesperson stepped out from the doorway and handed me a "10% Off" coupon.

"Everything in the store is 10 percent off today," he said. "And this is on top of the sale that we've been running all week."

Hawaii was in an economic downturn. Customers weren't spending freely. And shop owners were doing all they could to encourage people to spend.

The concept of using coupons to attract business has been around a long time—particularly in the food and home products industries. Coupons are the reason some people buy newspapers on certain days. Coupons are also why people purchase one product and not another.

Dale Kemper, a friend who owns a strip mall shopping center and operates a successful pharmacy, once told me that his best advertising tactic is to mass mail a coupon book to his local community. He tried flyers, display ads and many other advertising media, but the coupon booklet works best for him.

```
┌─────────────────────────────────────────┐
│  MONEY OFF COUPON                       │
│                                         │
│  10% Off      ╱‾‾‾╲      This Month     │
│  On Web      │  $  │      Only!         │
│  Design       ╲___╱                     │
│                                         │
│  Save on all your site development needs! │
└─────────────────────────────────────────┘
```

Fig 7-2. Coupons can attract more business.

His 16-page, saddle-stitched booklet is approximatey 3.3" high and 8.5" wide. He puts one or two products on each page. For his particular retail business, women are his best customers. They carry his coupon book in their purse. They carry it in their car. And they buy what he advertises.

A recent article in the *Wall Street Journal* described a university study to determine the affect coupons have on consumers. Researchers at three universities found that of the 310 billion coupons distributed in the U.S. annually, only 7.7 billion were actually redeemed—a mere 2.5 percent. But even though most (97.5%) go in the trash, coupons still influence what people buy.

The study revealed that coupons affect sales more than redemption rates indicate. It turns out that when consumers see coupons, even the non-coupon-clippers are more likely to buy a coupon-advertised brand product than they will a brand product not advertised in a coupon. In fact, purchases of a product advertised by coupon are just as strong with non-coupon users as they are with those who do redeem coupons, so, just distributing a coupon offer can boost sales. According to Ohio State University marketing professor, Robert Leone, "Coupons send more than just a discount signal to consumers." He says that a coupon also draws the consumer to read the rest of the ad.

These researchers also reported that people looking for specific coupons are affected by the messages conveyed by other non-related coupons. Incremental sales by non-coupon buyers increase just by their seeing the coupons. This offsets the reduced profit margin caused by the coupon-redeeming customers.

Another place coupons work is in promoting new products and services. Typically, the Sunday paper has a thick coupon stack and many people love to look through them. They know that here is where the new products and services are advertised.

Coupons work in retail. An article in *Marketing News* states that coupons will attract new users to a product and increase the long-term sales if they have headlines that focus on the benefits of the product or service.

Coupons can work in Web services, too. What if you offered a 10% discount during a "Get To Know Us" sale? The idea is to attract prospective buyers. What if you gave a free copy of a special booklet on Internet marketing if a customer returns your coupon with an order for any of your Web development services?

Use special holidays and seasonal events to promote your business with special dollars-off coupons. And consider sending coupons (or putting coupons at your Web site) in late spring to attract jobs over the summer.

Since the average service job is over $100, you don't need a huge response to make coupons worth the effort. Few service providers currently use coupons. Perhaps they should. Perhaps you should try cyber-coupons.

Rebates

Another tactic is the rebate. Rebates are common in automobile, telecommunication and video tape feature film sales. Why do these vendors offer rebates instead of just lowering their prices?

The strategy behind rebates is that sellers want prospects to be attracted by a lower price (money back) but be repelled by the bother of collecting. Actually, many people end up not asking for a rebate when it was the rebate that psychologically pushed them into buying.

```
REBATE
$   Return this!
    Get $10 back
    on your purchase
    fine print, fine print, fine print
                                        $
```

Fig 7-3. Rebates convert prospects into clients.

Consumer preference research shows that "prospect theory" drives rebate strategies. Thomas T. Nagle, of the Strategic Pricing Group in Boston was recently quoted in *Fortune Magazine* regarding the concept of rebates. He said, "People judge the loss of any given amount as more painful than they judge the gain of an equal amount as pleasurable."

What sounds complex is simply that people view spending a few more bucks as less painful if they have an opportunity to get some of their expense back. This psychology pushes them into jumping on rebate deals. They view rebates as a reduction in pain when buying.

Yet, according to prospect theory, once they make the purchase, the actual rebate becomes less important.

Once they buy, the rebate feels like a small gain for the time and effort it takes to collect. Most procrastinate and don't bother. A five dollar rebate offer on a $14.95 product looks good and causes people to buy. But taking the time to fill out and send in a five dollar rebate form just doesn't seem worth the effort. Many don't feel the time is justified for only a five dollar gain. And many delay past the deadline date printed on the rebate form.

Rebates are a profitable form of price discrimination. Cutting rates attracts both price-sensitive prospects and those who would pay a higher price anyway. If, instead of cutting price, you offer a rebate, many price-sensitive buyers will go for the deal and some will apply for the rebate. But less price-sensitive buyers will also go for the deal, yet they won't be as eager to return the rebate form. In effect, they pay the higher price anyway.

Think of it this way: If every buyer collected on every rebate offer, rebates wouldn't be worth a seller's effort. A price cut would work just as well. But, by exploiting the psychology of the buyer, you can make rebate offers quite profitable. This is a direct example where procrastination by others can add money to your pocket. Most rebate offers give the perception of price cutting without actually reducing revenue on the sale.

Send a Check

An interesting form of coupon that has been used quite successfully is the customer savings check. In this tactic, you design a check payable to your company. Make it for a fixed amount, and make it look real. Send it to prospects and existing clients with a marketing letter explaining that they can apply this check to the next job they bring to you that is for over some set price. In the fine print, state that only only one check may be applied to a job.

```
                    CHECK
                                Date: _____

pay to the order of: CyberBucks Web Services   $25.00
  twenty-five    and         00/100    dollars

 Apply this check to your next Web service job at CyberBucks.
            Total job price must be for over $150.
         (limit one check per job) (offer expires: _____)
```

Fig 7-4. Checks can be a powerful tool.

When people see a check in the mail, they usually hold on to it. Psychologically, it represents money. To you, it represents a reduction in your normal price. But it's a strong attraction to get clients and prospects to act.

Everyone likes to get a check in the mail. Send them a check and they'll send you more business.

Discounts and Allowances

Another approach is to alter the list prices of your products based on a discount or allowance. A *discount* is a reduction from the list price that you apply to a customer's purchase when they meet certain conditions. These conditions include paying cash instead of using a credit card, paying in full upon purchase, paying early on a purchase with net terms, buying a selected range of services, or buying during a seasonal promotion.

A customer may also qualify for a reduction from the list price by performing some activity. This is an *allowance*. It works like a discount. An allowance can be a special markdown for including your promotional banner at the customer's Web site. It can be a reduced price for participating in a community service project or becoming a member of a certain club or organization.

To some Web developers, the list price is simply a reference from which to discount. In this instance, services are rarely sold at list price. If this is how you operate, you're bound to encounter buyers who only care about the difference between what you advertise and what they actually pay.

Some companies advertise a new "low-price" every month to boost sales. But when one special deal runs into the next, soon customers expect the gimmick and won't buy until the next "special" is advertised. This results in little business growth, so carefully control the specials that you offer.

The value of discounting can be overestimated. Research reported in *Entrepreneur Magazine* shows that some sellers must lower prices 65% to substantially affect demand. This may be even lower in some industries, but pricing is specific to circumstance. Increasing demand is not as simple as just lowering price.

You must cover all the cost of your services sold, including marketing, advertising, and commissions. And the results of discounting are usually temporary.

Price changes are often used as a tactic. If customers base buying decisions on price alone, you can always be slower in completing a job, as long as you offer the same quality and information as your competitor, but at a much lower price—20% is a much lower price.

Discounts tend to reduce customer loyalty. Budget buyers are easily lured away when another shop offers a deeper discount. And the risk exists that discounting can undermine a service provider's credibility. Customers wonder what they would pay if competition hadn't pressured the seller into offering the discount.

Immediate discounting from your list prices can make a buyer wonder it they're really getting the best deal. Customers who push for discounts can get suspicious of your pricing once you cave in. They wonder if lower prices cause compromises in quality or service.

According to Lawrence Steinmetz, author of *How to Sell at Prices Higher Than Your Competition*, there is no evidence that long-term success goes to sellers who consistently discount. Steinmetz feels that slipped profit margins always catch up with you. He says that none of the top discount chains of 1962 are around today.

As shops become better at pricing, individual buyers usually aren't offered discounts. Yet, there is a time and place for everything. Subtle price reductions can help increase sales during slow business cycles. Try coupons and rebates, but discount with discretion.

Giving Volume Discounts

It's good business to offer a discount to clients who purchase more than one of an item or service. In Web development, discounts are offered for each page that is designed and linked to a Home Page.

Table 7-1. Example sliding scale for page design.

CyberBucks Web Services
Multiple Page Design Prices

Home Page	$230
1-5 connected pages	$110 each
6-10 connected pages	$100 each
11-20 connected pages	$75 each

(Each page limited to 200 words, up to three graphic images, and up to four links to the same or other sites.)

You begin by identifying the lowest price that you can charge for a service. Make certain that ALL of your costs are handled. If you don't incorporate your costs into the lowest quantity, you could lose money taking on a single page job.

Next select the highest price that you can charge for a single page. Between the two price points, you can assign a range of prices for volume page jobs.

Some service providers establish a minimum price because it costs the same to open a file, generate an invoice and collect payment regardless of the quantity of pages that are designed.

Put your sliding scale into a price table and make it available to your customers. It could move them to purchase more pages than they had originally planned.

Discounting and the Law

Be careful if you're thinking of discounting. A deep discount may constitute unlawful price discrimination. Section 2(a) of the Robinson-Patman Act relates retailer pricing policies to distributors and resellers. It says that it's illegal for a retailer in commerce to sell commodities of like grade and quantity at different prices for use, consumption, or resale, where the effect of the discount difference will substantially lessen competition or create a monopoly.

Software publishers sometimes get in trouble when they discount to their authorized dealers more than they do to a standard distributor. The differences must be "cost-justified" to the extent of the seller's actual cost savings incurred in making, selling, or delivering the product to a particular reseller.

Services can also considered a product. You can discount to one customer if that customer uses your output, but assumes a higher marketing cost. Just be careful not to overstep the line when discounting.

Cut Prices Carefully

According to conventional wisdom, if service isn't selling well, you can always consider lowering prices to create volume. But cutting prices by 50% may not increase your sales volume by 400% (which is usually what you'll need to net the same profit). Lowering your fees by 20% will require much more than a 20% increase in sales just to offset the revenue loss.

You can calculate the sales increase that you'll need to stay even after a price cut using this formula:

$$\% \text{ more sales needed} = \frac{[(\text{old price}) \times (\text{discount percent})]}{(\text{new price}) - (\text{service unit cost})}$$

Suppose you charge $80 for designing a simple Home Page. It is HTML text only, and your cost of service is $40. You consider dropping the design price by 10% (to a new price of $72). How much of an increase in sales will be required?

$$\frac{80 \times 0.1}{72 - 40} = \frac{8}{32} = 25\% \text{ increase in sales required}$$

Now work the same formula for a price cut of 30 percent. You'd need a whopping 150% increase in sales revenue to make this lower price work!

$$\frac{80 \times 0.3}{56 - 40} = \frac{24}{16} = 150\%$$

But, can you achieve 150% more sales revenue at the lower price? Lowering the price on one service could boost sales volume. But work the numbers first.

Many new shop owners work for less than they should because they want to develop business relationships. This is risky, because if you get known as a low-price shop, it's very difficult to break out of this mold. Once your clients are conditioned to a lower price, they will resist any change toward higher prices.

The Capacity Trap

There is one form of price cutting that is a trap that catches many experienced business people. This trap involves selling unused capacity to make sure that shop resources are fully utilized.

At first glance, this seems like a sound business decision. However, it could be a disaster. Here's why.

When you focus on just capacity, you're likely to look only at the cost of the hardware and software that sits idle. You tend to ignore the variable costs incurred when this equipment is used — operational wear and the added labor. If you offer your equipment at reduced price, you risk looking at sales, not profit.

Suppose you do cover operating costs and include a small profit on selling services at lower price to keep your systems fully occupied and productive. What about opportunity cost? If you agree to fill schedules with low-margin sales to keep resource use high, your shop may not be ready when high-margin sales occur.

In effect, you just made your shop a new competitor to itself. Prices will always seek the lowest level. When you start charging two prices for the same service, you compete against yourself! And customers aren't stupid. Once they figure out that you're willing to work for less, they'll make sure that you do.

You also risk losing your current, full-price customers because they'll hear about your reduced rates for others and become alienated against you. They'll demand the same service for the reduced price.

Giving a discount can work, but do it for a reason other than excess capacity. Instead consider discounting for volume purchases, or for special terms. It's actually better not to lower your price. Instead, offer more value. It may cost to provide added value, but you keep your full-price customers while also gaining new clients.

When Price Cutting Can Work

Reducing price to build market share often results in a short-term reduction in profit. You can minimize this effect by moving to increase market share only when one or more of the following conditions exist:

1. Customers only care about price. These customers will shift quickly to another shop with lower prices. They have the least loyalty of all the customer types. To attract and keep these customers, you need to offer a permanent price advantage. This is why some shops have a special price sheet for "corporate accounts" and a "counter" price sheet for walk-ins. You can make superficial changes in the style or brand of materials that you use, but you risk affecting the quality of your output product. You also risk upsetting current customers when the larger volume of work means that they get less of your attention.

2. The total market is growing. Here, you don't have to "steal the sheep" from your competitors. Concentrate instead on inexperienced buyers. A lower price attracts these clients as they make their first cautious move into on-line commerce.

3. Your reputation for quality won't suffer. If buyers measure quality by your response time and how you communicate, or by some other criteria, cutting the price of your services can attract more business.

4. Your competition probably won't retaliate. When your competitors are preoccupied with fighting "alligators" such as funding deficits, cash flow, unmet regulations, lower capable equipment, management and employee disputes, you can make a price move without their noticing, or being able to respond in like manner.

5. Your current market share is small. If you already have 50% of the market in your area, there's not much advantage in cutting prices. But, if you only hold 5% of the market, the potential for additional sales activity is significantly improved.

6. Your resources are underutilized. There's an economy of scale when you can make every square foot of your shop and every piece of equipment work to generate money. Idle equipment and idle employees are costly. Just remember the capacity trap!

7. The margin will remain high. If reducing prices to increase sales volume will reduce your variable cost per sale—the contribution margin (revenues less variable costs) should remain high.

If a majority of these conditions are present, it's likely that your price-cutting strategy will succeed.

How to Handle a Price Cut

Here are suggestions for handling a price cut.

Look at past history. If you didn't raise your prices when your competitors did, determine if your sales volume and profit increased or decreased.

Use a special money-off offer. Cite the actual dollar savings rather than the percentage of savings, so customers who know your prices will still be attracted to the special offer.

Offload excess capacity with "two-for-one" offers for a short time period. Just be certain to incorporate costs and profit. Again, remember the capacity trap.

Consider occasional discounting, but watch the effect on positioning. You don't want a price cut to "cheapen the image" of the service that your shop offers.

Experiment with formal price cutting in a few products or services. Don't make across-the-board cuts.

Don't automatically follow the price moves of your competitors. They may not have done their homework. Let them lose money on a deal, instead of you.

Keep the new break-even point clearly in mind when you consider lowering the price of any service.

When to Turn Down a Job

Some people will not be interested in added value and insist on a volume discount even when they have a single page to be designed. Here is where you must accept the reality that you can't do business with everyone. There are those who want more for their money than you can provide. The only way to deal with them is to simply decline the business. Simply say "No."

A smart service provider will turn away sales that aren't profitable. If taking the job conflicts with your long term goals (margin and profit), turn it down!

According to Phyllis Apelbaum in *INC* magazine, "When you turn down business for the right reason and in the right way, very often it will come back to you."

Sometimes, customers who are willing to pay at any price, are the most risky. If you quote high and they want your services anyway, consider this a red flag that they may not be able or willing to pay you when the job is complete. They may have already been turned down by someone else or their credit has been cut off. They didn't call you because they love your business name. Non-paying customers can be a cash flow nightmare.

Here's another situation where you may want to rethink taking on a job. Some money-hungry shops operate like blinded sharks gobbling up every job that comes along. Then the really BIG job comes. They jump on it with dollar signs forming in their eyes. But after dumping lots of money into the job, the customer decides to cancel the whole project. Will you be paid?

Perhaps a real-life example will make my point. I have a friend who owned the largest computer retail store in Hawaii. He was doing well over a million dollars a year and was on his way to financial stardom. Then he got a contract to sell and install hundreds of computers and network interfaces at the University of Hawaii and in the major hotels in downtown Honolulu.

He and his wife were elated. They ordered the equipment (over $750,000 worth) from the supplier and positioned it at their store for delivery and installation the following month.

But the recession of 1990-1991 hit, and it hit Hawaii especially hard. His buyers all put their work on hold. They didn't cancel the contracts. They put the jobs on hold citing severe economic times.

My friend tried to return the equipment to his vendor with a promise to re-order when his customers gave the go-ahead on the projects. The response from his supplier (who was also facing severe financial strain) was a lawsuit. Litigation cost my friend his business. He had jumped on a huge and promising opportunity, but it was too big for even his customers to handle when something went wrong. Perhaps he should have developed a contingency plan for Murphy's Law. But then, who expects the economy to go into the tank so quickly.

10 Reasons for Turning Down Work

Here are some very good reasons to turn down a job.

1. It's a lot of money. Money should never be the single reason that you accept a project. Watch and prevent over-committing resources and finances.

2. It will cut into your ability to market other work. You should spend at least eight hours each week marketing your business. If a project will cut deeply into this time—no matter how lucrative—rethink taking the job.

3. The first job was a pain. If the first job that you do for them is messy and frustrating to you, future jobs are likely to be the same or worse.

4. It's too easy getting this job. If it feels wrong, check it out carefully. Feels wrong? Probably is.

5. The numbers don't work out. If you can't make the margin, profit and ROI you want, then why do the job?

6. Payment will be on their terms. Remember you can't

afford to be the bank for someone else's cash flow. And you surely aren't a collection agency.

7. You'll tie up all of your resources. If you accept this job, perhaps you won't be able to take on the job you really want. Committing full energy to a single project could prevent you from being able to act on a better opportunity that's about to occur.

8. This customer is not in your top 20 list. You'll find that 20% of your customers generate 80% of your revenue, so why waste time on those that aren't top revenue producers.

9. You'd have to hire additional resources quickly. If you hire more people, what happens when the job is complete? Perhaps outsourcing is a better solution.

10. You'd have to invest in new hardware and software. Unexpected expenses can quickly drain your bank account. If this is a new business area, and one that you've not planned entering, then re-consider spending a lot of money for little financial return.

One final note on turning down work. When you decline a job, it's a nice gesture to recommend someone else who could do the work for the price that the customer wants. This not only creates goodwill with the client and with competitors, you could find this person coming back to you more willing to pay your price or wait until your schedule can accommodate their job.

Raising Your Price

Most Web service providers are reluctant to raise prices. They feel that it's much harder to raise a price than it is to lower a price. This feeling is supported by studies suggesting that about 72% of all consumer buying decisions are based on price alone. Yet, other studies conclude just the opposite. The question is: Which study do you believe?

Obviously, you must be very careful when raising prices. You probably shouldn't implement added features or time-saving devices if doing so will increase your list prices by 20% or more. This could exceed the "value threshold" of your customer base. They'll find your actions unacceptable and seek other alternatives.

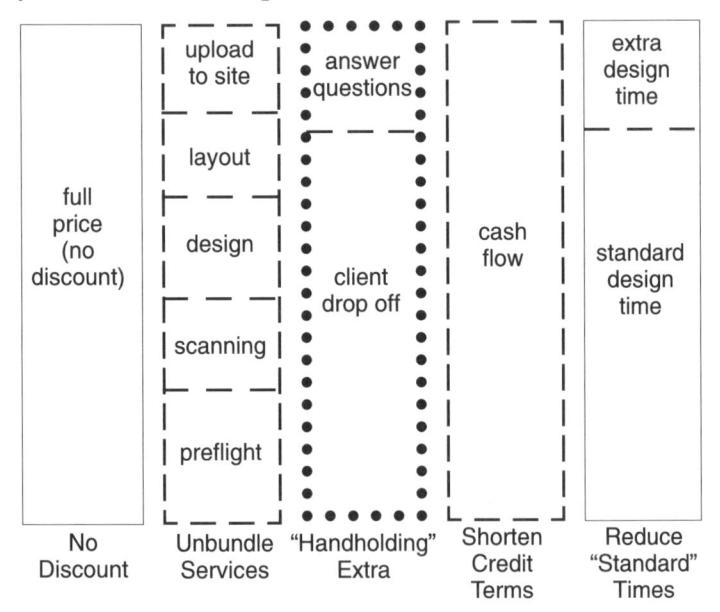

Fig 7-5. Various ways to raise your prices.

On the other hand, many shops literally "give away" labor income because they are afraid customers will balk if they increase their rates to a profitable level. You can only be generous if it doesn't curtail achievement of business goals. You are running your shop to make a profit. If not, close the doors and sell out. Otherwise, raise your prices so you can make that profit and get a decent return on any investment that you've made.

Carefully increase price. Besides alienating some customers, you could entice competitors to start offering the same services. High prices tempt competitors. If the temptation becomes too strong, they may add resources to compete in your market niche.

So when you raise prices, make each increase small. Work the numbers. You'll discover that a 1% increase in price can produce a 10% increase in profit. This is usually pretty close to reality because once you've developed your services, there's little added cost in raising price. But each increase is applied immediately to the bottom line.

Your best approach is to conduct an analysis of each service that you sell. Then selectively raise prices on only those services that warrant the action.

One effective strategy for holding market share while raising prices is to implement a 5% price increase every time demand rises by 10 to 20 percent. The 5% increase should be not enough to attract competitors.

A recent study found that a price 10-20% price increase has little affect on reducing purchases, but an increase of 40% or more will immediately prompt customers to seek alternativest. At one time, they went to another shop in town. Now the geographical region of purchase comfort is much wider.

How to Know It's Time

There are benchmarks that can indicate a price increase is necessary. These include, increased costs, shrinking margins, major improvements in a product or service, and the fact that you are entering a new market.

Some professionals feel that you should consider raising prices when your competitors raise theirs. Others feel that many customers expect price increases every January, so this is a good time to publish a new price list.

Another school of thought suggests that you raise prices if your service isn't selling as well as you'd like. Customers may not be buying because they think your low price represents lower quality work. To them, a higher price means better service. Here you can use the "you get what you pay for" mindset to your advantage.

Another good time to consider a price increase is whenever demand exceeds a certain benchmark. For example, when workload causes overtime for your staff, this could be a good time to raise prices.

One final note. If you made an error and have been underpricing your work all along, re-package the services and sell them at higher price.

If you aren't bold enough to implement a price increase, your shop may be in deep trouble. Savvy service providers successfully raise prices, even through recessions. The key is knowing if it's the right strategy for your company.

How To Handle Price Increases

Price increases are handled differently whether you are dealing with a new customer or a current client. For new customers, just charge more—the price increase is unannounced. But for your current client base, a price increase should be handled tactfully. There are several ways to approach the mechanics of a price increase.

You could position it, not as a price increase, but as a better service package with added value. Offer more service, bundle, or change the mix of service options.

On the consulting side, try to cut costs for existing clients so you don't have to raise your rates. Offer a package of services so you can shift your clients from a rate basis to a bundle of services basis. Just be certain that you cover your costs and profit expectations.

Some owners send a warm, personal letter to each current client reminding them of the successful projects that they've supported in the past. Then they tell them that they are upgrading several capital items (hardware, software, etc.) to provide better, faster service, that higher taxes are causing higher operating costs, or that they are experiencing higher labor costs.

Next, they hit them with a small (no more than $5 an hour) rate increase. They set the effective date for the price increase about four weeks ahead to give their clients time to take advantage of current low prices. They reassure their customers that they will continue to bill at the old rate for any projects started before the price increase takes effect. Then they assure them that they value their business and look forward to working with them on future new and challenging assignments.

This is the *"Oreo cookie"* or *"sandwich"* strategy. Lead with something positive, such as announcing a price cut on some service or increasing your level of guarantee. Then hit them with the price increase. Follow this with more good news such as giving them a period of time to initiate projects at the lower price.

Some shop owners mention specific projects that a client has talked about and may want to get started right away, before the price increase kicks in.

Other shop owners visit their top 10 customers to discuss "some things that are going on that will affect billing rates." They try to keep current customers at the old price—perhaps by a commitment to buy more services within the next year.

Another school of thought suggests that you avoid advising your clients of a new hourly rate. This group feels that most shops give customers a quote based on more than just an hourly rate (including a flat fee for work paid up front or added charges for changes), so focusing on a higher hourly rate is unimportant. They also suggest that you not worry about what new clients will think of your higher rates. Most will not be aware of the old rates (as long as you change the signs and paperwork properly). If they are referred by another client, and comment on your prices, explain why your rate increase was necessary.

Never announce a price increase to infrequent or occasional buyers. This could create a negative impression. These customers don't really need the information until they come to your for services again.

Quoting your new rate in a price increase letter may turn away major clients who are not comfortable paying by hourly rate, but who can accept a flat-rate estimate or a daily or weekly rate. Quoting an hourly rate instead of a flat rate to these customers can scare them away. Some are simply not comfortable working with professionals who charge by the hour. For these folks, it's better to put a job into perspective by expressing project costs as a total package price.

There are other advantages to quoting a flat rate. It's easy to build in fees and charges that would stand out like a sore thumb on a price breakdown sheet. If you quote a job 20% lower than what customers can find elsewhere, you can incorporate a price increase while still giving the impression that they are getting your service for "peanuts."

Once a site is designed, most shops charge for alterations and corrections. When working on an hourly rate basis, you can offer a lower hourly rate for handling changes. Your customer feels that they're getting a bargain (even though you still earn a good profit).

The key point here is that you should present your price increase as an increase in value, not as an increase in price. Try to use a price increase as an opportunity to build a better business relationship. Tell clients that they are important to you. Explain to them that you are improving or adding more service value. Then do it.

If you find your costs rising and must raise prices to compensate for this, then announce your new prices as an "interim market adjustment." This softens the blow and gentle lets your clients know that you are simply passing along the added costs that you've experienced.

Explain that you are reluctantly passing these external cost increases along to all of your clients.

If your client asks for a justification, show them your costs increases. Only do this if they ask. Don't share your profit and return on investment intentions. Instead show them that your productivity and hard work has enabled you to maintain your prices for much longer than would normally have been possible. And commit to giving more value for the new prices they will pay.

How Much Can You Raise Your Price?

Finding a customer's acceptance or resistance point is a challenge. It involves knowing the price sensitivity of your potential market, your competitors, and your customer base. An increase of $5 an hour may be palatable. Raising rates by $10 an hour may be too much. Typically an average price increase is 5-10 percent. Tom Winninger, author of *Price Wars*, feels that the threshold of pain for consumers is lower — between four and five percent. Businesses can accept 7-8% price increases.

Winninger cautions that you should not wait very long to raise prices. Two years is too long. Many clients expect a price increase every January.

If you're new and your business is evolving rapidly, shift immediately to a well-researched solid pricing rate regardless what increment you determine is appropriate. Just be certain that your customers still perceive sufficient value in your services. You can add value by bringing attention to what you already offer such as fast turnaround, a good record of on-line hits to client sites, or special multimedia designs done for major clients.

If your analysis and calculations indicate a $15 an hour increase is appropriate, move immediately to this new price. Avoid the step increases because these can cause confusion, and word will spread rapidly that one client got a similar job done for a better price. If you can justify the increase and give your customer base advance warning, boldly move forward and increase your hourly rate. But be sure to replace your printed and on-line signs and price sheets so everything matches what you tell your clients.

Some service providers say that the price is right when 20% of your customers complain that you're too expensive. This is a decision that you alone must make.

Subtle Ways to Raise Prices

You can effectively raise prices by eliminating discounts and by reducing credit terms. Just reducing the payment terms from 30 days to two weeks will cause a noticeable increase in cash flow.

You can also customize. If you find clients continuing to order a similar site design, bundle the various job elements into a new product template and sell this at a higher price than the "standard" design.

Or unbundle projects, charge a low price for the basic design and then charge a fee for each added element that your client selects.

Remember to charge for those seemingly small and not-so-small things that your client asks you to include or asks you to perform. These include adding another tiny image file, including a special link and being there at the end of a telephone or modem e-mail link when the client has "just a quick question."

And bill your client for services beyond what's normal. This includes quick delivery, working over the weekend or working into the evening.

Handling Objections to Price Increase

Price objections are the biggest problem you'll face when selling service. As you discuss a price increase with your team, you'll encounter some interesting objections from your own people. These are some common objections:

"We'll lose customers."

"The customer buys on price alone, not quality."

"Our quality isn't high enough, so we need to discount our price."

"We'll lose long term business."

"The competition will eat us alive."

To help your staff understand why a price increase is necessary, hold a company meeting in which you openly and honestly explain your pricing strategy. Show them how the customer gets more value because of time and productivity savings they will achieve by using your company for Web site development.

Conduct an "objection clinic" with your employees. Use role playing, and have them counter objections that a customer might make. Often the employees can create objection scenarios that your customers haven't thought of. This role playing experience is helpful in getting both your staff and your customers comfortable with any price increase. Banks and financial services use this technique when adding products, eliminating products, or changing fees. If it works for them, it can work for you, too.

The idea is to discover and address objections before a prospect thinks of them. Be proactive—not re-active. Address their concerns while you're still qualifying them as prospective customers.

Most concerns involve your shop's skills, project difficulty, the price you'll charge, and a fear that the prospect doesn't know enough to make an informed decision on which service provider to go with. By qualifying them carefully, showing them sites that you've designed and testimonials of happy customers. (You are asking for these aren't you.?), you can educate them on the process, and show them that you know how to do it right. Just be certain that you've qualified them as a bonafide prospect rather than a low-budget leech who draws your knowledge, then goes elsewhere to negotiate a better price from the educated position that you gave them. This has happened at least once to most service providers who live and work "in the trenches."

If a prospective customer claims that your competitor is charging less for the same job, explain that your shop can offer quality, service, and low price, and the client can choose any two. Tell them that your business cannot provide top quality, fast and accurate service and still charge a low price. It takes more resources and skills to do a fast, quality job. These cost-benefits are reflected in the prices that you quote. Ask them which of the factors they think the competitor is compromising on to be able to price lower.

Another ploy when hearing a price objection is to comment, "If price were not an issue, would you buy our service." Then see if there is a way to provide the service they want at the price they feel comfortable paying. Try to offer lower quality, longer response time, or a reduced scope of effort in the design.

Be slow to give concessions. They will try all they can to get the most for the least cost. Giving in too quickly will diminish the value of the concession.

If you lower your billing rates to match competitors, the prospect will wonder if they could have gotten you to go even lower. Instead of trying to justify your prices against a lower price competitor, explain how much skill and experience is required to do what they want. Then ask them why they think the competitor values their work and their own people less than you value yours. Gives them something to think about.

I remember reading about a shop owner who took a wavering prospect, who was badgering for a cheaper price, out to lunch. They stopped in at a cheap, "greasy-spoon" fast-food restaurant. When the prospect looked at the owner in disbelief, the owner said "Hey, this is the cheapest! Isn't this what you're after? Is the quality of this meal, the same quality that you expect on your project? What you pay, makes all the difference in the world." The point was made clear and dramatic.

If you think your prospect is comparing your price with a discounter, ask them if there are other expenses that could occur in the long term if they went with a lower priced shop. Explain that you have competitors who try to win business with lower prices. Ask them what they think these low price competitors sacrifice in order to offer those low prices. Suggest that they may be skimping on design quality, on follow-up service or some other thing that you don't. The key is to question every component of the job to be certain that the prospect is comparing apples-to-apples.

Some believe that there are no price objections. There are only value questions. Stress value, not price. You can offset a higher price by demonstrating value. So, don't defend your price. Promote your value. In the end, it's up to you to convince your customer that you provide more value for the buck than your competitor.

Choosing the Right Price

Determining the right price for your service takes time and work. Yet, the closer you get to the "right" price, the greater the impact on your bottom line. It takes only 1% improvement in price with a steady sales volume to produce a 12.5% increase in profit. Thus, a small step toward better pricing can be worth plenty.

Perform the analysis. Develop a draft set of prices. Then compare these against the objectives and strategic and tactical pricing plan that you've developed. Do a break-even analysis, and a margin curve analysis for each service. Collect market intelligence on potential clients and existing competitors. Determine the likely reactions that your existing customers and competitors will take when you make your prices known. What value do they place on your service? Look at the different ways that clients value your service. What are their perceptions of you and your shop?

Include in your analysis the expected impact each price change will have on your other services. What is the price sensitivity of your client base. Remember price elasticity from Chapter 3. Price elasticity is the percent change in the number of sales that you'll get after a 1% change in your price. On average, the number of sales will drop by two percent. But perhaps you didn't have the right price from the start? Clients will shop around and assess the value of your services given the alternatives. Then they will mentally establish a price threshold over which they will be reluctant to go.

Identify an optimal service package and pricing structure. Decide whether you should offer coupons, rebates or discounts. Adhere to local, state, and federal regulations so you avoid legal trouble.

Suppose you are planning volume prices for scanning and placing images on site pages. If it costs your shop $2 to handle each image, set your single image price at, say, $7, then $5 more for a second image, $4 more for a third and $3.50 more for a fourth. Offering image scan and placement for a flat $7 each could turn off some buyers. People expect quantity discounts. So develop a pricing schedule that handles volume sales and keeps the client interested in buying more, while still covering your costs and generating as much profit as possible.

Once you feel that you have a good price list, develop a contingency plan for potential adverse consequences. If you know that a price increase will upset certain clients, carefully work the increase into your operation. And learn the best way to handle price objections.

How will competitors react to your pricing changes? You'd prefer not to start a price war. Consider second- and third-order effects on your pricing decisions. What would you do if you were a competitor? If you raise your prices by 5%, what will your competitors likely do? What if you cut prices by five percent?

Once published, monitor your new prices to see how clients and competitors react. If clients begin to collect and use your coupons and rebate offers more, you know that you're at the high end of their value threshold.

Assess your client's emotional response to your prices. When we released our first pricing tables, we set our price at $49. We held them there even when marketing and advertising agencies told us we should be able to get over $1,000 for the information. Our market was (and still is) the independent entrepreneur struggling to make a decent living in a mostly-anti-business world. By doing so, we've received hundreds of testimonials and a loyal following of customers who appreciate our efforts and buy every upgrade to our tables.

Like yourself, we had to analyze whether the return was worth the cost. If you find your clients cost more to service than you can earn, then you must re-think your prices. You must also re-think the life-time value that these clients give to your company.

Don't lock yourself into a price. Cast your pricing strategy in "Jello™"—make your plan semi-rigid. There are always circumstances that require a slightly different approach to pricing—an opportunity, or a threat. When you bid jobs, price your work based on how much it will cost to perform on that particular job. Often the cost to perform on one job is greatly different than the cost to perform on another similar job.

Finally, develop a policy of periodically reviewing your pricing structure. Don't be afraid to modify your price as market conditions change. Pricing is an on-going process. It doesn't end the moment you publish your Web service prices.

Problems in Web Service Today

Web service providers are dealing with a number of real-life problems today. The issues include:

1. Clients demand the impractical or impossible. Web design is unique and not the same as printed page design. The process is different and the page layout is different. Some clients have a hard time understanding this reality.

2. All browsers are not created equal. Color that looks great when viewed with one browser, may not look good with another browser. Even the text layout seems to change according to the browser.

3. Design takes a lot longer. Web design is a learning experience for both client and designer. Projects just seem to take longer than they do with traditional desktop publishing.

4. Many still want a local shop. Some clients don't trust someone they can't see or talk with. While some Web developers are successfully working with clients half a continent away, others find clients difficult to convince if you aren't in their immediate vicinity.

5. Clients want to re-use old printed copy. Many clients think old printed copy will work in a Web site design. Often, old material requires significant editing and rework to make it Web-suitable. Content is a big problem to many site designers. So are re-used graphics.

6. Clients need more marketing info. Clients need help in marketing and advertising their businesses on-line. They need coaching on what to put on each page and how to link pages so the message flows properly. This makes Web designers also marketing consultants.

Much of your time will be spent informing your client what can and cannot be done with a Web site. These people become much easier to work with once they understand the current limitations of the Web.

Summary

This chapter was a gold mine of valuable pricing tactics. In Chapter 8, you'll learn critical business numbers and ratios that can indicate trends and signal the health and wealth of your company.

8
Managing by the Numbers

"To keep prices right is the trickiest problem in this new economy."

Analyzing Financial Numbers

There is a certain symmetry to financial statements. After you've looked at a hundred or so, you see that the revenue that a shop earns can be partitioned into various factors such as costs, taxes, and profit. In fact, these typical expenses can be partitioned out by percentage.

Web service shops have a relatively low material cost (toner, paper, disks, etc.), but a high production cost (labor intensive). Earlier, you learned how to calculate gross margin. From gross margin you subtract sales, general and administrative expenses to get gross profit.

Sales costs for a shop are typically between eight and 12 percent of total sales revenue. G&A expenses include the indirect costs —the costs just to do business.

The federal government and several private research groups monitor financial data for the major industry groups. (Desktop and Web services are not considered industry groups, yet.) The income and expense category percentages that they report depend greatly on the type and size of business. For example, G&A for software company, Corel was 19.6 percent. Adobe managed 8.4% G&A. The best G&A value that I could find was 3.2% for Microsoft. Typically, the larger the company, the lower the G&A as a percent of total sales income.

This means that a small Web services shop with one or two employees will likely spend much more on G&A than a large shop employing over 10 employees. This is also why there's such a push to control operating costs — in particular, general and administrative expenses. Cost cutting is crucial to optimizing profitability. And operating expenses can be what separates the high- and low-profit performers.

If you subtract sales costs and G&A expenses from gross margin, you can determine your operating (gross) profit. This is your pretax profit. If you have debt expense, this must be deducted from your operating profit to get gross (pretax) profit. Depending on debt load, interest expense is usually between one and five percent. Since most shops don't have to deal with this, I didn't show interest expense in the tables.

After applying your shop's tax rate to pretax profit you get net profit (the bottom line). Most shops face a tax rate (federal and state) of about 40% on the pretax profit. Does 1.2% in net profit look low? In most industry groups (including printing, prepress, and desktop publishing), the bottom line profit is typically between 0.2 and 3 percent. Now you see why excessive taxes hurt business. Net profit represents the funds that you use to grow your business. These cover new capital purchases (assuming you don't want to go in debt).

Once you establish your shop's financial profile, you can use this information to make interesting comparisons. For example, you can use the percent ranges to analyze each job that your shop performs to see which projects represent wheat and which represent chaff. You'll probably discover that 80% of your profit comes from only 20% of your customer base.

There are also indicators that can tell you how much money you'll make this week or month. They can also tell you if you'll run out of cash by the end of the next pay period. They are the critical numbers that determine if you'll sleep well tonight, or toss and turn in a sea of anxiety. The following are key things you can watch in monitoring the health and prosperity of your business.

The Critical Number

Every business has one. It could be the number of minutes of FTP time expended during a day. It could be the number of Web pages designed that week. It could be the number of proposals submitted that week. It can be just about anything. but it's the single critical number that determines if you'll earn a profit.

For restaurants, it could be the length of the customer line waiting for tables at 7:30 pm because the owner knows the average profit per table. For a manufacturer, it could be the weight of raw steel shipped the day before knowing the cost per finished pound of product. A hotel could monitor the occupancy rate because anything above a 70% break-even will generate pure profit.

You must decide your shop's critical number, and then focus on it so you get beyond break-even and into maximum profit generation. All other numbers are affected by this single yardstick. Find it. Work to improve it, and you'll win.

Cash on Hand

One important number is cash on hand. Many shops operate from payday to payday, from bill payment day to bill payment day. Cash is the most pressing need to most entrepreneurs. There never seems to be enough. And it's what you spend much of your day chasing after. Cash on hand refers to the amount of actual dollars you can get your hands on — checking and savings accounts, credit card cash advances, and the hard currency kept in your petty cash drawer.

It's always comforting to know that there's a cache of cash tucked away for emergencies.

Income

Income is how much actual money flows into your business within a specified period of time.

Be careful not to fall into the trap of counting a sale as income before payment has been received. The best approach is to firmly maintain that "a sale in not made, until a sale has been paid."

Expenses

Here you monitor the bills to be paid. If you can shift some vendors to accept credit payment terms, you can significantly improve your cash available. But in the end, all bills must be paid.

Monitor your expenses at least monthly. List each expense not only in dollars, but also as a percent of your total cost. Watch for trends. Are expenses in any area going up? Should they?

As sales increase, service expenses go up. Because of net payment terms, bills can continue to rise even after sales begin to taper off. This is why many shop owners compare purchase orders (job orders) with expenses every week.

Are sales softening while expenses remain high? Start tightening your belt. Weekly monitoring enables faster corrective response.

Cost of Services Sold

In a service business, labor comprises the largest part of the cost of services. As you discovered in earlier chapters, cost of services sold is a prime candidate for actions to lower costs and thereby improve gross profit.

Remember, a small change in costs of services sold can have a large impact on your gross and net profit.

Expense as Percent of Gross Income
Another technique is to calculate and then monitor the expense versus gross income ratio (expressed in percent). Simply divide your costs by your gross sales income to establish a baseline value. Watch for a rising ratio in any expense category. It could indicate trouble.

You could establish a ratio for each expense and then monitor which expenses are likely to vary. This lets you quickly spot trends (positive or negative).

Accounts Receivables
Since Web service providers are busy, it's easy to get preoccupied and overlook delinquent clients. As these customers gradually take longer and longer to pay their invoices, you become their lending bank. This affects your cash flow and the available cash on hand.

Watch aging on your accounts receivables. For resellers, an average, 72% of their accounts receivables are 30 days or less outstanding. Only 8% are aged past 90 days. This is positive for these businesses. It shows that they don't have a problem collecting on credit accounts. Learn and then monitor your own accounts receivable aging. You want to keep payments current.

Carefully examine accounts receivable clients. Then take action quickly when payment isn't made on time. Review the section in Chapter 7 on getting paid. This can be a real problem with shop owners. Be alert. And act decisively and quickly when due dates are missed.

Monitor these credit payment trends at least weekly:
1) the receivables that are due in 30 days or less,
2) the receivables that are up to 30 days late,
3) those between 30 and 60 days late,
4) those over 60 days late.

Remember, the longer you delay going after the deadbeats, the less likely you're going to get paid.

Some owners closely track the ratio between the total number of accounts that are current and the total number of accounts that are overdue.

They also monitor the ratio of dollars in receivables that are current to the dollars in receivables that are delinquent. Any change in the ratio raises a caution flag suggesting a closer examination of the factors.

Inquiries Received

This refers to the number of calls that you receive each period (week or month). You want to see if your promotion and publicity actions are working. A rising number of calls or a rising number of hits at your site are positive signs that your efforts are working.

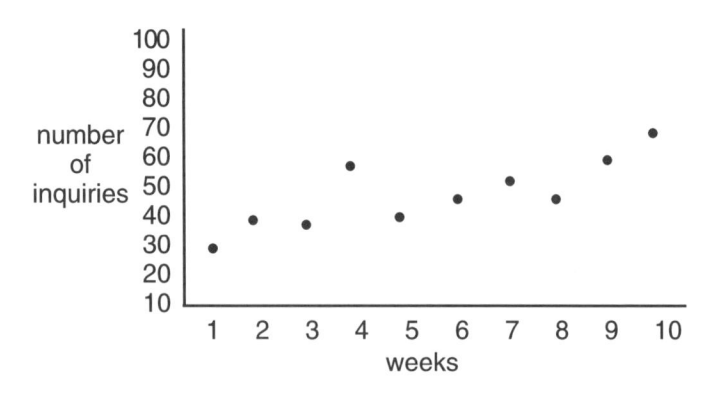

Fig. 8-1. Tracking inquiries within a time period.

By asking each caller where they heard or read about your company, you can determine where to best put your marketing and advertising dollars.

Purchase Orders (Sales)

Keep tabs on the number of purchase orders or sales that you get each month.

Also track the total dollar amount of monthly sales as well as the average sale value. By plotting this data, you

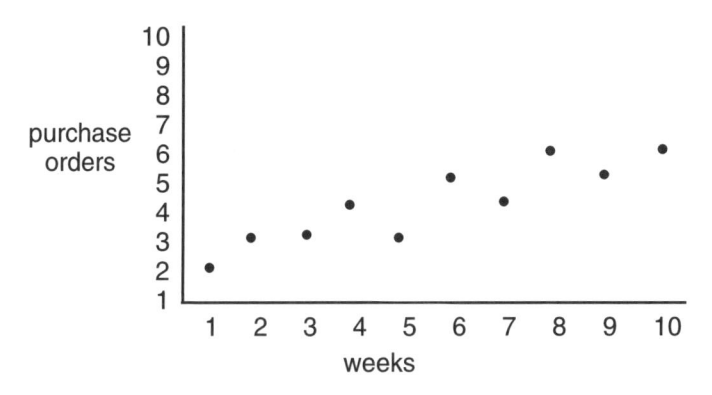

Fig. 8-2. Tracking purchases within a time period.

can see trends, growth and the affects of various pricing and advertising actions that you have made.

Conversion Ratio

Here you calculate the number of inquiries that are converted to sales. Two thousand hits at your site are useless if you don't have a fair number of actual transactions (sales), too. As shown in Figure 8-1, a conversion ratio chart can help you spot trends and help you in your decision-making process.

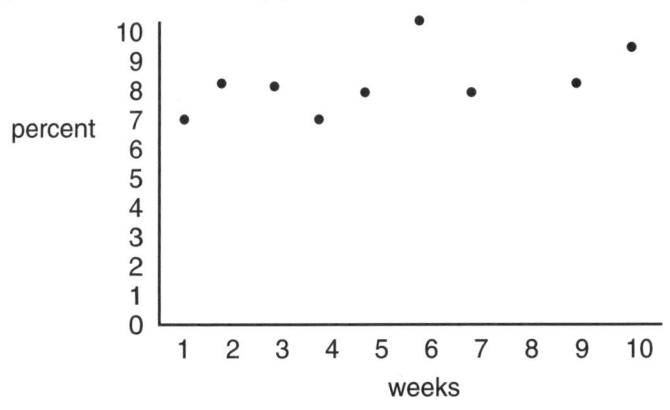

Fig. 8-3. Conversion ratio is a key measurement.

Typically, you'll get a 1-2% response to a direct marketing mailing. But a targeted market mailing can achieve 40% response and at least a 50% purchase result. This yields a 20% sales-to-mailing ratio.

To apply this to your business, first determine what your own conversion ratio is, then monitor it for improvement. Each time you do a mass mailing, change your Web site, offer a special, get unexpected publicity, or do any unique promotion, keep track of the number of telephone calls, e-mails or mail inquiries. Then count how many of these become actual sales (job projects).

Number of Customers

One gauge of company growth is the number of clients serviced each year. By counting and charting this factor, every month, you can see if your share of the market is growing or shrinking.

You could discover that the number of customers serviced in a particular month follows a yearly trend. In some industries, business often slows down from July through August, and then picks up again in September. By monitoring the numbers, you can make intelligent decisions about cash needs, training and vacation times.

Hours of Service Sold

This is an indirect way to monitor productivity. By knowing how many hours can be sold, you become proactive in trying to bill all the hours possible. You may decide to sell certain products or services only on selected days because computer systems, scanners, printers, or even clients are more available then.

Perhaps a special on fixed design Home Pages based on three or four template options will increase your hours of service sold. Perhaps you'll differentiate your services and sell hours to certain customers at special pricing levels.

You select the mix of service work that you want to handle. Then have your team focus on selling out the available hours in the first level, then selling out the available hours in the second tier, and so on. This way, you can sell two or three weeks of work in advance and maximize the capacity of your shop. By focusing on selling the hours available, you may decide that special rates for second shift or weekends is worth the effort.

Average Sale Amount

Here you monitor the average dollar amount on all of your sales. Then as other selling opportunities occur, you can quickly decide if you want to accept that job or if you should really push to increase the scope (and total price) of the job so its final value is above the average. Knowing this number helps you mentally push to increase the average dollars per sale for your shop.

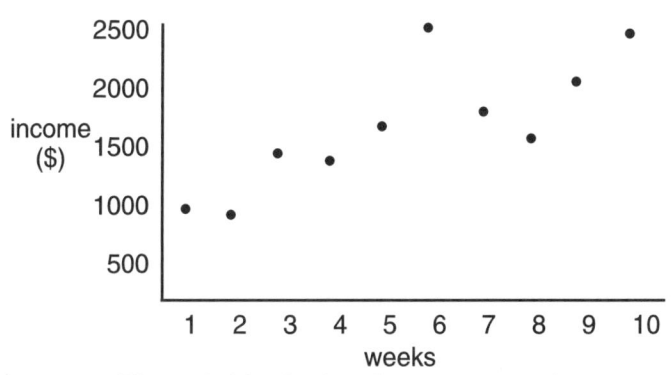

Fig. 8-4. Monitoring the average sale.

In direct mail selling, costs are such that it often does not make sense to process order for $10 or less. Many sellers try to achieve an average sale of $25 or more. By focusing on a higher average, you can significantly increase your annual revenue. It's all a matter of where you put your emphasis and how you package your products and services.

Gross Profit

Remember, this is your profit after expenses, but before taxes. Gross profit is a good way to track earnings and spending. Once your baseline is established, do all you can to increase your gross profit number.

If you borrow operating funds at 8% annual interest, you must earn a minimum 10% gross margin on your annual sales just to break even with the interest expense on the loan. This is why most companies try to stay debt-free. If you have a low gross profit margin, you may find your shop losing money overall.

Develop a *gross profit to net sales* ratio. Each month divide gross profit by total sales. Then monitor the decimal equivalent of this ratio. If the number goes down, costs are increasing more than sales revenue. If it goes up, costs are less relative to sales revenue. Again a spreadsheet is ideal for this calculation.

It's easier to monitor percentages than it is decimals, so express the ratio as a percent, and you have *percent gross profit*. Divide gross profit by total sales. Then multiply this number by 100 to get percent gross profit.

Net Profit

Here's where you see how much money is left over after everything has been deducted. Net profit is an exciting figure to watch. It's the dollars that you use to generate bonuses and rewards for your team. And it's the dollars that you put away for those rainy days when sales just don't go as planned.

Like gross profit, you can divide net profit by total sales and multiply the result by 100 to get *percent net profit*. This is actually the value that you want to watch. It's easier to see that net profit has gone from 1.6% up to 4.7% in the last quarter, than seeing that it went from $1,687 to $4,956. Monitoring percentages is easier, and faster to read and absorb.

An article in *Entrepreneur* magazine recommends that you set aside 3-4% of your marketing budget for unexpected marketing opportunities. You could earmark part of your net profit for this, instead.

If net profit doesn't come out what you want or expect, go back over the other monitoring steps to determine what went wrong. Then act quickly to reverse any negative trend.

Project Turnaround Time

Project turnaround refers to the actual time it takes to complete projects. If you can determine a rough standard for each task that you do, you can estimate turnaround time on any project.

You can also assess the impact of rush job requests by impatient clients. Our *Desktop Production Standards* reference lets you generate time standards for any task, using your computer to do the calculations.

Knowing how long it should take, and how long it actually takes helps you make better pricing decisions.

Projects Pending (Backlog)

This defines how many jobs are in progress or are about to enter the work stream. By monitoring this number, you can schedule resources, and determine when jobs are coming in faster than your staff can handle them. Rather than face irate customers, tracking this lets you act quickly to increase staff, subcontract work out to others, or turn down jobs.

By charting the number of uncompleted orders on a weekly basis you can spot backlog problems early enough to prevent problems. Perhaps a freelance floater can be on call to work off the overload. Perhaps you'll want to discuss overtime with your staff. The key is knowing when you are about to have a problem. Then acting on this information.

Revenue Per Employee ($/FTE)

Tracking the dollars in revenue per employee is one of the most valuable productivity and profit models you'll discover. With it you can establish a productivity factor for your shop and for each of your employees.

Table 8-1 shows a form that you can put into a spreadsheet and use to monitor individual and shop productivity. Notice that it partitions each month into working days. There is a column for each employee in your shop or profit center. The form is used to record dollars billed and hours worked. By monitoring these numbers, you'll be able to determine who is the most productive (and profitable) and if your pricing is in line with strategic and tactical planning.

Table 8-1. Productivity Summary Form

	PROFITABILITY $/FTE PRODUCTION SUMMARY				Month___
EMPLOYEE Billed Hours Out Worked	EMPLOYEE Billed Hours Out Worked	EMPLOYEE Billed Hours Out Worked	TOTAL DAILY	TOTAL HOURS	FTE HOURS	$/FTE

Rows 1–31, with callouts:
- "Highlight around dates that comprise each week."
- "MUST consider non-billable hours spent when evaluating $/FTE"

TOTAL

AVG $/FTE

On the right are columns that summarize the activity for each day. One column lists the total daily income, another lists the total hours worked, another lists the total number of FTE hours worked, and the last records the dollars of income per hours FTE worked ratio.

You could add a third column that normalizes each employee's output to a standard 8-hour full time equivalent (FTE) day.

At the bottom of form, the total dollars billed and hours worked for each employee are summarized. Then the hours are divided by the number of possible 8-hour work days in the month to get an equivalent FTE hour rating for each worker. This is divided into the total dollars earned to get a $/ FTE for each employee.

Some people prefer to print out the form and complete it manually. Each month they use a color "highlighter" pen to outline the dates that constitute each working week. Then the form is filled in for the days containing billable work.

You could design this form to record weekly subtotals during the month with a final tally at the end of the month.

By associating the columns that list dollars billed and hours worked with the dollars earned per hour worked, you focus on the income that each employee earns for the shop.

At the end of the year, the total income per employee is added and the total hours worked per year per employee are added to get annual values. The total hours worked are divided by a value representing the total hours possible to get an equivalent FTE rating for the year. For example, if Employee 1 worked 1,040 hours of 2,080 hours possible for an 8-hour worker, they worked half time and are assigned a ratio of 0.5 to represent one half what an FTE would work. If they earned $30,000 for the shop during the year their productivity represents $60,000 FTE (30,000/0.5) for your business. On the other hand, if they generate only $10,000 in billable income, they represent $20,000/FTE in productivity (10,000/0.5) and this is low. They may not be as productive as other employees.

If all workers have essentially an equal amount of non-billable work to perform each day, then all of them can be compared with each other to determine who is more profitable to the company, and the shop in general can be compared with itself to determine if it is becoming more or less productive over time.

Monitoring Schedule

Below is a recommended monitoring schedule for business information. Once each quarter, ask yourself if you're limiting yourself to those essentials that are necessary to track day-to-day business results or if you should find and track some other critical numbers.

Table 8-2. Schedule of Monitoring Points

	daily	weekly	monthly
total sales	X		
deposits		X	
sales by service		X	
cost of services			X
expenses			X
gross profit		X	
net profit			X
receivables			X
payables			X
cash flow		X	

This schedule based on recommendations by several sources that were found during research for this book. It's not the only schedule possible. But start from this and develop your own monitoring points.

Cash Flow

Cash flow relates to how much money you take in and then pay out. It establishes the amount of money available to run your business. It's the lifeblood of your company. Without it, your shop will whither and die.

You can be drowning in orders, yet be facing a shrinking cash position. If you have too many jobs relegated to accounts receivable (money due because credit was extended), you may not have enough funds to handle payroll, or to pay for that new system when it gets delivered. Cash flow is critical. Here's some great ideas for getting an instant cash flow status.

First, forecast what you'll need for the year. Looking at cash requirements for a 12-month period smoothes out the seasonal cycles and the impact of delayed payment on projects.

Next, factor in all of your known expenses including estimated taxes, insurance and license fees. You particularly want to know how much money you'll need for those quarterly payments. If there will be a shortfall, you want to know well in advance.

Then project your money requirements on a monthly basis. On a spreadsheet, make a detailed account of each month's anticipated income (receipts) and expenses (disbursements). This monthly forecast will help you prioritize projects. If a project slips two weeks and the invoice doesn't get delivered to the client as planned, what affect will this have on your cash flow.

Next, make a *daily cash control log* to record all money coming in and going out. You want to know how much cash you have available right now—today!. When your bank statement comes in, reconcile it with your checkbook right away, so you know how much cash is in the bank. Table 8-3 shows a daily cash flow monitor that you can use to help in this process.

Table 8-3. Daily Cash Flow Monitor

Daily Cash Flow Log

Day: _____ Date: _____

I. Cash and Investments (as of)

	This Morning	Yesterday
Total Cash on Hand	_____	_____
Other Available Funds	_____	_____

II. Payroll (as of)

	This Morning	Yesterday
# Employees	_____	_____
# FTEs	_____	_____
Last Payroll	$_____	$_____

III. Receivables

client	amount due	date due	default
a. <name>	_____	_____	_____
b. <name>	_____	_____	_____
c. <name>	_____	_____	_____
d. <name>	_____	_____	_____
a. <name>	_____	_____	_____
e. <name>	_____	_____	_____
f. <name>	_____	_____	_____
g. <name>	_____	_____	_____
h. <name>	_____	_____	_____

TOTAL RECEIVABLES: _____

IV. Projects in Process

project	% complete	expected completion date
a. <name>	_____	_____
b. <name>	_____	_____
c. <name>	_____	_____

d. <name> _____ _____
a. <name> _____ _____
e. <name> _____ _____
f. <name> _____ _____
g. <name> _____ _____
h. <name> _____ _____
TOTAL EARNINGS TO DATE: _____

V. Payables Due Today
    vendor   amount due
a. <name> _____
b. <name> _____
c. <name> _____
d. <name> _____
a. <name> _____
e. <name> _____
f. <name> _____
g. <name> _____
h. <name> _____
TOTAL PAYABLES: $_____

VI. Cash Available After Expenses: $_____

By generating this report each morning, you will see where the dollars go. You'll spot trends early, and you'll detect potential profit problems before they surface. For example, you could notice that cash collections are tending down, leaving more in accounts receivable than you want. If a payment is just one day late, you want someone working the problem.

By sharing this report with your staff, you'll keep everyone on the same page and focused on bringing in the bucks. If you detect a need for more cash, you can act early to increase your credit line, reach deep into your own pocket, or seek alternative funding.

If you detect an upward trend in available cash, this may be the time to consider investing in that new computer system, or expanding shop services.

Analyzing Profit in Competitor Bids

Here's an interesting way to use percentage breakdowns to compare competitor bids. This is a quick way to see if a competitor is losing his shirt by underbidding just so they can "get their foot in the door." They may plan to "get well" on design changes and upgrades.

If you assume that your competitor uses similar equipment (hardware and software) and has the same or similar labor costs that you do, then you can enter the winning bid into a spreadsheet and quickly determine approximately how much revenue that shop won (or lost) on the bid.

For example, assume that you bid $10,000 on a particular site design project but were beat out by a competitor who submitted a winning $7,000 bid.

Table 8-4 breaks down the $10K and $7K bids into costs. The competitor bid a lower price but has the same outlay for materials and production service (shop labor). This means that after the cost to service the job are handled, this shop is already at the edge of the hole, and it gets worse as you look down the column. By the time you factor in the cost of sales, G&A, and interest, this competitor is losing over a thousand dollars just by bidding and accepting the job.

Table 8-4. Analyzing project award profit.

	Our Bid		Competitor	
Price	10,000	100%	7,000	100.0%
Service Cost	7,000	70%	7,000	100.0%
Gross Margin	3,000	30%	(000)	(0%)
Sales Cost	1,000	10%	700	(10%)
G&A	600	6%	420	(6%)
Pretax Profit	1,400	14%	(1,120)	(16.0%)
Tax (40%)	560	5.6%	0	(0%)
Net Profit	840	8.4%	(1,120)	(16.0%)

Amazing! By taking a single data point (their winning bid) and dropping the bid value into your price breakdown spreadsheet, you can readily see that this competitor bid far under their break-even. They're losing $1,120 just by taking on that job!

Perhaps it's a good time to send a letter to the client that awarded the job to them and send cards to all of the competitor's other customers telling everyone that your shop will still be open six months from now should they quickly need another source for service — (after the IRS closes the door on this failing competitor).

The sad truth is that there are far too many service shops who low-ball price and consistently operate on the razor's edge of survival simply because they don't understand business principles. No matter how you cut the pie, you still must pay for hardware, software, and the professionals who make a project happen. For most shops, the numbers will pencil out remarkably similar.

Bidding below break-even only speeds a shop's eventual demise. Unfortunately, many shops are doing this without even knowing it. Knowledge is power. The challenge is to get your knowledge to produce profit.

How Much CanYou Actually Earn?

Since the desktop publishing revolution began 10 years ago, desktop service providers have struggled to find the best price to charge for their work. The massive layoffs that began in the late 80s pushed thousands into small one-person businesses. Today, in entrepreneurial states such as California, the majority of businesses have three or fewer employees. Based on our survey data, the vast majority of shops are sole proprietorships, earn less than $50,000 a year, have one full time employee, and occasionally hire part time help. Desktop publishing, graphic design and Web design and development are the most common services provided.

When these entrepreneurs started by eagerly filing their fictitious names and doing their first project, they had the skills to do the work. Most did not have the skills to operate a business. Being an entrepreneur is exciting, yet challenging. It can also be risky to your life savings. Sound pricing is the key to making profit.

For example, the first thing most start-up business owners do is call their competitors to see what everyone else is charging. They use what little information they get through this difficult and time-consuming process to set their prices below everyone else, assuming that customers will come in droves. When they don't, reality sets in and these entrepreneurs begin the long process of learning how to operate a service business.

Their first vision of sugar plums is typically to assume that if they charge $20 an hour they can make a decent living. With approximately 2080 working hours in a year, they should bring in $41,600—about $10,000 more than the average worker in California. Table 8-5 shows their thinking.

Table 8-5. Maximum Possible Income
(at 2080 hours per year)

Billing Rate	Possible Income
$10	$20,800
20	41,600
25	52,000
30	62,400
40	83,200
50	104,000
60	124,800

Looking at these numbers, they are ecstatic! This discovery is the greatest thing since sliced bread! What they forgot are their costs, taxes and productivity.

If you operate your own business, you cannot be productive all the time. Part of your day is spent seeking more work. And part of your time is spent trying to get paid. Remember the "30-60-10 Rule" and the fact that most small shops are only 30-50% productive (generate billable hours only 30-50 percent of the time). These owner-operators are paying themselves much less than they admit.

As shown in Table 8-6, the maximum possible income changes drastically once productivity and payroll are factored into the formula. At a billing rate of $10 an hour and assuming 2080 hours of work a year, this person is far below the poverty level in actual possible income. With only 30% productivity, they actually earn only $6,240 a year. They can't even pay their expected $16,640 annual salary.

Table 8-6. Maximum Possible Income at Various Productivity Levels.

Billing Rate	Hourly Pay	Average Productivity	Payroll	Possible Income
10	8	30	16,640	6,240
25	10	30	20,800	15,600
32	10	30	20,800	19,968
40	10	30	20,800	24,960
40	10	40	20,800	33,280
50	10	30	20,800	31,200
50	15	40	31,200	41,600
50	15	50	31,200	52,000
60	15	30	31,200	37,440
60	15	40	31,200	49,920
60	15	50	31,200	62,400
100	15	50	31,200	104,000

If they raise their shop rate to $25 an hour, they can earn $15,600 a year. But they can't pay themselves $10 an hour. At a $32 an hour shop rate, they still can't cover payroll. So they work longer hours while continuing to calculate income at 40 hours a week, or they jack their prices to $40 an hour. At $40 an hour, the numbers suggest that they can cover payroll and have a few thousand dollars left over. When they raise their rates (assuming they can and still get business), the dollars left over increase. The picture is getting quite respectable. But then they factor in expenses—including taxes.

Even in a home office, there are costs to running a business. You must still pay for the equipment, software, supplies, telephone and added utilities. In reality, you should expense out a portion of the mortgage or rent, association fees, trash collection, and cleaning. Your overhead costs will run between 10% and 50% of revenue.

Then consider taxes. In 1940, Americans paid around 3% of their income back to the government in the form of taxes. Today, a sole proprietorship will pay around 40% in taxes (25% to the federal government and another 11% to the state). Even a Class C corporation will face 19% taxes to the feds and close to 10% to the state. This means that the small independent business person faces a hefty tax on every dollar earned. This is in addition to the normal operating costs.

As a new shop, they feel they cannot afford to offer benefits such as health, life, vision and dental insurance. They can't even afford to take a vacation for the first few years.

Once the shop owner-operator adds overhead costs and taxes to their spreadsheet, the numbers begin to change drastically as shown in Table 8-7.

Table 8-7. How Much Am I Actually Earning?

Actual Income Compared with Billing Rate

Billing Rate $/hr	Maximum Revenue Possible	Actual Income/Expenses (at 30% productivity)	Taxes Fed/State (25%)	(30%)	Benefits $/year	Left Over For You $	Your Actual Hourly Pay
10	20,800	6,240	1,560	1,872	none	2,808	$1.35
20	41,600	12,480	3,120	3,744	none	5,616	2.70
40	83,200	24,960	6,240	7,488	none	11,232	5.40
50	104,000	31,200	7,800	9,360	none	14,040	6.75
50	104,000	52,000	13,000	15,600	none	23,400	11.25

This table tells the real story. And it suggests several things that you can do to improve your take-home pay. First, at low shop rates, you simply cannot operate a business. Costs will be much more than $1,560 a year. Even at $20 an hour, expenses and taxes force your effective pay down to only $2.70 an hour. Things begin to brighten when the shop rate is increased to $40 an hour. Still the costs keep your effective pay to less than minimum wage.

At $50 an hour, a 30% productive shop can bring the owner $6.75 an hour. But, if this owner can increase productivity to 50%, the business now looks like a business, and the owner-operator is beginning to earn enough to survive. The important fact to notice is that going from 30% to 50% productivity (a 67% increase in billable output) increases the actual income by 67% from $31,200 to $52,000, AND the dollars left over by 67% from $14,040 to $23,400! This means that every percent improvement in productivity drops directly through to the bottom line in added profit.

Now imagine what you could earn if you could set your shop rate at $60, $70 or even $100 an hour! You can if you provide those unique services that customers are willing to pay premium prices to get.

Summary

This chapter gave you the tools you need to monitor and consistently improveyour income. In the next chapter, you'll learn street smarts that will help you find and achieve more business.

9
Street Smart Ideas

"The only barrier is you."

The following subjects don't directly pertain to pricing, but they do directly relate to your ability to sell service. Therefore, I've included them in this chapter on tactics. Here you'll find jewels here that could help you win that next Web development project.

Networking For Business (How to Work a Room)

Networking. Fishing for contacts. Mining for prospects. This activity is critical to business success. The best way to market your business is by "word of mouth." And the most successful way to accomplish this is by personal contact—talking up your company with others who may need your services—networking yourself and your business. Whether we like to or not, we must learn how to talk with others about what we do. We need to develop contacts and exchange information. So, here's how to network your Web service business.

Selecting the Group

The first step is to carefully select the group that you will network with. People join professional organizations to meet and talk with others about issues that are specific to their field or to learn what useful business techniques others have found. Many join to find job opportunities, to measure success, or to enjoy the prestige that an organization has among other professionals. Choose a group relevant to your business.

Networking groups have been around for years, although only savvy individuals knew how to fully exploit this resource. I've heard about Rotary clubs, Lions clubs, Soroptimist clubs, and other organizations as long as I can remember. These groups are dedicated to providing community service. We also have groups specifically organized for networking business—groups such as Le Tip, Professionals in Networking, and Women's Business Network. These groups were formed with a specific goal in mind — getting more business. They don't exist to provide service to the community. They exist for their members to network with and sell to each other. Even the Chamber of Commerce puts on social meetings so members can network. So let's prepare for and attend a networking event.

Preparing for the Encounter

Read books and articles on group dynamics during the networking process. Then practice to become skillful at interacting with people. Learn how meetings work and how you can best participate. The goal is to make you and your business visible and to get jobs. The objective is to collect the business cards of at least three hot prospects by the end of each event. You'll work to collect as many cards as you can, but you want some promising business opportunities for your time and effort. And you want to make you and your business visible. You want people to remember you, so the next time they see you, they walk up and greet you warmly. Try to develop business relationships in which each participant can win. Help them, and you help yourself.

When the event is over, your prospects will have one important representation of you — your business card, so design one that is colorful and professional. If you walk into a group meeting with both hands full of brochures and cards, you'll look like a amateur. Keep the brochures at your office, or out in your car. You'll use these later when you follow up. But bring about two-dozen business cards with you. And have some more out in your car. Usually one will be used as you sign in. Many groups have a raffle or drawing during the event and people participate by dropping their business card into a jar at the registration table. Keep your business cards in one pocket. Use the opposite pocket to hold the cards of people that you meet. It's awkward to hand someone what you think is your card, only to notice that it's someone else's.

Before you arrive, practice how you'll describe your business. Once the networking event begins, you want to spend as much time getting contacts. So be ready to describe what you do in a few important words. Know the kinds of problems that your business can solve for others. Each moment is precious, and you don't want to waste time rambling. So focus on benefits.

Dress for the event. If you're in doubt, err on the formal side. If the dress code is unclear, dress up. This lets you project position, power and wealth. It will also give you more confidence. Many people wear something unusual such as a bright pin, scarf or tie—something that will help people remember them.

Ready, Set, Network

When you arrive, you'll typically have to sign in at a registration desk. Be friendly and act enthusiastic. You'll likely be asked to print your name on a tag that you'll pin or stick to your clothing. The best place to put this is on your right chest. As Americans, we shake hands with our right hand. It's easier to look up slightly following the hand shake and read a person's name tag as you look into their eyes. And print large and carefully so it's easy for others to read your name.

Don't pick up anything at the registration desk (unless you need a program schedule). The idea is to keep your hands free so you can shake hands and still hold a drink or snack. You'll be able to pick up brochures and announcements when you leave.

If you're shy, get there early. There's little pressure before most of the people arrive so you can practice your networking with relatively few people. Look for wallflowers who are also uncomfortable in groups. Statistics show that 95 percent of us are uncomfortable in a room with strangers. But, learn how to be gregarious. Seek out and be friendly with people standing on the periphery. They're probably timid since it's their first visit, too. They could be your best contact that day.

A good technique is to attend a networking event with a friend from a noncompeting business. This gives you someone to talk with as you get started, and you can cross-promote each other. Act enthusiastic and friendly during the event; you'll seem enthusiastic and confident. Practice introducing each other before you arrive.

Working the Room

Everyone at a networking meeting is there for the same reason. So mingle. Circulate. Your objective is to cover the entire room or area. And you want to meet everyone. If you spend three minutes with each person, you can make 20 contacts in a hour. Spending just two more minutes with each person there lowers your "hit" ratio to only 12 people. The larger the gathering, the less time you have to speak with each person you meet.

And spend even less time with those you already know. Greet them, smile and shake hands. Make a short friendly statement and then move on. Spend extra time with the "hot" contacts. Your goal is to make contact, generate interest and move on. If you can, arrange appointments to call or visit a hot contact. Make small talk brief, but important. Answer questions succinctly and quickly. You've a lot of gold to mine in that field and you want to work over as much ground as you can.

Walk up to people, extend your hand and introduce yourself. Read their name tag and use their name as you speak. Ask about their business, it's location and products, and what they do there. Exchange business cards freely. Then close the conversation with a statement such as: "Well, it was really nice meeting you, here." And move on. Both of you are there for the same reason, so everyone quickly learns the rules. Meet. Greet. Exchange (cards). Move on.

As you walk away, write a short note on the back of their card describing something unique about them or their business. You'll use this later when you follow up after the event.

You'll be wearing both buyer and seller hats since everyone else is also trying to sell. Be polite. Never snub anyone. And never say a bad thing about anyone or any business. You never know if that person you speak with is connected to the person, product or business that you're bad-mouthing. Instead, project a positive and winning attitude. If you refer someone, be certain that the person mentions your name as the source of the referral. You may even want to call the person that you're sending a referral to. When you see that person later, ask if the referred person called and how the call turned out.

As you mingle, keep your ears and mind alert. Listen for problems and opportunities. Go out of your way to meet as many people as you can. If you come up to several people who appear otherwise engaged, wait for a lull and then lead in with, "Excuse me, but I'd like to meet you both." Then introduce yourself and exchange cards. The networking has begun.

Step out of your comfort zone and take a chance. You've only added business to gain and nothing to lose.

Every contact doesn't have to become a sale. Useful information, referrals, trends and business tips can be just as important. The idea is to become visible to the group, gather intelligence, and to meet potential customers. Get them to know you so they'll recognize you the next time you meet. Once they get to know you, they'll be more likely to buy from you.

Follow-Up

After the event, the next important step is to follow up on the contacts that you've made. Within two days, send each person a promotional piece on your Web development services and a personal note telling them how much you enjoyed meeting them. Mention the unique thing that you wrote down on their card—their terrific hair, attire, watch, smile, etc. And then include something of personal interest to them such as an article on a subject they mentioned, the name and number of a prospect they could contact, or a URL where they may find information useful in their own business.

Remind them where you met, what you talked about and who you are. You could write: "It was really nice meeting you at the Chamber of Commerce gathering on Tuesday. I like your idea for a newsletter Web site. Here's some info about the work I do. Let's keep in touch." Or you could say: "Enjoyed our chat. Thought this might interest you. Let's get together." That's how easy it is.

If they've given you information during the event that was beneficial to you, tell them that you appreciate it. If they offered you advice on how to get in to see another prospect, and you managed an appointment, thank them and tell them that you're meeting with that person. If they gave you the address of a useful information site on the Internet, check it out, and acknowledge how much it helped you. Everyone likes to feel helpful, so tell them how you used their idea and how good you feel about them for telling you.

Suppose you want to call a networking prospect. The best time to phone is before 9 a.m. since most people don't go into meetings until then. If they're not in, leave your name, the link (met at recent Chamber meeting), and the time you'll call back. Ask them to let you know if the time is inconvenient and to suggest a better time. The idea is to make contact and speak person-to-person.

Today, networking is a key event for owners who want to get ahead in business. It's often uncomfortable when you start, but as you learn the ropes, networking becomes easier, and much more successful. As the Chinese fortune cookie note says: "A wise man knows everything. A shrewd man knows everyone."

Listening for Profit

In chaotic times, the entrepreneurial "playing field" becomes littered with the debris of failed businesses. Yet, one wonders how many companies could have survived and even prospered if their owners had listened to the marketplace. Not "heard" the marketplace. "Listened" to the marketplace!

Listening is the primary source for conflict. It's also the chief cause of lost profit potential.

There's a story in the Bible about 10,000 Philistines, who were slain with the jawbone of an ass. It's likely that at least this many sales opportunities are lost each day using the same weapon. Sometimes people talk too much and listen too little.

Listening is not easy. It's a skill—an art. And it should be learned, honed, and nurtured. Listening is a remarkable key to achieving business and personal success. Yet, poor listening is a problem that many service providers don't recognize and accept. Most people think that they listen quite well—that listening is a natural gift. But while they hear a speaker's voice, they often fail to listen to the actual message.

During arguments between couples, one person may exclaim "You don't listen to me!" Mothers correcting their children may demand "Open your ears and listen to what I'm saying!" Mothers and wives can be outspoken. A client will communicate by firing you. They'll find another source for their information —a source that "understands"—a Web service company that "listens."

The problem is that many people just don't recognize the other person's point of view. They don't give concentrated, active and attentive focus on what a speaker is saying. A message must be received AND understood before true communication can occur.

The point is: You can't learn when you're talking! Listening is vital to every aspect of business. It lets you gain valuable information, understand others, recognize problems, and discover solutions. It's also your tool for finding business opportunity.

Listening focuses on hearing and acknowledging. Listening is not easy. It takes work. It's complicated and strenuous. And it takes mental effort.

We can hear four to five times faster than we can speak. This means that while someone is talking, our mind can fill in the time between words with other thoughts, ideas, opinions, and conclusions. This causes some people to interrupt and complete sentences for a speaker. It causes them to close their mind. It causes them to lose opportunity and repeat sales.

Poor listeners can misinterpret directions, hear a problem incorrectly, ignore valuable information, and overlook true meanings behind statements.

The key to better listening is you. Better listening can directly affect your bottom line. If you understand this, then you will desperately want to improve. This means that you will earnestly work to develop your ability to concentrate on a speaker. With a positive attitude you can accept that each person is worth listening to. And then work hard to improve your ability to listen.

Craving appreciation is a basic human need. Listening is one of the highest forms of appreciation. Listening with attention and sincerity enhances the self-esteem of the speaker. It also enhances the perception of you as an open, friendly person.

Complete listening leads to complete understanding. Understanding leads to respect. Respect leads to motivation. Motivation leads to purchases. Purchases lead to profit. It's in your best financial interest to become a better listener.

Some service providers seem defensive and protective. When working with their staff (or prospective clients) they evaluate, direct, and manipulate. When asked questions, they return a controlled response. They are not open and sincere.

This causes others to sense hidden agendas and strategic game-playing. Clients begin to mistrust the person and the business. They become cautious. Most of them go elsewhere.

Successful service providers develop a business environment that is supportive. They listen to their staff. They listen to their clients. They share problem solving and level with their customers. If they can't produce a site design within a desired time frame, they tell the customer. They suggest solutions, even if those solutions involve another service provider. These owners put the client first. Contrary to mere rhetoric by others, these owners actually make customer service paramount in their business strategy.

The customers sense this. They feel comfortable with the service provider. This motivates them to tell others and to suggest new Web development opportunities. It can lead to much larger and more profitable projects.

Several years ago, I learned an acronym for remembering the key points in good listening. The acronym is "LADDER." Here's how it goes:

The "L" stands for *LOOK*. *Look at the person speaking*. Keep your eyes focused on them. By looking directly at them, you convey dynamic interest. This helps you clarify the content of their message. It also lets you observe facial expressions and judge intent.

"A" stands for *ASK*. To keep the conversation from bogging down and a person from rambling, *ask questions* periodically. Asking questions beginning with "where," "when," and "who" can result in a single word answer. These are called "closed" questions. If you ask questions, beginning with "why," "what," or "how," you'll usually get an open-ended response. The "open-ended" question provides more information.

The first "D" in "LADDER" is for *DON'T*. *Don't interrupt*. Many people have a tendency to jump into a conversation with their own ideas. This is precisely the problem in poor communication. Stepping on a person's thought is just as rude as stepping on their toes. People avoid contact with interrupters. So, bite your tongue, and wait your turn. Let them finish their idea or sentence before you add to or clarify the message.

The second "D" also stands for *DON'T*. *Don't change the subject*. This is another way to alienate a customer. You can insult them if you immediately switch the conversation to another subject. Let them complete and close on their thought before you switch tracks and go off in another direction.

"E" represents *EMOTION*. If you are conversing with another person and they become emotional, *don't overreact*. Martial art experts know that the moment you become emotional, you lose control of the situation. Lose control, and you lose the ability to influence the other person. Instead, when listening, hear them out. Concentrate on the message and not the debate.

Finally, "R" stands for *RESPOND*. Show that you are listening. Your demeanor, your posture, and your facial expressions convey your acknowledgment. Sit or stand straight. Look attentive. Don't slouch. While they're talking, occasionally nod your head in agreement or move it slowly side to side in sympathetic understanding. Contribute an occasional "hm-mmm" or "uh-huh" to show that you received the message. An occasional question can help you focus on the message and show the speaker that you're listening.

To listen better, use a LADDER—**L**ook. **A**sk. **D**on't interrupt. **D**on't' change the subject. Control your **E**motions. **R**espond to the speaker through gestures, short utterances, and questions. Each rung of the ladder is important.

Several years ago, I was in the office of the general manager of the Westinghouse plant in Sunnyvale, California and was pleased to observe statesmanship that distinguishes a leader from a manager.

A minority activist group was threatening to demonstrate in front of all the entrances to the plant because the group felt minorities were being denied defense contractor jobs. The leader of the group demanded an audience with the top person at the plant. He was invited to the general manager's office.

When he arrived—with a half dozen other activists—he stormed into the office without an introduction, acting like an irate union steward. He was a large, angry-looking man. He shouted, he cursed, and he threatened. He leaned over the manager's desk and attempted to bully the manager into submission.

The general manager sat silently behind his desk listening to the verbal tirade. He looked directly into the eyes of the leader of the group, ignoring the rest of his "henchmen." He listened quietly and focused intently on the speaker. His eyes never narrowed in anger. He kept his composure.

When the activist had completed his outburst, the general manager spoke in a soft, but firm voice. He told the visitor that he believed that the inability of minorities to get government contracts existed because many minorities didn't know how to generate a good proposal so they could qualify to get on a bidders list and compete for jobs.

Then he told the activist that he would like to go back to his corporate management in Baltimore and ask for $100,000 to set up a training program to help minorities in the local area learn how to solve the real problem. He asked the activist if this idea was acceptable to him.

The anger melted from the activist like butter in a hot frying pan. I could see the calm flow over the man and his body relax. In a mellow, low voice, he told the manager that his idea was "very nice." Then he thanked the general manager several times, shook his hand, shook my hand, and calmly left the office with his group. They were smiling as they departed. They had met a person who actually understood their frustration—a person who listened to them.

The manager followed through and did what he had suggested. He obtained funding, and he established the training program as he had said.

The minority group never demonstrated at the Westinghouse plant. In fact, they used this manager as an example of the treatment they wanted from all of the other defense contractors in the area. The managers at the other plants refused to see the group and were boycotted, picketed, interviewed and photographed by the media. The negative press alone cost thousands of dollars in lost revenue and prestige.

One business manager had listened, didn't get emotional, and responded. He was perceived a great leader. That day, he won my respect and the respect of many other people. He is the kind of leader-manager that we need—that we should all strive to become.

You can improve your ability to listen by taking the time to focus. Increase your listening span. Adopt your thought speed so you can give full attention to the speaker. Avoid hasty evaluations and restate the message to ensure understanding. Don't overreact to the delivery or the content of the message. Listen for ideas and feelings, not just facts. Listen "between the words" for the emotion behind a statement.

Collecting market intelligence is a critical part of our business life. And there's no better way to do this than by listening. As an old Chinese proverb states: *"To be heard, there are times you must be silent."* Listen and become a sponge that absorbs information. Then act on the information that benefits you and your business.

We each have two ears, but only one mouth. Some think this is because we should spend twice as much time listening as we do talking. Others claim that it's because listening is twice as hard as speaking.

Listening is an art, a science, a skill. To be good at it takes practice. Practice doesn't make perfect. Practice makes permanent. Only perfect practice makes perfect permanent. Focus on the right skills and develop the right habits.

If there's one "secret weapon" for business success, it's listening. Listen. Learn. Recognize profitable niches. And then act quickly to market to those niches before your competitors arrive. Listening is the ultimate expression of respect for your client. It's also the ultimate tool for finding new Web service opportunities.

"His words were few and didn't glisten.
Yet he profited much because he could listen."

The message is clear: To enhance your profit picture, don't just hear. LISTEN!

Body Language in Business

In business, entrepreneurs consistently look for tools to help maximize profit. An interesting method for selling clients on you, your company and your services involves nonverbal communication—those subtle messages conveyed by your posture, facial expressions and gestures—in fact everything about you and your workplace. These include your appearance, mannerisms, dress, hair style, jewelry, desk mementos—even the color on your office walls, because all of these things produce sensory messages about you. People buy based on their senses, and everything that you can do to positively affect their senses can and will affect your ability to sell. This goes for your Web site, too. It is a visual representation of you and your company.

Psychologists claim that the impact you make on others comes from what you say (7%), how you say it (38%), and by your body language (55%). Since how you sound also conveys a message, 93% of emotion is communicated nonverbally.

The master speaker, S.I. Hyikowa once commented that "In this era of television, image is more important than substance." Some believe that Richard Nixon won the presidency because he was a master at using color to convey character. He wore a dark blue suit at a television debate in which the set background was light blue. The light blue background with Nixon in his dark blue suit produced an aura of honesty, integrity and sincerity. He won that election.

It's often not what you say that makes an influence on others; it's what you don't say. The signals that you send nonverbally suggest attitude, understanding, empathy and ethics.

The moment you meet a prospective client, they judge you by what they see and feel. The process takes less than 10 seconds but the impression is permanent. Whether you make or break a sales opportunity can literally depend on the silent signals that you send during this first contact.

Fig. 9-1. Body language tells you when they're closed to business.

It's critical for entrepreneurs today to understand and use body language. Once you understand what to look for, you can read your client like a book. Oriental business people are expert at recognizing and using nonverbal signals. This ability makes them formidable negotiators. Most American's fail to recognize and use body language, although women are inherently better at sensing emotion and intent than men.

Body language is communicating without words, with unspoken messages. The human body can produce over 700,000 unique movements. These movements have been partitioned into about 60 discrete and symbolic signals and around 60 gestures. A nodding head can signal yes. Pointing two fingers at your eyes can mean "watch me." Running your fingers through your hair can indicate frustration. A smile or a grin is a universal signal for happiness. Likewise, crying signals sadness or, in conjunction with a smile—extreme delight.

However, some nonverbal signals can mean different things. Crossed arms can indicate defensiveness. It can also be a comfortable way to stand or sit. Touching the nose can suggest doubt in what the person is hearing. It could also be a response to an itch or soreness from a recent cold. Likewise, an unbuttoned jacket can signify openness and cooperation. But it could also be an overweight person trying to fit into an old jacket. The same hitch-hiking arm extended with thumb pointed up can give a negative message in other cultures.

However, each nonverbal signal is a flag. It's not a complete message. Look for a pattern of signals that all have the same meaning. The body language should match the verbal expressions. It should also match the context of what is happening in the situation. So look for body language in clusters of signals with common meanings. Once you understand body language, you can use this knowledge and sell using your voice *and* your body.

Let's start with the handshake. A handshake can be soft, firm, brief, long, and sometimes painful. The way you shake hands gives clues to your personality. Aggressive people have firm handshakes. People with low self esteem often have a limp handshake. Politicians typically shake one hand while holding the same hand or elbow with their other hand (so you can't twist away, I suppose). Domineering men often squeeze the hand when greeting a woman. The clever woman will move her index and little finger in toward her palm preventing a crushing handshake. This negates his dominant act and keeps her in equal control.

As a business person trying to sell, you should adopt a handshake that is firm, yet not crushing. You want to convey confidence and professionalism, not dominance.

Next, comes posture. A slouch conveys lack of confidence. Standing straight with your weight balanced on each foot makes you look confident and relaxed. When you sit, sit up straight; don't slouch.

Rather than saying "Trust me," convey the message "I can be trusted" by how you use your body. Honest people have a mannerism that conveys honesty. Even animals sense this. One particular mannerism is how the palms are shown. Holding a hand out to a dog with the palm down conveys dominance to the dog. It may snap back if you're a stranger. Shaking hands with your palm down conveys the same thing. Showing an open hand with palm up conveys honesty and sincerity. To an animal it conveys trust. Hands thrust into pockets convey hidden agenda or secretiveness. Show the palms. Help build trust.

Fig. 9-2. An open palm is a good signal.

The open hands with palms visible should be accompanied with an open posture and a sincere facial expression. Your arms should be unfolded, not crossed in defensiveness. And your eyes should be steadily focused on your client. Darting eyes suggest deceit. Looking left as you speak can convey truth. Looking right when you speak can convey dishonesty. Always refrain from looking down when you speak.

And get rid of the sunglasses. Dark glasses prevent a customer from seeing your eyes and "reading your soul." It's been said that a person's eyes cannot hide a dishonest intent.

My best advice to women is to go with your feelings. Women have an innate ability to receive messages to both their right and left brains simultaneously. They can sense, and they can feel emotion in others. A woman can "tell" if you aren't sincere. Unfortunately, some women don't follow their instincts. This has gotten them in trouble. Your "sixth sense" is the part of you that tunes in on nonverbal messages. Learn how to read and use these messages in business, and you'll substantially increase your sales success.

When you face a client, use honest, open gestures. Outward and upward movements of the hands are positive actions. Putting the tips of the fingers on one hand against the tips of the fingers on the other is a form of "steepling" that conveys confidence. Clasping your hands behind your head as you lean back in a chair can suggest arrogant confidence and turn people off. Placing your hands on each side of your waist is called "standing at the ready." It conveys confidence and attracts others. This is why many catalog models are photographed in this pose as they show off new outfits.

Unbuttoning a suit jacket in front of a customer will signify an open attitude—that you're willing to talk, to negotiate. Taking off your jacket is really powerful. And rolling your shirt sleeves part way up suggests that you're ready to get down to the final price.

As you talk with a prospective client, watch their body language. If they cross their arms, use positive signals and words that will cause them to unfold their arms and become open to your sales approach. If their arms and legs are uncrossed and their hands are open, you're on track. When you notice them "mirroring" your movements and gestures, you've got them locked on your sales presentation. Mirroring indicates that you are in maximum communication mode with the other person. If you move your arms apart, opening your palms, and they do the same, you are acting as one—in synch. The messages and the words of the sale are being received and accepted by the other.

Fig. 9-3. Watch for "mirroring" of your gestures.

Apply a technique called "tracking." Mirror their body language. Then gradually move them toward a more positive posture and psychological openness. As they shift their posture to mimic yours, their attitudes will shift, and you can close on the sale.

If they begin to cover their mouth, touch their nose or touch near an eye, they are withdrawing. Something that you said has turned them off. You must back up and resell using another approach. Gently re-focus on the prospective client. Encourage them to share their concern. Open your palms to them and occasionally touch a palm to your chest as you speak. This is a strong signal of honesty.

I was "told" by a deaf person that you can tell if a signing person is actually deaf by observing if they touch themselves. A hearing person will "sign" words, but seldom touch the body. A deaf person often touches their chest as they "sign." The same gesture accompanies sincere statements by hearing and non-hearing people. Touching a palm to the chest usually doesn't occur unless a person is making an honest comment.

Avoid fidgeting or appearing nervous. Even if this is the first serious prospect in a week, you must act as though your business plate is relatively full. If they appear defensive or hostile, don't react in like manner. Use all positive signals. Lean slightly forward to put energy into the conversation. Open your hands and spread your arms with your palms up.

The old adage "Don't point" can be repeated here. Pointing at a person is an aggressive act. In my classes on communication skills, I present dozens of magazine photographs showing political leaders pointing at each other or chopping their hands down in a defiant gesture. These people antagonize. They don't sell.

Think of your customer as wearing a traffic signal. Positive nonverbal messages signal "green" to go ahead and approach a close on the sale. If the client's body language transitions from positive to defensive or non-believing, the signal is "yellow" and caution must be observed. Slow down and advance carefully. Try to get them to exhibit openness. A defiant, arms and legs "double-cross" with a scowl on their face is a definite "red" signal. You cannot close a sales unless you have a "green" light. If you can get your prospective client to mirror your movements they'll be in synch with your presentation and receptive to closing on a sale.

If you are still unable to close, thank the person for stopping by. Approach sales like renting an apartment. It typically takes five showings before a rental is achieved. Likewise, it can take up to five inquiries before you close on a sale for Web services. If they're number four, the next person in the door should be the one that buys. And the person who decided not to buy today, will consider you again if they leave with a positive impression of you and your company. Impress them with your professionalism and integrity.

Finally, don't get discouraged when a prospect decides not to buy. Your attitude can affect future sales. Take "turn downs" in stride. Use your body in the selling process and keep upbeat. If you believe in your services and the quality of your work, others will too. A positive, honest message conveyed by your nonverbal body language will win far more jobs than you think. Using body language to move prospects from suspicion to open and receptive attitudes can sway "fence-sitters" into buying. You can also use body language to calm hostile clients who are upset with mistakes or miscommunication even when it's actually their fault.

Learn more about body language and nonverbal communications. Then look in the mirror. Watch how you appear when speaking on the phone or talking with someone else. Look for the signals of openness. Watch customers and follow their cues. Smile from within and without. They'll sense this and be won over.

Those who are in the Web services business to rip others off, should get out of the business, because as buyer's become aware, they'll use body language to read the insincere service providers like a book.

Getting Paid

A *"deadbeat"* is a client who doesn't mail the check as agreed. Credit is fine when you're receiving it. But it can be a cash flow nightmare when you're the creditor.

Slow paying customers represent the nemesis of the struggling shop owner. Poor bill-paying behavior can quickly cause cash flow problems. The more clients that you have paying on credit, the more cash flow problems you can have.

Often your best customers are individuals or small sole proprietorships. While they usually pay in cash, you can increase sales from them by offering credit.

Credit comes in two forms: 1) payment in full *(net pa*y) after an agreed time and 2) payment using a credit card. With net pay you should receive all moneys within a set time period—14 days, 30 days or some other agreed period—after delivering work output to your client. It's imperative that both you and your client agree on the terms of purchase and what level of service will be provided. (Our *Desktop Production Standards* book includes a complete chapter on contract standards. In it is a shopping list of all the places where Murphy could be hiding in any business transaction. By covering all of your bases, you minimize problems later.)

A common dilemma for service businesses is that there's no way to take back a service once it's been provided. This is why many shop owners operate on a "1/3, 1/3, 1/3" basis. One third of the bill is paid upon signing the contract or work order. One third is paid upon delivery of a first draft (or some action halfway through the project), and the remaining one third is paid upon delivery of the final design (perhaps uploading it to the ISP server and viewing it from a browser).

What you'd like them to do, is use their credit card for each payment. It's convenient and psychologically easier for them to use—as compared to physically writing out a check.

Charge card sales are good because the funds are usually credited to your bank account within 24 hours. Since most people use "plastic" today, offering credit card sales should increase work volume. When we secured our merchant account to offer credit card purchases, our sales increased by 50 percent.

But credit card purchases have their own risks— charges backed out months later and occasional credit card fraud with little or no recourse. A customer who buys your services with a credit card, can renege on the sale and decline the charge—depending on the credit card account—up to 12 months after the date of purchase. And individuals who buy using stolen credit card information sometimes get away with the fraud if the crime involves a low dollar amount. Usually credit card companies force the seller to absorb low-dollar fraud losses and don't go after the criminal. When a person in Maryland bought one of our books using stolen credit card information, we tracked the criminal down, but Mastercard refused to prosecute because the sale was under $300. The actual card owner in Texas cried "fraud" when they saw the charge on their bill. The credit card company reversed the charge and our company was forced to absorb the loss. Prosecuting in an out-of-state court for a $60 loss is like throwing $100 dollar bills out a window in a brisk breeze.

Fortunately, credit card fraud represents less than 3% of sales for most companies. The most common problem service providers face is getting some credit customers to pay on time. Slow payment directly affects cash flow. It doesn't take very many "deadbeats" to drain your resources and threaten your own business survival. Sales may look nice on a ledger report, but only sales paid are sales (actually) made.

To successfully add clients while maintaining positive cash flow, ration credit like a miser tips a waiter—only when necessary, and to the least extent possible. Consider allowing credit purchases only for customers who represent volume business. Then check their credit history carefully before agreeing to terms. Credit customers tend to buy more products or services, but their ability and willingness to pay are critical. If you can, consider credit only for those clients who consistently bring you jobs with high profit margins.

I have a policy that all first-time customers must pay in cash or by credit card. Later, if they come back with follow-up work or new projects, I consider extending credit—but only if they ask for it.

Before you accept credit sales, collect copies of credit applications from every source that you can find. Adopt the "good things" on these forms, and generate a credit application that is custom to your business.

Then, before agreeing to a credit relationship, check out the applicant. Your best references on a potential credit customer are the companies that they already buy from on credit. Check with the applicant's bank, and contact credit reporting agencies to learn about their payment history. Place a higher weight on the most current information. Where possible, call the references.

I use the "Reverse 3" technique with my credit account applicants. I ask them to list three credit references. Then I call the references in reverse order—last one listed is called first. The last reference may have more reliable information for you than the first (most popular). This technique works well in hiring, too.

If a customer's credit history seems solid, discuss the terms for which you will conduct business. Establish ground rules before any work is performed. Don't jump on a 30 day payment schedule—called "net 30." Try to get agreement on a "15-day pay" instead. The sooner a customer pays, the better your cash flow.

Consider offering "price breaks" for paying early. Some shops give customers an additional 1 percent discount if they pay their bill within 15 days instead of 45 days as required by their credit agreement. Some owners print a statement on invoices to government organizations that the buyer can deduct 2% from the invoiced amount if they pay before the net due date.

Most government organizations require their contracting officers to take advantage of any discounts that are available. I've used this technique and received payments for sales to the U.S. Government Printing Office two weeks after receipt of invoice—unheard of in most "small business - big government" transactions.

And, include a penalty clause in your credit agreement to cover late payment. Charging for past due invoices should be a standard practice. Most credit customers will delay as long as possible in paying their bills. This helps their cash flow. It hurts yours.

Position your invoices at the top of their stack of accounts payable bills, by putting a prominent notice on your invoice that a late fee of one and one-half percent will be charged for payments made past the due date. If payment is delayed past the due date, immediately re-invoice them and include the late fee. Stamp on the new invoice, "PAST DUE."

Some clients will honor the late fee. Others will ignore it, so call them and politely ask them about the discrepancy between the invoice amount on your last invoice and the amount they actually paid. Regardless what they use as an excuse, tell them that you value their business, but you expect payment according to the agreed terms. Ask what you can do to prevent this delay from happening again. You don't want to become a thorn in their side, but you do want to make it very clear that you expect to be paid according to the terms of the invoice. Explain that you cannot afford to be a cash flow bank for them. The reason for a late fee is to ensure that they pay on time.

In your terms and conditions statement on the reverse side of your work order or customer agreement form state that, should legal action be necessary to collect on the account, the losing party must pay the attorney fees and court costs of both parties. Do everything possible to motivate customers to pay early—or at least on time.

When a project is delivered, give the customer your invoice at the same time. If it's local, get the person receiving the hard copy of the Web pages to check them for suitability. Upon acceptance, have them mark the invoice accompanying the shipment "OK TO PAY." Then immediately put the invoice into their payment system. It can take two weeks to move an invoice through the bureaucracy of a large company to final cutting of a check. I've encountered an amazing delay getting payment from some large, well-known companies. Their excuses run the gamut.

"Well, the buying department must approve the invoice for payment first, and that can take some time."

"We only cut checks on every other Friday."

"The invoice has already been paid!" This can mean the invoice has been accepted by the receiving office and submitted to Accounts Payable for payment. Mailing of the actual check can take another week or two.

Some large companies simply pay when they want to pay. They will readily agree to a payment schedule, but their Accounting Department operates by its own rules. However, since most accounting people understand cash flow and its affect on a small business, many are willing to work with you. You only need to ask.

When you complete a project for a large company, fax the invoice to their accounting office at the same time you notify the client that the project is complete. Then follow up the faxed invoice by mailing a copy. Faxing can expedite payment by several weeks.

Before you accept credit, be certain that both you and your customer are clear on what you will do and how you will be paid. Put in writing what will occur if payment is not made or if payment is made with a check that is returned for insufficient funds. Then monitor your customer's payment behavior, and take action as soon as danger signals occur.

After completing a project with net-pay terms, mark your calendar and then call your customer a week before the due date to thank them for the business and to confirm that everything was completed and the invoice delivered properly. During the conversation, remind them when payment is due, and suggest that they take advantage of your discount policy for early payment. Most accounting managers want the discount.

Watch credit customer for signs of financial trouble—missing payment dates, unreturned telephone calls, stonewalling by their accounting department, delaying comments such as "... check's in the mail," or catching them in a "white lie."

If payment is due in 14 days, make your first telephone call on day 15 to get the check number and confirm its mailing. If you receive a check that later "bounces," immediately call the customer to arrange their delivering a cashier's check that will be "good." If they want you to "run the check through again," agree to do so but explain to them that an added charge will be levied for processing a returned check. Most banks charge between $15 and $25 for re-processing checks. Get immediate payment of this added charge.. Be sure to charge them for resubmitting any returned check.

When you feel that a debtor is in financial danger, call or visit them. Be pleasant, but professional. Explain that you have not been paid and that this is not their typical behavior. Ask them if there is someone else that you should speak with to correct the credit delinquency. Be firm. Communicate a strong message that prompt payment is normal and expected. The more professional clients will contact you BEFORE a due date is passed to arrange extended payments.

Convert delinquent clients, to "cash-plus" where they can continue buying services from you but must pay cash-on-completion plus a portion of the delinquent balance for each service purchased. Once they pay their account current, use "cash-up-front" for the next several jobs and then return them to a credit status if you feel comfortable that their payment problems are over.

Your best chance for collection occurs when an account is less than 30 days past due. Therefore, become the "squeaky wheel" to a laggard client and perform most of your collection activity within the first month after an account becomes delinquent.

Start with a telephone call. Then send a friendly note attached to a copy of the invoice. If this doesn't work, call and begin verbal needling. Make it clear that you want payment. After a week, send a formal appeal for payment in full. A week later, send a telegram demand for payment. The next day, call to determine when their check can be expected. If they stall, send a demand letter by Certified Mail. Clearly state what was agreed and what is and is not happening. Hint that you may be open to a payment plan, but (without threatening) be clear that their immediate response is urgent. You want to pin them down to a commitment for payment.

If all else fails, "play hardball." Send a certified "Pay Up Or Else" demand letter. Explain that you intend to initiate legal action for non-payment if you do not receive moneys in full within 14 calendar days after the date of your letter. Call their local Better Business Bureau to report the payment delinquency.

If your "deadbeat" customer refuses to budge, send them a letter by regular mail indicating that you intend to prosecute for non-payment. Attempt to call them to convey this same message. Wait two weeks. Then file a law suit in small claims court. This will cost under $50 in most states. If the amount is more than $5,000, hire an attorney and file a civil suit in the court the attorney recommends. (Hopefully, your sales contract includes a statement that they pay all legal fees if they lose in court.) This will be a difficult process if your customer is out of state or out of the country. For these customers, I implement a partial payment up front, and progress payments all during work on the job.

Consider using a collection agency. Use one that is bonded and/or licensed, has been in business a long time, and happily offers references that you can check.

Don't let delinquent clients cause red marks on your cash flow spreadsheet. Go after the deadbeats. All Web service providers struggle when irresponsible customers don't pay on time. By affecting one, they affect all. Be willing to work with delinquent clients. But keep them honest, responsible, accountable, and—even more important—paid current.

Summary

There you have it. You've now learned the tips, the tricks and the techniques for success. There's plenty of opportunity and plenty of business waiting for you out there. As companies struggle to establish their own Web sites, demand is swelling for people with your abilities.

High profit niche jobs do exist, and the opportunities in and around the Internet are immense. You can carve out your own niche in this huge opportunity pie by creating value for potential customers. This means, developing the skills and then finding ways to use your skills and current technology to generate more value for your clients—higher valued relationships with their customers, their suppliers and with their investors. Help your clients make money, and they'll help you make money. It's all in adding value. As I've said earlier, value is not what you think your services are worth. Value is what a customer will buy.

The coming year can be a bonanza for you. This book provides the tools you need to significantly increase your income. All you need do is read, study and apply.

So keep your core profit generator going while you look for niche opportunities in this emerging world of on-line commerce. May you find much success and profit in the Web service profession.

"Now go, and be the (Web)master of your own fate."

Index

"Oreo cookie" strategy - 213
$/FTE - 32
10-plus-10 strategy - 181
30-60-10 rule - 29
80/20 rule - 164
accepted reference markup pricing - 135
accounts receivable - 227
adding loss leader jobs - 170
adding products & services - 170
allowance - 199
analyzing financial numbers - 223
analyzing profit in competitor bid - 240
average distribution costs - 121
average dollars per sale - 111
average sale amount - 231
average variable cost per sale - 111
B-E - 112
B-E quantity - 113
BHC
    defined - 39
    single Home Page site - 57
    Six page site design - 60
    keyboarding - 49
    laser proof printing - 53
    scanning - 50
    ftp Web page to site - 55
    Web page layout - 52
    Web site design - 47
billing - 183
body language in business - 260
break-even
    on advertising - 116
    sales quantity method - 113
    sales-volume method - 110
break-even analysis - 110
break-even order size - 121
break-even point - 112
budgeted hourly cost
    calculating - 44
    defined - 39
    pricing - 135
budgeted hourly rate - 39
burden rate - 24
business objective - 128
calculated markup pricing - 134
capacity trap - 204
cash flow - 237
cash on hand - 225
charging - 183
check, sending a - 198
Clayton Antitrust Act - 74
collecting competitor information - 86
competition, analyzing - 85
competitor, beating them - 180
competitor, pricing assumptions - 175
contribution margin - 113
conversion ration - 229
cost
    hidden - 28
    maintenance - 27
    purchase - 27, 105
    sales & support 28
cost of goods sold - 96
cost of ownership - 27
cost of services sold - 226
cost of services sold - 27
cost of services sold - 97
cost-plus pricing - 135
cost-volume curve - 137
cost-volume pricing - 136

costs
    direct - 21
    fixed - 18
    general & admin - 25
    how vary - 64
    indirect - 22
    overhead - 22
    variable - 20
counter price sheet - 135
coupons - 194
critical number - 225
customer
    commodity - 124
    solutions - 124
cutthroat pricing - 175
cutting prices - 202
daily cash control log - 237
dead sites - 77
demand
    estimating - 75
    how to evaluate - 82
    responding to - 83
demand curve - 77
differentiation value - 163
direct costs - 21
discount - 199
discounting and the law - 202
distribution costs - 121
donating services - 169
economic value - 163
elasticity
    defined - 78
    elastic - 78
    factors affecting - 80
    inelastic - 78
    of demand - 79
    unitary - 78
elasticity factor - 78
expense as % gross income - 227
expenses - 226

Federal Trade Commission Act - 74
financial
    number of customers - 230
    analyzing numbers - 223
    accounts receivable - 227
    analyzing bids - 240
    average sale amount - 231
    cash flow - 237
    cash on hand - 225
    conversion ration - 229
    cost of services sold - 226
    critical number - 225
    daily cash control log - 237
    expenses - 226
    expenses as % gross income - 227
    gross profit - 232
    gross profit to net sales ratio - 232
    hours of service sold - 230
    how much can you earn - 241
    income - 226
    inquiries received - 228
    monitoring schedule - 235
    net profit - 232
    numbers - 223
    percent gross profit - 232
    percent net profit - 232
    projects backlog - 233
    purchase orders - 228
    revenue per employee ($/FTE) - 234
    turnaround time - 233
fixed costs - 18
flat rate pricing - 40
full cost pricing - 134
G&A - 25
GAAP - 95
general & administrative - 25

generally accepted accounting principles - 95
getting paid - 267
gross margin - 96
gross profit - 96, 232
gross profit margin - 109
gross profit to net sales ratio - 232
hassle factor - 185
hidden costs - 28
hours of service sold - 230
how much can you earn - 241
income - 226
income statement - 96
incremental cost pricing - 134
indirect costs - 22
inquiries received - 228
jobs
    10 reasons to turn down - 208
    when to turn down - 207
listening for profit - 253
maintenance cost - 27
margin analysis - 118
margin curve - 119
margin of safety - 48
marginal cost - 118
marginal revenue - 118
market
    affect of size - 70, 71, 72, 73
    analysis - 66
    measuring share - 166
    monopolistic - 67
    monopolistic-competitive - 69
    oligopolistic - 68
    purely competitive - 68
    research - 83
    size - 69
    type - 67
markup - 107, 109
markup pricing - 132

margin of safety - 48
monitoring schedule - 235
MOS - 48
net profit - 96, 232
networking for business - 247
non-verbal comms - 260
number of customers - 230
objective - 128
operating expenses - 96
optimal order size - 120
other charges - 185
overhead - 22
overhead factor - 24
page design - 8
page layout - 8
Pareto Principle - 164
percent gross profit - 232
percent markup - 108, 133
percent net profit - 232
price
    choosing the right - 219
    quoting - 167
    selling - 108
    reducing - 192
    countering cutthroat - 175
price cutting
    handling a - 206
    when works - 205
price elasticity - 83
price fishing - 167
price points 160
price raise
    described - 209
    how to handle - 212
    handling objections - 216
    how much to - 215
    subtle ways to - 216
    when it's time - 211
pricing
    "one-half" pricing - 147
    2.5X pricing - 144
    2X pricing - 143
    3X better, 3X below - 147

pricing (continued)
- accepted as customary - 155
- competing head-on - 149
- competition-oriented - 190
- competitive - 189
- competitor-oriented - 146
- composite - 162
- cost-oriented - 131
- customer-set - 154
- desired pay plus - 143
- flat rate - 40
- floor price plus some - 141
- going rate - 156
- in the "zone" - 152
- leadership - 151
- loss-leader - 154
- market-oriented - 150
- match the competition - 146
- net revenue marginal analysis - 143
- net revenue, inventory sell off - 143
- new service - 150
- only prices with commas - 144
- overcoming problems - 186
- penetration - 151
- penny - 159
- percent capacity plus margin - 142
- policy - 188
- pricing by expertise - 145
- right the first time - 187
- shop-oriented - 141
- single price, any customer - 143
- skimming - 150
- straddle pricing - 148
- strategy - 123
- strike zone - 153
- subjective - 156
- tiered - 157

productivity
- measuring - 32
- ratio - 104
- calculating - 30
- defined - 29
- factors affecting - 38

productivity factor - 30

profit
- defined - 98
- analyze clients by - 163
- break out top - 172
- improving - 122

project turnaround time - 233
projects backlog - 233
purchase cost - 27
purchase orders - 228
quoting completion time - 168

raising prices
- described - 209
- how to handle - 212
- handling objections - 216
- how much - 215
- subtle ways to - 216
- when it's time - 211

rebates - 197
reducing prices - 192
reference value - 163
return on assets - 104
return on investment - 102
revenue per employee ($/FTE) - 234

ROA
- calculating - 106
- defined - 104

Robinson-Patman Act - 73

ROI
- calculating - 102
- defined - 102
- on marketing/sales - 103

rush rates - 169
sandwich strategy - 213
selling price - 133

SG&A - 26
Sherman Antitrust Act - 74
site
    design & development - 6
    maintenance - 11
    management - 11
    promotion - 10
skimming - 150
standard markup pricing - 134
strategies, smart - 163
strategy, 10-plus-10 - 181
tactics, pricing actions - 186
targeted
    profit pricing - 138
    return-on-investment pricing - 140
    return-on-sales pricing - 139
value pricing - 71
variable cost percentage - 111
variable costs - 20
volume discounts - 201
Web consulting - 5
Web service
    cost elements - 17
    donating - 169, 171
    freebies - 171
    market for - 65
    problems in - 221
    profitability - 13
    selecting - 127
WOW content - 71
WOW formula - 188

Useful Periodicals

Interactive Age	http://techweb.cmp.com/ia
Interactive Week	http://www.interactive-week.com
Internet Underground	http://www.underground-online.com
Internet World	http://www.mecklerweb.com/mags/iw/
	http://www.iw.com
NetGuide	http://www.netguidemag.com
New Media	http://www.macromedia.com
ONLINE	http://www.onlineinc.com/onlinemag/
WebDeveloper	http://ww.webdeveloper.com
WebWeek	http://www.mecklerweb.com/mags/ww/
Wired	http://www.wired.com

Useful Organizations

Electronic Frontier Foundation	eff@eff.org
The HTML Writer's Guild	http://www.mindspring.com/guild/
The Internet Society	isoc@isoc.org
The Society for Electronic Access	sea-member@sea.org
The World Wide Web Organization	http://www.w3.org

Useful Sites

Business@Home	http://www.gohome.com
Enterpreneurs on the Web	http://www.eotw.com
Intl Small Business Consortium	http://www.isbc.com
Internet technical issues	http://www.ttalk.com
Small Business Administration	http://www.sbaonline.sba.gov
Smart Business Supersite	http://www.smartbiz.com
The Small Business Advisor	http://www.isquare.com
Web marketing	http://www.wilsonweb.com
Webmaster reference library	http://www.webreference.com
WebSearch	http://www.web-search.com
Women in Business	http://www.gridley.org/~imaging
Women's Business Resource	http://www.athenet.net/~ccain
Women's Wire	http://www.women.com

Order Form

Name: _____
Company: _____
Address: _____
_____
City: _____
State/Province: _____ ZIP/Mail Postal Code _____
Telephone: ( ) _____ Country: _____
Fax:: ( ) _____ e-mail: _____
SHIP TO: _____
_____
_____

BOOK(S) ORDERED:

QTY	ITEM	EACH	PRICE	TOTAL
___	Language of Computer Publishing	$24.95	_____	_____
___	Pricing Guide for Desktop Services	$34.95	_____	_____
___	Pricing Guide for Web Services	$29.95	_____	_____
___	Pricing Tables: Desktop Services	$49.95	_____	_____
___	Desktop Production Standards	$49.95	_____	_____

PRIORITY SHIPPING

quantity	U.S.	Canada	Other Countries
1 book	$5	$7	$15
2 books	$6	$10	$28
3 books	$7	$12	$34
(more	(CALL)	(CALL)	(CALL)

Sub-Total _____
Sales Tax (CA only) _____
Shipping _____
TOTAL (U.S. funds) _____

Make CHECKS payable to:
Brenner Information Group

CREDIT CARD ORDERS: *(Visa, Mastercard, or Discover)*

Card Number: _____
Expiration Date: _____
Name on the card: _____
Signature: _____